Trauma-Informed Christian Ethics

Series Preface
The T&T Clark Enquiries in Embodiment, Sexuality, and Social Ethics series features
textbooks and coursebooks for seminary, graduate, and advanced undergraduate
learning. Books in this series adopt an intersectional approach using tools of
social analysis to conceptualize, interpret, and analyze the ethics of sexuality
and embodiment, broadly construed, integrating theory and praxis, doctrine and
lived faith, and ideology and material existence. The series promotes progressive
scholarship intended to advance critical understandings of sexuality and gender.

*Trauma-Informed Christian Ethics: Bearing Witness through Love, Justice, and Solidarity in
Community*, the second volume in this series, takes seriously the Christian call to bear witness
to the inherent dignity of every person especially in circumstances of systemic injustice and
oppression. Stephens presents practices of attentive presence, historical clarity, and meaningful
participation as ways to concretely address difficult moral problems, including sexual violence,
racism, climate change, and institutional betrayal. Stephens brings a distinctly Methodist
approach, arguing that personal and social holiness are one and the same. Importantly, he models
for readers from social contexts of privilege how to attend to social disparities through models
of solidarity and accountability. This text models the call to get proximate with those impacted
by trauma so that through empathy and Christian love one can actualize social change.

This text is a must read for religious practitioners, students, and scholars. Its rich theoretical
and theological foundation support practical wisdom for "How we can love our neighbors in
traumatic times?" It teaches the reader and the communities to which the reader is connected
how to become trauma informed. The text uses multiple genres to explore the moral life such
as scripture readings, case studies, ministry profiles, and selections from ecclesial teachings. In
particular, the discussion questions in each section create a dialogical text that encourages readers
to reflectively engage the content in a fully embodied way. Stephens has written a theoretically
rich text, while providing critical tactics that bring attention to the mind, body, and spirit.

Monique Moultrie, Georgia State University
Kate Ott, Garrett-Evangelical Theological Seminary

Trauma-Informed Christian Ethics

Bearing Witness through Love, Justice, and Solidarity in Community

Darryl W. Stephens

t&tclark

LONDON • NEW YORK • OXFORD • NEW DELHI • SYDNEY

T&T CLARK
Bloomsbury Publishing Plc, 50 Bedford Square, London, WC1B 3DP, UK
Bloomsbury Publishing Inc, 1359 Broadway, New York, NY 10018, USA
Bloomsbury Publishing Ireland, 29 Earlsfort Terrace, Dublin 2, D02 AY28, Ireland

BLOOMSBURY, T&T CLARK and the T&T Clark logo are trademarks of Bloomsbury Publishing Plc

First published in Great Britain 2026

Cover design: Lara Himpelmann
Cover image © Elianna Gill via Unsplash

A catalogue record for this book is available from the British Library.

Library of Congress Control Number: 2025943384

ISBN: HB: 978-0-5677-0042-1
          PB: 978-0-5677-0043-8
          ePDF: 978-0-5677-0045-2
          eBook: 978-0-5677-0044-5

Series: T&T Clark Enquiries in Embodiment, Sexuality, and Social Ethics

Typeset by Integra Software Services Pvt. Ltd.
Printed and bound in Great Britain

For product safety related questions contact productsafety@bloomsbury.com.

To find out more about our authors and books visit www.
bloomsbury.com and sign up for our newsletters.

CONTENTS

TABLES

PREFACE

How shall we love our neighbors in traumatic times? In a world of suffering and conflict, neighbor-love (*agape*) is a rarity. Which neighbors can I risk loving—and how? Social strife, political wedge issues, alternative facts, and disparate worldviews cloud our vision for the moral life. Who can we trust? And what about loving my neighbor *as myself*? How shall I care for my own needs while caring for my neighbor? Multiple factors challenge our individual and collective well-being, including pandemics, social isolation, systemic racism, sexual assault, climate change, ongoing warfare, and forced migration. Loving our neighbors is particularly challenging across systemic barriers of economics, class, and race. Wealth inequality and patterns of economic and racial segregation keep us apart.

Christian social ethics equips us to address tough moral problems—concrete realities woven into the fabric of our social relations and institutions. I use the term *systemic injustice* to mean various forms of social oppression—patterns of unjust exclusion, domination, discrimination, segregation, and apartheid from which Jesus came to free us (Lk. 4:18-19). Furthermore, God's incarnation in Jesus is not just for humanity's benefit but for the entirety of God's creation. "For God so loved the *cosmos* that he gave his only Son, so that everyone who believes in him may not perish but have eternal life" (Jn 3:16). We cannot talk about poverty without also talking about racism, mass incarceration, and immigration, for example—and each of these challenges to human flourishing also affects the environment. None of these complex moral problems is isolated from the others. Christian moral living requires us to engage in social analysis of structures of oppression, contributing to the common good and the flourishing of all creation.

As many people struggle to survive, the idea of Christian ethics can seem an unnecessary luxury—yet it is vital to our human flourishing. When Jesus was asked about the responsibilities of life with God, he answered by quoting the Torah: "You shall love the Lord your God … and your neighbor as yourself" (Lk. 10:27, quoting Deut. 6:5 and Lev. 19:18). Then the lawyer testing Jesus pressed further with his interrogation, asking, "And who is my neighbor?" (Lk. 10:29). The ensuing parable about a roadside rescue by a member of the despised class is well known—so familiar that we may lose sight of its shocking message. The neighbor turned out to be not the dying man in the ditch but rather the Samaritan traveler "who showed him mercy" (Lk. 10:37). They shared the bond of neighbor-relatedness. Yet, the moral demands on each proved drastically different. Christians, as well as persons of other faiths or of no faith tradition, can benefit from this wisdom. Whether or not you share my Christian faith, I hope this book deepens your appreciation for the contributions of Christian ethics to the task of living lovingly, justly, and in solidarity as neighbors.

Loving our neighbors requires that we learn about these challenges to human flourishing and stand in solidarity with those persons directly affected. We need many diverse perspectives to shed light on this reality. As a heterosexual white male in the United States, I benefit from many social and economic privileges and have not experienced significant marginalization. Thus, I cannot provide all these perspectives on my own. My social location shapes, informs, and limits my understanding of social ethics. So, in this book I draw on personal accounts and writings of diverse persons with a variety of roles, locations, and perspectives: laity, deaconess, deacon, elder, and bishop; African, Latina, African American, Asian American, white, and Native American; married and single; parents and those without children of their own; old and young.

We all bring diverse perspectives to this book. Some of us are trauma survivors, dealing with significant trauma histories from childhood and adulthood. Some of us are members of communities that have experienced collective trauma or members of racial, ethnic, and tribal groups who carry epigenetic markers of trauma, passed from generation to generation. Many of us are members of communities that have caused the systemic oppression of others, directly contributing to individual and collective traumas. All of us are neighbors to trauma survivors. How we exercise our moral agency in this capacity—bearing witness to our neighbors through love, justice, and solidarity—is the topic of this book.

We have varied reasons for learning about trauma-informed Christian ethics based on diverse roles and vocations. Some readers are preparing for or already in the role of pastoral ministry, with responsibility for teaching and caring for a congregation. Others are pursuing or living out a vocation of consecrated, licensed, ordained, or other authorized role of ministry in contexts that extend beyond congregational leadership. Many readers are "religious professionals"—paid or unpaid, clergy or laity—who make a difference in communities around the world through their leadership in faith-based activism, non-profits, churches, mosques, synagogues, and other institutions and agencies. Some readers are laypersons, helping professionals who understand their work as serving others and whose work ethos is shaped by their faith in Christ. Still other readers may come to this text with a perspective beyond Christianity, seeking to learn a trauma-informed way of living in the world, and willing to translate the language of Christian faith into their own vernaculars of faith and culture.

This book is distinctive in the way it employs trauma studies as a partner for Christian social ethics, drawing on multiple disciplines to understand trauma and to adapt trauma-informed practices. However, it is not a guide for first responders. It is not designed to address immediate crisis intervention or acute primary care for victim-survivors of trauma. Furthermore, this book is not a guide to primary care by religious professionals, instead complementing existing resources that focus on pastoral care for victim-survivors. This book is also not primarily a work of theology or biblical studies, though it is informed by these conversations. Rather, this book adopts a trauma-informed approach to the way we understand and practice Christian ethics.

As a reader, you have the freedom to choose how you engage with this book. You are part of an audience that ranges from subject matter experts to first-year college students to seminarians to priests, pastors, deacons, and lay leaders in local congregations. For those engaging in scholarly research, the footnotes and bibliography provide detailed references to the literature. For readers bringing practical questions from a perspective of lived faith, the practices of discipleship discussed in Part Two provide a good entry point to this book. Throughout the book, you will note places to pause and engage questions for yourself—whether alone, in a study group or classroom setting, or with friends and colleagues in your faith community.

Whatever your picture of God and reason for engaging this text, I hope that this book deepens your understanding of Christian moral witness. I invite dialogue and partnership with other traditions. I write to Christians and all persons of good will—of other faiths or of no religion at all. For Christians, I explore how to live out our faith in Christ in ways that contribute to human flourishing (Jn 10:10) and the reconciliation of the entire world to God (2 Cor. 5:18). For persons of other faiths, I find common connection in the transcendent reality we call God. I aim to contribute to dialogue and mutual understanding, strengthening our moral community. For all readers seeking to live morally and contribute to the common good, I provide an ethic that can be practiced in community regardless of one's own faith commitments.

All are welcome on this journey.

Discussion Questions

1 Consider your social location and relative privilege to those around you. How does your location shape your experience of the world?

2 What are the most pressing moral issues facing your community?

ACKNOWLEDGMENTS

The book owes much to many, and it is difficult to pinpoint its origin. Thank you to Choi Hee Ahn, director of the Boston University School of Theology Anna Howard Shaw Center, who invited me to speak on the topic "Imagining God's Justice" at the annual Women in the World conference in 2013. While it seems a long time ago, this keynote address prepared the ground for the larger project, which intersected with my work supporting victim-survivors of clergy sexual misconduct at the General Commission on the Status and Role of Women in The United Methodist Church. Gratitude also goes to Mary Cheng, Praveena Balasundaram, and other staff at United Women in Faith, who entrusted me to write the 2021 Spiritual Growth Mission Study, *Bearing Witness in the Kin-dom*. This study serves as the core (Part Two) of the present book, and I appreciate permission to reuse and adapt this material. A special word of thanks is due to those persons who shared their stories of ministry with me: Garlinda Burton, Liz Fulmer, Eunice Musa Iliya, Cindy Andrade Johnson, Tweedy Sombrero Navarrete, HiRho Park, Jenny Phillips, and Marilyn Zehring. I would also like to thank Pamela Brubaker and Jane Dutton for allowing me to quote from their sermons. This research followed appropriate human subject research protocols, and all interview participants gave informed consent for their words to be published.

There are many friends and colleagues I would like to thank. Much appreciation to members of the Society of Christian Ethics who provided feedback on my presentation, "Bearing Witness to Survivors of Sexual Assault: A Trauma-Informed Ethic of Love, Justice, and Solidarity," January 2021. Thank you, as well, to colleagues in the Diaconal Studies project, who provided feedback on my presentation, "Developing a Trauma-Informed Diaconal Praxis," during a consultation in April 2023. I also extend my appreciation to members of the theology and ethics group of the Oxford Institute of Methodist Theological Studies, who provided critical feedback on the chapter "Climate Change and Empire" in August 2024. Additionally, key individuals offered feedback and encouragement at different stages of manuscript development. My appreciation is by no means limited to those few named here: Karen V. Guth, Mark Harris, Patricia Beattie Jung, Ellen Ott Marshall, Rebecca Nyros, Kevin J. O'Brien, Mike Schutz, Rose Shepley, Linwood Smith, and Josie Stephens. Thank you especially to Kate Ott for a careful reading and insightful feedback on the manuscript during the latter stage of development and to the anonymous peer reviewer engaged by Bloomsbury/T&T Clark, who provided detailed, constructive feedback on every chapter of the manuscript. These readers provided immensely helpful and insightful critique—more feedback than I was able to incorporate into the final project. The remaining deficiencies of the manuscript are all my own.

A work spanning so many years draws on much prior writing and preparation. The following articles and chapters of mine are reused with permission:

A portion of Chapter 1.1 is adapted from "Reenvisioning Christian Ethics: An Introduction and Invitation," *Religions* 2020, 11(2), 74, https://doi. org/10.3390/rel11020074.

Chapter 1.2 is adapted from "Trauma-Informed Pedagogy for the Religious and Theological Higher Education Classroom," *Religions* 2020, 11(9), 449, https://doi.org/10.3390/rel11090449.

Chapter 1.3 is based on "Bearing Witness as Social Action: Religious Ethics and Trauma-Informed Response," *Trauma Care* 2021, 1(1), 49–63, https://doi. org/10.3390/traumacare1010005.

Chapter 1.4 is an adaptation of "Developing a Trauma-Informed Diaconal Praxis," in *Diaconal Studies: Lived Theology for the Church in North America*, ed. Nessan and Stephens, 133–46 (Regnum Books International, 2024).

Chapters in "Part Two: Practices of Discipleship" are based on *Bearing Witness in the Kin-dom: Living into the Church's Moral Witness through Radical Discipleship* (United Methodist Women, 2021).

Chapter 3.1 is a revision of "Bearing Witness: A Trauma-Informed Approach to Christian Ethics," *Journal of Feminist Studies in Religion* 39 no. 1 (2023): 155–74, https://dx.doi.org/10.2979/jfs.2023.a893198.

Chapter 3.3 incorporates material from two articles: "A Deacon's Eye for Healing Congregations," *Currents in Theology and Mission* 42, no. 3 (2015): 213–19; and "Community Healing after Spiritual Leader Misconduct," in *Responding to Spiritual Leader Misconduct*, ed. Lauren D. Sawyer, Emily Cohen, and Annie Mesaros, 181–6 (FaithTrust Institute, 2022).

Heartfelt thanks to my editor Anna Turton at T&T Clark/Bloomsbury for her confidence in this project, diligence in securing quality peer reviews, encouragement for creating the series *T&T Clark Enquiries in Embodiment, Sexuality, and Social Ethics*, and patience in awaiting a long-delayed manuscript. Thank you also to assistant editor Jack Curtin for his care and skill in guiding this manuscript to publication. Finally, much love and appreciation for my supportive family: Myka, Zeke, and Cecily.

ABBREVIATIONS

ACE	Adverse Childhood Experience
CDC	Centers for Disease Control and Prevention
Covid-19	Coronavirus Disease 2019
DARVO	Deny, Attack, & Reverse Victim and Offender
IPCC	Intergovernmental Panel on Climate Change
LGBTQIA+	Lesbian, gay, bisexual, transgender, queer, intersex, asexual, and others
MSF	Doctors Without Borders/Médecins Sans Frontières
NIV	New International Version
NRSV	New Revised Standard Version
PTSD	Post-traumatic stress disorder
SAMHSA	Substance Abuse and Mental Health Services Administration
UMC	(The) United Methodist Church
UMPH	United Methodist Publishing House
US	United States (adjectival form)
USCCB	United States Conference of Catholic Bishops
WCC	World Council of Churches

Introduction

This introduction to Christian ethics provides a constructive account of living in love, justice, and solidarity in a traumatized world. Grounded in God's love for all of creation, this book offers hope for individuals and communities seeking to live as neighbors. Bearing witness recognizes the inherent dignity of every person. It expands the love commandment to address systemic injustices and oppressions through practices of attentive presence, historical clarity, and meaningful participation. This trauma-informed approach to Christian ethics equips us to address tough moral problems, including sexual violence, racism, climate change, and institutional betrayal. Together, as neighbors of many faiths, we can imagine God's will for a more just world and join in bringing it about.

Christian ethics is rooted in baptism, in which we are welcomed as children of God. The baptismal vow "to resist evil, injustice, and oppression in whatever forms they present themselves" leads Christians to work together for a more just world as we grow in the life of faith, both individually and together.[1] We find ourselves part of a larger community, the church, bearing witness to Christ and each other. The moral witness of the church is our human participation in God's good work. Human dignity, basic goods, justice for victims, and full flourishing of creation are essential commitments of this witness. Attention to flourishing in community prompts us to imagine God's justice and notice when we fall short. These ethical commitments stem from God's gracious activity in us through the Holy Spirit and our response through a life of discipleship. All of this is rooted in God's salvific work to make new all of creation.

Christians often contrast faith and action, separating our testimony about what God has done in our lives from our own ethical actions and decisions. However, the two are intertwined, God's grace and our response. As any child knows who has sung, "They will know we are Christians by our love," our treatment of others is a witness to our faith. Or, as one New Testament author put it, "faith by itself, if it is not accompanied by action, is dead" (Jas 2:17, NIV). As a Methodist theologian and ethicist, drawing on John Wesley's understanding of God's gracious presence and our

---

[1] *The United Methodist Hymnal: Book of United Methodist Worship* (UMPH, 1989), 34.

response as a theological framework for the life of faith,[2] I view human moral agency in light of God's grace-filled action in the Holy Spirit. Personal and social holiness are one and the same. We grow in faith together: as individuals, as a church, as a community, and as the world that God so loves.

This book examines how belief in Christ leads to participation in God's saving action so that all of creation may flourish. Christian ethics helps the church and its members to bear witness to the will of God for a more just world. Thus, this book explores moral witness as both an individual and collective process that considers context, establishes a justice-focused framework, and inspires action. Addressing issues such as eugenics, the Doctrine of Discovery, and racial discrimination, this approach to Christian ethics takes responsibility for past unjust actions, propelling us toward more faithful witness in the future. Furthermore, as active participants in the establishment of just practices in church and society, we must consider how our faith impacts the world and what is needed now. These facets of the moral life are explored through scripture readings, case studies, ministry profiles, and selections from ecclesial teachings. Discipleship and community provide the context for living out Christian ethics.

Kin-dom

Family imagery helps us understand our connectedness to God and each other. Jesus chose this image when he taught his disciples to pray, "Our father in heaven, hallowed be your name" (Mt. 6:9, NRSV). We are God's children. God is our father—not a distant patriarch but an intimate, divine "daddy." The image of God as loving parent is not bound by our gendered ways of thinking, either. In Isaiah, God speaks of Godself: "As a mother comforts her child, so I will comfort you" (Isa. 66:13a). God, our loving parent, brings all of humanity into familial relation. We are kin in Christ.

Ada María Isasi-Díaz, a trailblazing *mujerista* theologian, proposed *kin-dom* as a metaphor for the reign of God and our human relatedness within this new reality. The word *kin-dom* indicates more than kinship. It signals not only a family relationship but also something bigger, something with political significance. It is a modern interpretation of *basileia*, a word traditionally translated as kingdom or reign. Jesus's first sermon proclaimed the dawning of the kin-dom of God on earth. In the gospel of Mark, the first words out of Jesus's mouth refer to this political reality: "The time is fulfilled, and the *basileia* of God has come near; repent, and believe in the good news" (Mk 1:15). Kin-dom was no tangential emphasis, no brief aside before getting to the good news. Jesus was not just clearing his throat before calling for us to repent and believe. The nearness of the kin-dom *is* the good news. This is what Jesus taught us to desire when praying to God: "Your *basileia* come, Your will be done, on earth as it is in heaven" (Mt. 6:10, NRSV). Thus, *kin-dom* refers to a reign built not by kings but on the radical notion that if we recognized

---

[2]John Wesley, "The Scripture Way of Salvation," in *John Wesley's Sermons: An Anthology*, ed. Albert C. Outler and Richard P. Heitzenrater, 372–80 (Abingdon, 1991). For a detailed exposition of Wesleyan theology, see Randy L. Maddox, *Responsible Grace: John Wesley's Practical Theology* (Kingswood, 1994).

the kinship of God's creation, we would take care of each other as we do our own family.[3]

The political implications of Jesus' arrival, proclamation, and prayer caused immediate jubilation and concern—depending on one's social location. Anticipating the birth of her son, Mary sang out, "My soul magnifies the Lord, and my spirit rejoices in God my Savior ... He has brought done the powerful from their thrones and lifted up the lowly ..." (Lk. 1:46-47, 52). The political leaders of Jesus's time found this imminent kingdom / kin-dom of God threatening. Learning of his birth, Herod the king sought to kill the infant Jesus, causing Mary and Joseph to flee to Egypt with their child (Mt. 2:13-16). Later in Jesus' life, after three years of public ministry, the Roman governor of Judea, Pilate, responded with lethal force, executing Jesus, "king of the Jews," as an enemy of the Roman state (Mt. 27:11). The cross on which Jesus was killed—the equivalent to a modern-day electric chair—symbolizes both salvation and Christian resistance to state-sponsored violence. In Christ, God's kin-dom is proclaimed and embodied above all earthly powers.

Now we have gone from preaching to meddling. This is dangerous rhetoric. It is one thing to promote human kinship. It is another thing entirely to incite political rebellion—or so it would seem. Yet, the gospel of Christ is inherently political. Jesus, according to his own testimony, came to bring good news to the poor, to proclaim release to the captives and recovery of sight to the blind, to let the oppressed go free, and to proclaim the year of the Lord's favor (Lk. 4:18-19). One cannot speak out against poverty, mass incarceration, inadequate health care, systemic injustice, and inherited debt without treading on politics. These issues touch the entire human family, God's family. Jesus promised to upend conventional power arrangements. No one would be unaffected. To proclaim release, recovery, freedom, and forgiveness is central to the good news of Jesus Christ and is a political project. This is kin-dom work. For Jesus, this risky agenda led to his arrest, torture, and death. A choice to follow Christ is just as political and equally risky.

Bearing Witness to God and Neighbor

Christian ethics is about being shaped by and living into the kin-dom of God. Through the moral witness of the church, we participate in God's gracious response to suffering and injustice. This deliberate effort is rooted in Christian faith. It is based on what we believe about God and God's intention to reconcile all creation. As members of the kin-dom, we may act individually but never alone. We live as God's family. Christian ethics is responsive to the groans of humanity and all of creation. Our trust is not placed in ourselves, our leaders, or any human institution. We do not attempt it under our own power but by the power of God working through us. Individually and together, we join with each other in what God is doing in the world. We bear witness to God's gracious presence in ways that make a material difference

---

[3]Ada María Isasi-Díaz, "Kin-dom of God: A Mujerista Proposal," in *In Our Own Voices: Latino/a Renditions of Theology*, ed. Benjamín Valentín, 171–89 (Orbis, 2010), 179.

to all of creation, all persons, and especially victim-survivors of trauma and those who are most vulnerable.[4]

There is more than one way to bear witness to the will of God for a more just world: we can witness both to what is right and to what is wrong in the world. Personal faith-sharing provides first-hand witnessing to God's will done on earth. When we testify to our faith, we provide a first-hand account of what God in Christ has done and is doing in our lives. "We declare to you what was from the beginning, what we have heard, what we have seen with our eyes, what we have looked at and touched with our hands, concerning the word of life" (1 Jn 1:1). This is an evangelistic proclamation, telling our neighbor about our experience of God.[5] There is another way to witness to God, though. More often, people (ourselves included) do not conform to God's will, and we must call out actions, traditions, and structures that work against the kin-dom. Thus, we can also bear witness to God's will thwarted on earth. Bearing witness in the face of injustice draws attention to the distance between human experience and God, often due to human failings. When reality falls short of what we know of God's vision of righteousness, we must be present for and with each other. This form of witness often requires us to cross boundaries of culture and geography through discipleship and mission.[6] We bear witness to the reality of suffering so that it may no longer be so.

To bear witness to another's story, particularly stories of suffering and harm, is a remarkably loving thing to do. Bearing witness does not stop at listening. When we bear witness, we become an ally, an upstander, proving neighbor like the Samaritan assisting the man he found beaten on the side of the road. The reality of the gospel is found in relationship. Regarding the body of Christ, composed of many members, Paul declared, "If one member suffers, all suffer together with it; if one member is honored, all rejoice together with it" (1 Cor. 12:26). This is true both within and outside of the church. We live in an interconnected world.

When we bear witness habitually, intentionally, and with a preferential option for persons who have been marginalized or oppressed, we begin to realize God's kin-dom. The journey of bearing witness engages us not only in the work of love but also in the work of justice, inviting us into solidarity and community. The struggles of my neighbor affect me. As Martin Luther King Jr. stated so eloquently, "Injustice anywhere is a threat to justice everywhere."[7] We are in it together, each with different

---

[4] Traci West adopted the term *victim-survivor* to draw attention to the moral agency of those harmed by violence and sexual abuse. Traci C. West, *Wounds of the Spirit: Black Women, Violence, and Resistance Ethics* (New York University Press, 1999), 1. See also Carolyn Bratnober, "Traci C. West: Disruptive Activism, Ministry, and Scholarship," in *Challenging Bias against Women Academics in Religion*, Women in Religion, vol. 2, ed. Colleen D. Hurting, 111 (Atla Open Press, 2021), https://doi.org/10.31046/atlaopenpress.46.

[5] For approaches to evangelism resonant with this book's trauma-informed ethics, see Charles Kiser and Elaine A. Heath, *Trauma-Informed Evangelism: Cultivating Communities of Wounded Healers* (Eerdmans, 2023); and Elaine A. Robinson, *Godbearing: Evangelism Reconceived* (Pilgrim, 2006), 92.

[6] My approach has much in common with "relationship-based mission." David W. Scott, *Crossing Boundaries: Sharing God's Good News through Mission* (Wesley's Foundery, 2019), 76.

[7] Martin Luther King, Jr., "Letter from Birmingham City Jail," in *A Testament of Hope: The Essential Writings and Speeches of Martin Luther King, Jr.*, ed. James Melvin Washington, 289–302 (HarperSanFrancisco, 1986), 290.

gifts and perspectives. May we learn from each other and witness together through the kin-dom we share as children of God.

Discussion Questions

1 Bearing witness to the experiences of our neighbors requires more listening than speaking. In what ways is listening an expression of love?

2 Think of an experience when someone listened deeply to you during a difficult time in your life. What did you find meaningful about their act of bearing witness?

3 When we are attentive to suffering, we bear witness to "God's will thwarted." Have you ever thought about social injustice in this way? What difference does it make that we are "in it together" in an interconnected world?

Trauma and Christian Ethics

Trauma is the wound to body, mind, and spirit resulting from unspeakable, life-threatening horror. The widespread existence of trauma has only been recently recognized and studied. Since the mid-1990s, the concept of trauma has had a growing influence on multiple disciplines of theological study, particularly pastoral care, systematic theology, biblical studies, and practical theology. To love our neighbors, to truly seek the best interests of our neighbors, we must enter relationships in ways that do not compound the trauma histories already present. We must do no harm—or at least strive to minimize the harm we might do inadvertently. Furthermore, we can do good. By bearing witness to survivors of trauma, we can contribute to healing and wholeness.

The field of Christian ethics is indebted to Traci West for her early, insistent, and continuing work to address the trauma of sexual violence against Black women. West has researched and written about the emotional and spiritual impact of traumatic violence against women since the 1990s. She was one of the first Christian ethicists to engage Judith Herman's research on trauma.[8] Specifically, her book, *Wounds of the Spirit*, provides a model of resistance ethics to support and enhance the agency of Black women victim-survivors of intimate partner abuse and sexual violence. West proves a valuable conversation partner for developing an explicitly trauma-informed approach to Christian ethics, and I devote an entire chapter to her work (Chapter 3.1).

This book is deeply informed by the work of Judith Herman, a psychiatrist and pioneer in trauma studies. Herman asserted that "trauma is truly a social problem"

---

[8]West's pioneering work of bridging trauma studies and Christian ethics is not widely recognized in a field Shelly Rambo described as dominated by "white, Christian, cis-gendered scholars from North America"—herself included, though she made no mention of West's writings. Shelly Rambo, "Foreword," in *Feminist Trauma Theologies*, ed. O'Donnell and Cross, xv–xviii (SCM, 2020).

requiring "justice from the larger community."[9] Through interviews, she learned that "first and foremost," survivors need "recognition of their humanity" in order to heal.[10] The path to healing for survivors is thus relational, involving self, perpetrators, bystanders, and the larger moral community. Furthermore, Herman encouraged bystanders "to ally with survivors in the name of human dignity," that is, "to take action in solidarity with those who have been harmed."[11] Taking cues from Herman, this book synthesizes trauma studies and transformative models of Christian social ethics for the purpose of strengthening moral community.

In this book, the connections I draw between Herman's understanding of trauma and the themes of dignity, love, justice, and solidarity resonate with the work of other Christian social ethicists. For example, Rebecca Todd Peters' *Solidarity Ethics* is "rooted in the mutual recognition of the human dignity that everyone possesses."[12] Recognition of mutual dignity supports the work of solidarity, allowing for "moral equality" in relationships between persons of diverse backgrounds and social locations "to work together toward the common good."[13] Such is the case when bystanders desire to join in solidarity with trauma survivors. Elizabeth Vasko's *Theology for Bystanders* explores "compassionate solidarity" as an antidote to "unethical passivity," or apathy.[14] The bystander's compassion must respect the other's dignity, be moved by empathy, remember past exploitations, and seek change: "true solidarity has as its goal radical social transformation and emerges in the practices of mutuality and compassion."[15] Thus, solidarity involves a transformative encounter between persons of unequal power—social, political, and otherwise. From a Roman Catholic perspective, Marcus Mescher's *The Ethics of Encounter* explores the dynamics of these relationships in much the same terms—dignity, love, justice, solidarity—and emphasizes the role of imagination in helping individuals transcend their distinct social contexts.[16]

The present book shares with Herman, Peters, Vasko, and Mescher a social context of relative privilege. It also shares with these authors a concern for attending to the ethics of social disparities, particularly how to engage in relationships of solidarity across differentials of power and privilege. Each of us addresses our writing primarily to readers who often experience a degree of relative power and agency in relation to the neighbors they encounter. Thus, Peters addressed persons benefiting from first-world economies of neoliberal globalization, explaining, "the ethic of solidarity can be understood as a form of liberation theology for the privileged."[17] Vasko's focus on *bystanders* is also meant to draw attention to disparities of suffering and social privilege, addressing the responsibilities of those who witness the suffering

---

[9]Judith L. Herman, *Truth and Repair: How Trauma Survivors Envision Justice* (Basic Books, 2023), 3.
[10]Herman, 79.
[11]Herman, 37.
[12]Rebecca Todd Peters, *Solidarity Ethics: Transformation in a Globalized World* (Fortress, 2014), 10.
[13]Peters, 41.
[14]Elisabeth T. Vasko, *Beyond Apathy: A Theology for Bystanders* (Fortress, 2015), 86, 219.
[15]Vasko, 86, 201, 204.
[16]Marcus Mescher, *The Ethics of Encounter: Christian Neighbor Love as a Practice of Solidarity* (Orbis, 2020), 79–80, 114–16.
[17]Peters, *Solidarity Ethics*, 116.

of others.[18] Likewise, I focus on the ethical responsibilities of the bystander rather than the victim—though many people find themselves in both categories at different points in their lives.[19] Inevitably, my readers occupy diverse relationships of relative power and privilege as they bear witness, using their power on behalf of and in solidarity with survivors of trauma.

Attentive readers will already notice significant themes and influences shaping my approach to Christian ethics. Scripture shapes my understanding of the moral life. In particular, the double love commandment provides a starting point for theological reflection. A presenting issue is, "How do I love my neighbor as myself?" Appropriate self-regard provides important balance to the task of ethics. I also presume that God is active and involved in the world and in our lives. Grace, the responsive and proactive presence of the Holy Spirit, animates and empowers us to live ethically. My use of the term *kin-dom* signals an engagement with liberation theology—particularly the work of Isasi-Díaz, who coined the term *mujerista* to describe theology and ethics emanating from the lived experience of Latinas. Yet, my engagement with liberationist, womanist, feminist, and *mujerista* perspectives is complicated by my social location as a white male. Thus, I adopt an intersectional and multidisciplinary approach to Christian ethics to address the world's complexity. I write with the tools of Christian social ethics, attending to the roles and responsibilities of individuals, communities, and institutions.

Moral philosophy provides inspiration. I embrace H. Richard Niebuhr's prompt for moral theology, asking "What is going on?"[20] Context matters. Love is not an abstraction but rather an action in real places at particular times. To love our neighbors requires an awareness of what is going on in the world. This awareness quickly exposes politically charged issues. We must pay attention. Niebuhr developed his conception of the Christian moral life around the image of "the responsible self." Along with Niebuhr, I recognize the social nature of the self. The moral life is not a solitary endeavor. Thus, for Christian ethics, I emphasize discipleship in community and presume the church as an important context of formation, accountability, and action. The church's moral witness expresses Christian ethics nurtured and amplified through a community of faith. More broadly, a trauma-informed approach to Christian ethics contributes to the nurture and development of moral community in society.

Discussion Questions

1 How does the "bearing witness" model differ from other approaches to Christian ethics, such as rule-based or virtue-based ethics?

2 What are your initial thoughts about what it means to be a bystander, ally, or person bearing witness to someone else?

---

[18]Vasko, *Beyond Apathy*, 7.

[19]West emphasized the victim-survivor's own resources. In contrast, Jennifer Beste emphasized limitations to the victim's capacity for moral agency in her exploration of the theological and ethical implications for communities of faith and those bearing witness to victims. Jennifer Erin Beste, *God and the Victim: Traumatic Intrusions on Grace and Freedom* (Oxford University Press, 2007), 107–28.

[20]H. Richard Niebuhr, *The Responsible Self: An Essay in Christian Moral Philosophy* (HarperSanFrancisco, [1963]1978), 60.

3   The terms *dignity, love, justice,* and *solidarity* will feature prominently in this book. Write down your initial definitions and understandings of these words. How do you think these concepts are differentiated and connected?

Outline of the Book

The three parts of this book examine theoretical foundations, practices of discipleship, and contemporary challenges, respectively.[21] **Part One: Foundations** provides the basis for bearing witness as a trauma-informed approach to Christian ethics. The first chapter, **Reenvisioning Christian Ethics,** articulates my underlying convictions and assumptions and examines social location. My understanding of Christian ethics is real, perspectival, dialogical, collaborative, and purposeful. Correspondingly, I describe the work as awe-filled, discerning, responsive, participatory, and hopeful. Thus, I invite intersectional, interdisciplinary, and intercultural approaches as we partner with all members of global society to promote the common good, shared justice, and full flourishing of all creation. The next chapter, **Trauma-Informed Response,** introduces psychological trauma and the paradigm of trauma-informed care. Trauma is not confined to individual experiences of single horrifying events— trauma can be collective (community-wide, for example, Covid-19), epigenetic (inherited or intergenerational), social-cultural (e.g., racism), complex (involving a series of events), or vicarious. This chapter also discusses care for caregivers, who must deal with their own traumatic pasts as well as the secondary effects of encountering, bearing witness to, and supporting traumatized individuals and communities. The chapter **Bearing Witness** constructs a framework for trauma-informed Christian ethics from a wide range of disciplinary and faith perspectives. The work of trauma response and recovery involves transcendent and moral facets, as described by Judith Herman and the Substance Abuse and Mental Health Services Administration. This chapter invokes a broad understanding of spirituality, transcendence, and faith, drawing on Christian, Jewish, Muslim, Buddhist, Sikh, and Humanist traditions. Bearing witness becomes a social action, a moral response with inherent religious dimensions and spiritual implications, with the potential to address personal, systemic, and political aspects of trauma response and recovery. The fourth chapter **Diakonia** explores points of connection between trauma-informed response and diaconal praxis and methodology. This discussion provides guidance for diaconal workers bearing witness to individual victim-survivors, equipping both to participate in social change movements for justice, healing, and possible reconciliation.

Part Two: Practices of Discipleship explains and illustrates each moment with concrete examples from the life of faith, both individual and communal. The chapter **Grounded Being** reckons with our created existence. Moral witness is grounded in

---

[21]To develop a trauma-informed approach to Christian social ethics, I engage with multiple disciplines from diverse perspectives. This approach requires me to cover a lot of ground in one volume. Throughout this introductory textbook, I provide tools and illustrations to equip and inspire my readers to imagine how they will practice trauma-informed Christian ethics in their diverse contexts. The combination of foundations, practices, and challenges presented in this book equips readers for this task.

prevenient grace and the belief that each and every human being is created in God's image and loved by God. Recognizing each other's dignity spurs commitments to equality and human rights, despite the risks that this moral witness may entail. The next chapter, **Attentive Presence,** moves from recognition to empathy, expressed by loving the neighbor in the present. Empathy uncovers suffering and prompts a concern for meeting basic human needs, especially for the most vulnerable. The concept of *diakonia,* service to others through discipleship, illustrates how bearing witness in the present moment leads to consideration of past and future moments in the church's moral witness. The chapter **Historical Clarity** reckons with the past. Coming to terms with the reality of brokenness and our complicity in it involves a process of grieving as well as repentance, which is an exercise of memory. Repentance requires practices of justice involving personal and communal restitution, healthier mindsets, more equitable structures of power, and new forms of accountability within the church and other institutions. The chapter **Meaningful Participation** reckons with the future. Joining in solidarity, we can participate in challenging and transcending structures of violence. Inspired by God's will for a more just world, we can imagine a future of reconciliation and *shalom* in which all creation will flourish.

Part Three: Contemporary Challenges dives deeper into specific ethical issues using the framework of bearing witness. The chapter **Racism and Sexual Violence** addresses race, racism, and violence against Black women, engaging the intersectional work of Traci West. The chapter **Climate Change and Empire** turns full attention to humanity's relationship with the rest of creation, viewing the earth itself as a victim-survivor of human-induced traumas. Motivated by neighbor-love and guided by grace, the process of bearing witness attunes us to God's will and helps us imagine God's intention for creation. The chapter **Abuse and Betrayal** addresses sexual violence and institutional betrayal in church settings. Prioritizing the needs of victim-survivors, healing congregations can become places of courage rather than harm, offering restitution and repair after abuse.

The book concludes with reflections on **Strengthening Moral Community.** Trauma-informed ethics is ultimately the work of a community of persons bearing witness to trauma as a political project of social justice and liberation.

Discussion Questions

1 Consider why you will read this book. What questions do you bring to the text, based on your needs and vocational context? If you are a student assigned to read this text, reflect on how this book addresses specific course learning goals.

2 Consider how you will read this book. Which parts will you read in detail and which parts will you skim or skip altogether? Where will you begin? If you are a scholar or graduate student, dive into the footnotes. If you are a church leader or reflective practitioner, consider starting with Part Two, Practices of Discipleship. Be smart about your choices!

PART ONE

Foundations

1.1

Reenvisioning Christian Ethics

The responsibility of Christians to join with members of global society for more rigorous ethical thought, reflection, and action is more important now than ever. We live in an age of "wicked problems"—foremost among them are anthropogenic climate change and widespread experiences of trauma. A wicked problem has complex causes; it cannot be solved but only addressed in better or worse ways.[1] We also live in an age of alternative and contested facts. Moral disagreements arise not only from differences in values and commitments but also from differences in perception about scientific knowledge and historical events. When the real recedes from view, morality has precarious standing. How shall we reenvision Christian ethics in this context?

Christian ethics is more accurately described as a field of inquiry, study, and practice than an academic discipline. The study of ethics includes historical, descriptive, critical, constructive, and applied projects on countless topics. Christian ethics includes diverse methods, approaches, theological perspectives, starting points, purposes, and partner disciplines, such as theology, philosophy, and sociology. While informed by theology and philosophy, my approach most clearly falls within the stream of discourse known as Christian social ethics, given my attention to the material circumstances and embodied realities of persons, cultures, and institutions within specific historical contexts.

This chapter envisions Christian ethics as a liberative endeavor open to the insights of multiple disciplines and attentive to social location. I begin by revealing my basic assumptions, underlying convictions, and worldview. This self-examination is aided by encounter, dialogue, and material collaborations with others. I am intentional about engaging with persons inside and outside my immediate spheres of religious conviction and social perspective. Then, I discuss the way social location shapes moral agency and responsibility. There are barriers of power and privilege to participation in God's kin-dom of mutuality, especially for persons who are not part of a marginalized community. Thus, participation in an ethic of liberation demands different responsibilities of persons within and outside of marginalized communities.

---

[1]Willis Jenkins, "Working with Politics," in *T&T Clark Handbook of Christian Theology and Climate Change*, ed. Conradie and Koster, 70–82 (T&T Clark, 2020), 72.

Christian Ethics

My understanding of Christian ethics is real, perspectival, dialogical, collaborative, and purposeful. Correspondingly, I describe the task of Christian ethics as awe-filled, discerning, responsive, participatory, and hopeful. I reenvision Christian ethics as a confluence of intersectional, interdisciplinary, and intercultural approaches expanding beyond the academy, the church, and religion itself as we partner with all members of global society for the common good, shared justice, and full flourishing of all creation.

Real and Awe-filled

Envisioning necessarily presumes that there is something to see. Christianity is a religion based on the belief in one God in three persons, embodying divine truth and love. My understanding of Christian ethics is premised on a reality shaped by this unity—what Howard Thurman described as "the sound of the genuine" and what H. Richard Niebuhr understood as "that transcendent absolute for whom ... whatever is, is good."[2] The one commonality, the one link connecting all of reality—the genuine and the absolute—is God. "The world is an intelligible whole in which all things are related to one another and to God."[3] Christian ethics is about something experienced as real and, on some level, understandable. Thus, not only do I seek some degree of commonality, no matter how distant, between various approaches to Christian ethics, I also expect some coherency—not in the sense of coming to the same answers from different angles but in the sense of contributing to our thinking about a shared reality, despite differences in how we may experience it.

My ontological realism should not be confused with a strategic compromise to be "realistic" or an identification with a particular school of thought, such as Christian Realism. It is a more basic conviction, an awe-filled sense of creaturely relation to our Creator, who shapes the arc of the universe—that orienting "center of value" at the heart of H. Richard Niebuhr's "radical monotheism."[4] Christian ethics shares this realism with theology: it "allows human beings to advance particular descriptions and normative claims about what is most essentially real or true."[5] I believe God and God's presence are real, intelligible, yet never fully understood. I stand in awe even as I am drawn into relation with the transcendent. Thus, I prioritize with Niebuhr the question "What is going on?" and expect a glimpse of something real in response.[6]

---

[2]Howard Thurman, "The Sound of the Genuine," *The Spelman Messenger* 96, no. 4 (1980): 14–15, https://radar.auctr.edu/islandora/object/sc.001.messenger%3A1980.03/; H. Richard Niebuhr, *Radical Monotheism and Western Culture: With Supplementary Essays* (Harper & Row, [1943]1970), 112.

[3]Robin Lovin et al., "Introduction: Theology as Interdisciplinary Inquiry: The Virtues of Humility and Hope," in *Theology as Interdisciplinary Inquiry: Learning with and from the Natural and Human Sciences*, ed. Robin W. Lovin and Joshua Mauldin, xxiv (Eerdmans, 2017).

[4]Niebuhr, *Radical Monotheism*, 100.

[5]Christian Scharen and Aana Marie Vigen, with contributors, *Ethnography as Christian Theology and Ethics* (Continuum, 2011), 3.

[6]H. Richard Niebuhr, *The Responsible Self: An Essay in Christian Moral Philosophy* (HarperSanFrancisco, [1963]1978), 60.

My approach to Christian ethics presumes an underlying reality in God, no matter our differing perspectives.

Perspectival and Discerning

An assumption of shared reality does not necessarily imply a shared understanding or identical experience of that reality. Philosophy is filled with stories illustrating the difficulty of truth and perception, from Plato's cave to the folktale from India about six blind men describing an elephant. Humanity's unrelenting desire for knowledge continually chafes against the limitations of our perspectives, which are the only windows we have available to see the real, "For now we see through a glass, darkly ..." (1 Cor. 13:12, King James Version). Our glimpses of the real and true are necessarily partial and incomplete. Just as all theology is contextual, all Christian ethics is perspectival. Like human personality, each person has a perspective that is in certain respects, like all others, like some others, and like no other.[7]

Acknowledging the perspectival nature of moral vision does not commit me to recognizing every perspective or interpretation therefrom as equally valid or ethically binding, though. A perspectival approach does not mean that "anything goes."[8] Recognizing the validity of differing perspectives no more leads to extreme relativism than recognizing an underlying reality leads to absolutism. It does, though, raise the possibility of error. My own perspective could be wrong, misinformed, or myopic—particularly so when warped by the forces of social privilege and refracted through hegemonic power.[9] There is a need for discernment. Perspective, though limiting, provides vantage for critical discernment; in fact, it is the only vantage for critique I have. There is no "view from nowhere." To exercise critical discernment is to stand somewhere while acknowledging the limitations of my own perspective.

Reenvisioning presumes that what is seen can be seen anew, in a different and perhaps more helpful way, and for this, we need assistance from others. James Gustafson described "the fault of rationality" as misconstruals of reality based on my limited perspective, compounded by my refusal to "submit them to criticism and correction by others."[10] I hasten to add, we particularly need criticism and correction from persons with perspectives that differ from our own. For example, as a white, cisgender male of comfortable economic status in the United States, I must be open to the corrective insights of Black womanist ethicists, for example, who draw on moral struggles and oppressions that are not part of my own experience (Cannon 1988, 5–6). For this reason, a perspectival and discerning approach to Christian ethics must also be collaborative and participatory.

---

[7]Emmanuel Y. Lartey, *In Living Color: An Intercultural Approach to Pastoral Care and Counseling*, 2nd ed. (Jessica Kingsley, 2003), 34, drawing on Clyde Kluckhohn and Henry A. Murray, eds., *Personality in Nature, Society, and Culture* (Knopf, 1948), 35.

[8]Scharen and Vigen made a similar point addressing the fear of relativism in relation to prioritizing human experience, particularly embodied knowing, as a source for Christian theology and ethics. Scharen and Vigen, *Ethnography*, 61.

[9]See, for example, Elizabeth Sweeny Block, "White Privilege and the Erroneous Conscience: Rethinking Moral Culpability and Ignorance," *Journal of the Society of Christian Ethics* 39, no. 2 (2019): 357–74.

[10]James M. Gustafson, *Ethics from a Theocentric Perspective: Volume One: Theology and Ethics* (University of Chicago Press, 1981), 300–1.

Collaborative and Participatory

Collaboration is at the heart of Christian social ethics; it is not optional. This shared work, or co-laboring (*colaboración*), involves individuals as well as entire communities in the task of Christian ethics. Emilie Townes, for example, emphasized that "dismantling the cultural production of evil … must be a group project."[11] It is in our struggle for wisdom and survival, "en la lucha," as Ada María Isasi-Díaz described it, that we encounter the real.[12] Christian ethics can be an emancipatory praxis. When Christian ethics is done in a participatory community, when we partner with each other to gain perspectives unavailable to any one person, we build networks capable of transcending our limited perspectives. For this task, we need each other.

Christian ethics is not just for students in the classroom or members of a scholarly guild. Our collective task requires bringing faith communities and the wider public into our discursive and scholarly spaces, not merely as subjects of research but as interlocutors defining and shaping what it means to do Christian ethics.[13] Churches and practitioners (clergy, social workers, community organizers, journalists, bus drivers, and many others) are essential conversation partners. Furthermore, the task requires that we engage the community, roll up our sleeves, and view everyone around us as potential collaborators in this most practical endeavor, learning to hear and live in harmony with the sound of the genuine. We might even be audacious enough to attempt "pragmatic solidarity with those who suffer," as we join in the struggle.[14] However, participatory collaboration is a means, not a guarantee, of widening perspectives and gaining greater insight into what is really real or, as Townes phrased it, "the true-true."[15] Crowdsourcing can quickly degenerate into group think, ossifying one's own perspective through echo chambers of like-minded individuals. Both outcomes are possible. Reinhold Niebuhr's depiction of "immoral society"[16] may be just as appropriate as Paul's depiction of the church as a body with many members (1 Cor. 12:12). Collaboration is a shared task that demands dialogue and response.

Dialogical and Responsive

Christian ethics is an ongoing task subject to continual revision, requiring critical dialogue, shared material projects, and appropriate responsiveness. Material collaboration should lead to constructive dialogue across differences, offering

---

[11]Emilie M. Townes, *Womanist Ethics and the Cultural Production of Evil*. Black Religion / Womanist Thought / Social Justice Series (Palgrave Macmillan, 2006), 160; see also Elizabeth Soto Albrecht and Darryl W. Stephens, eds., *Liberating the Politics of Jesus: Renewing Peace Theology through the Wisdom of Women*, T&T Clark Studies in Anabaptist Theology and Ethics (T&T Clark, 2020).

[12]Ada María Isasi-Díaz, *En la Lucha / In the Struggle: Elaborating a Mujerista Theology* (Fortress, 2004).

[13]Scharen and Vigen, *Ethnography*, xxii.

[14]Scharen and Vigen, 24.

[15]Townes, *Womanist Ethics*, 161.

[16]Reinhold Niebuhr, *Moral Man and Immoral Society: A Study in Ethics and Politics* (Charles Scribner's Sons, [1932]1960).

mutual critique and deeper insight. Whether through communicative ethics,[17] cross-disciplinary intersections,[18] or interdisciplinary conversation,[19] a dialogical approach open to mutual critique enables continued learning. David Hollenbach's "dialogic universalism" is a good example of this kind of learning.[20] Students of Christian ethics must engage in dialogue and mutual critique not only with each other but also with scholars, the official teaching offices of churches,[21] the lived contexts of churches and denominations,[22] "communities of shared practice,"[23] marginalized communities,[24] new realities,[25] the earth,[26] and a combination thereof.[27] Perspectival insights can lead, for example, to awareness of intersectionality and other social realities laden with power[28] and to valuing the particularity and countermemory of marginalized groups.[29] The task of Christian ethics demands that we be appropriately responsive within this mutually critical dialogue.

Responsiveness implies vitality and relationship. Unresponsiveness is an indication of death. To respond, then, is to be alive in some way. Responsiveness shows an awareness of others and a capacity to be open to their influence and to be changed through that interaction—fundamental insights of process theology. Responsiveness is necessary for relationship. Not all relationships are healthy, though. Appropriate responsiveness implies recognition of the other and sensitivity to context, needs, and power dynamics. Appropriate responsiveness demands different things of different persons. Recognizing my own social location as a cis-hetero white male, appropriate responsiveness demands my humility.[30] For others, from different social locations,

---

[17]Seyla Benhabib, *Situating the Self: Gender, Community, and Postmodernism in Contemporary Ethics* (Routledge, 1992); Jürgen Habermas, *Moral Consciousness and Communicative Action*, Studies in Contemporary German Social Thought, transl. Christian Lenhardt and Shierry Weber Nicholsen (MIT Press, 1990).

[18]James M. Gustafson, "Conclusion: The Relation of Other Disciplines to Theological Ethics," in *Intersections: Science, Theology, and Ethics*, 126–47 (Pilgrim, 1996).

[19]Patricia Beattie Jung and Aana Marie Vigen, eds., with John Anderson, *God, Science, Sex, Gender: An Interdisciplinary Approach to Christian Ethics* (University of Illinois Press, 2010); Lovin and Maudlin, *Theology as Interdisciplinary Inquiry.*

[20]David Hollenbach, *The Global Face of Public Faith: Politics, Human Rights, and Christian Ethics* (Georgetown University Press, 2003), 10–16.

[21]Charles Curran, "Humanae Vitae: Fifty Years Later," *Theological Studies* 79, no. 3 (2018): 520–42, https://doi.org/10.1177/0040563918784769.

[22]Darryl W. Stephens, *Methodist Morals: Social Principles in the Public Church's Witness* (University of Tennessee Press, 2016), 195.

[23]Willis Jenkins, *The Future of Ethics: Sustainability, Social Justice, and Religious Creativity* (Georgetown University Press, 2013), 99.

[24]Miguel A. De La Torre, *Doing Christian Ethics from the Margins*, 3rd ed. (Orbis, 2023); Traci C. West, *Disruptive Christian Ethics: When Racism and Women's Lives Matter* (Westminster John Knox, 2006).

[25]Robin W. Lovin, *Christian Realism and the New Realities* (Cambridge University Press, 2008).

[26]Cynthia D. Moe-Lobeda, *Resisting Structural Evil: Love as Ecological-Economic Vocation* (Fortress, 2013); Rasmussen, Larry.L., *Earth Community, Earth Ethics*, Ecology & Justice series (Orbis, 1996).

[27]Melanie L. Harris, *Ecowomanism: African American Women and Earth-Honoring Faiths*, Ecology and Justice Series (Orbis, 2017).

[28]Grace Ji-Sun Kim and Susan M. Shaw, *Intersectional Theology: An Introductory Guide* (Fortress, 2018), 107.

[29]Townes, *Womanist Ethics*, 23.

[30]Compare to Lovin et al., "Introduction," xxix; Scharen and Vigen, *Ethnography*, 17–18.

the task of Christian ethics may demand boldness, courage, fortitude, and audacity.[31] Constructive dialogue and appropriate responsiveness, especially across differences, are means by which our vision can be improved, adjusted, or otherwise clarified— even as we acknowledge the limitations inherent in our individual perspectives. The constructive possibilities of reenvisioning Christian ethics as dialogical and responsive also imply a sense of purpose and hope.

Purposeful and Hopeful

Finally, Christian ethics has a normative dimension. The task is purposeful. Though our individual motivations may differ widely, we do not enter this dialogue or participate in mutual critique without some aim. Whether seeking *eudaimonia*, rest in God, or full human flourishing, we each participate in the collaborative effort of Christian ethics for a reason. These reasons are diverse and multiple, motivating some to witness to an eschatological community of peace[32] and others to disruption[33] and hopelessness.[34] For example, Traci West described the necessity of Christian ethics: "when racism and women's lives matter."[35] Whether grounded in a present sense of hopelessness[36] or a conviction that academic scholarship might make some positive difference in this world,[37] the ongoing work of Christian ethics entails some kind of vision for a better future. Thus, Christian ethics is ultimately a hopeful task involving academic study, ecclesial practice, and partnership with all members of global society. Our shared task involves the common good, systems of justice, and the full flourishing of all of creation.

Discussion Questions

1   Consider the conceptual pairings above: real and awe-filled; perspectival and discerning; dialogical and responsive; collaborative and participatory; purposeful and hopeful. Do you agree with the logic behind each pairing? In what ways might you disagree?

2   Consider alternative visions for Christian ethics. For example, some Christian approaches to the good life presume a reality shared only by the elect, the saved, or the community of true believers. Other approaches are universal rather than perspectival. Still others emphasize rules (deontology) rather than dialogue or obedience rather than collaboration. Which parts of the author's reenvisioning surprised you or challenged you the most?

---

[31]Alice Walker, *In Search of Our Mother's Gardens: Womanist Prose* (Harcourt, 1983), xi.
[32]Stanley Hauerwas, *The Peaceable Kingdom: A Primer in Christian Ethics* (University of Notre Dame Press, 1983).
[33]West, *Disruptive Christian Ethics*, 68–71.
[34]Miguel A. De La Torre, *Embracing Hopelessness* (Fortress, 2017).
[35]West, *Disruptive Christian Ethics*, xi–xii.
[36]De La Torre, *Embracing Hopelessness*, 5–6.
[37]Lovin et al., "Introduction," xxxi.

Obstacles to Solidarity in the Kin-dom

Several obstacles can inhibit an approach to Christian ethics that aims for solidarity in the kin-dom. In North America, many Christians live out their religious convictions by practicing evangelism and many others by emphasizing social justice. However, Nancy Ammerman, a sociologist of religion, found that the most common understanding of the purpose of the church and its ministry is to serve people in need, to treat others as you would like to be treated (Mt. 7:12).[38] A problem with the Golden Rule, when invoked by the privileged, is that it centers the viewpoint of privilege rather than need. A more liberating approach would be to treat others as you would like to be treated, were you in their shoes. Even better would be to treat others as they would like to be treated: "aid must be recognized by the oppressed as aid"[39] The latter formulation requires entering into mutual relationship with our neighbors and supporting their agency to choose for themselves.

Relative privilege and power skew the possibilities of mutuality, a characteristic of relationship in the kin-dom. According to Ammerman's research, Golden Rule Christians cross all theological and racial divisions; their focus on doing good is not ideologically based but rather rooted in material difference.[40] Golden Rule Christianity, as observed by Ammerman, is primarily about charity for those in need: the "haves" sharing with the "have nots." This paternalistic posture impairs the ability of persons of relative wealth, power, and social resources to be in solidarity with others.

The same problem of paternalism is often present in evangelical approaches to the faith. Evangelism is an essential aspect of the *missio Dei* and is not inherently contrary to solidarity. Evangelism does not have to be rooted in an exclusive truth-claim. However, as practiced by Christians who are not afraid to claim the word *evangelism*, this activity is often accompanied by a mindset of superiority. When one claims an exclusive access to divine knowledge and Truth, any differing claim by others is either false or a disguised form of the Truth one already knows. Either way, there is nothing to learn from others. Such soteriological certainty impedes forming relationships open to mutual transformation. When combined with other forms of privilege, such as wealth or political power, the asymmetry in encounters with others is exacerbated, undermining the possibilities for solidarity.

Christians promoting a social justice approach to the faith must also be vigilant about relative power, privilege, and paternalistic patterns. When persons with relative power swoop in with preconceived notions about how to fix the problems of the other, marginalized communities are further disempowered. A truly justice-oriented response would need to prioritize the humanity and needs of the marginalized, supporting them in solidarity rather than supplanting their agency. The commandment to love your neighbor as yourself begs important questions: not

---

[38]Nancy T. Ammerman, "Golden Rule Christianity: Lived Religion in the American Mainstream," in *Lived Religion in America: Toward a History of Practice*, ed. David D. Hall, 196–216 (Princeton University Press, 1997), 197–8.

[39]Darryl M. Trimiew, *Voices of the Silenced: The Responsible Self in a Marginalized Community* (Pilgrim, 1993), 103.

[40]Ammerman, "Golden Rule Christianity," 199–200.

only, "Who is my neighbor?"—the question posed to Jesus—but also, "How do I love my neighbor?" What is the morally responsible way to love our neighbors in a world of trauma?

Discussion Questions

1   Of the three most common ways that Christians in North America live out their faith (evangelism, social justice, and Gold Rule), which best characterizes your own convictions? Which best characterizes the way your congregation or community of faith lives out its convictions?

2   What is paternalism? How is it an obstacle to relationships of mutuality?

3   Consider ways that your community provides for those in need, for example, food and clothing banks, soup kitchens, overnight shelters, job placement centers, and so on. How are those on the receiving end of these services involved in decision-making about these services? For example, do current or formerly homeless persons serve on the board of the homeless shelter?

Moral Responsibility

With the question "What is going on?" H. Richard Niebuhr began his inquiry into the moral life of the responsible self in community. The ethical task then involves interpreting what is going on in the world, in light of God as our ultimate center of value, to discern the fitting response. A trauma-informed approach helps us discern how to love our neighbors in fitting ways that open the possibility of solidarity in the kin-dom. To do so responsibly, however, requires attention to the obstacles of power, privilege, and paternalism that inhibit true solidarity with victim-survivors of trauma. For this, we must attune ourselves to listen to the voices of the silenced— whoever they may be in relation to ourselves and the moral communities we inhabit.

Social location has everything to do with responsibility and interpretation of what is going on. Darryl M. Trimiew's *Voices of the Silenced: The Responsible Self in a Marginalized Community* offers a critique and adaptation of Niebuhr's essay on moral philosophy from a perspective much different from Niebuhr's. Trimiew, a Black scholar of Christian social ethics, argued that his "marginalized self" has a different perspective and different responsibilities from Niebuhr's "empowered self" (xiii, 2). Trimiew's exploration of responsibilist ethics in marginalized communities serves as a necessary corrective to Niebuhr and, since my own social location shares much with Niebuhr, provides invaluable guidance for my attempt to engage liberation ethics as a member of a non-marginalized community. Trimiew also warned that the distinction between oppressed and oppressor is not neatly drawn: "some people are both victims and victimizers" (20, 114n57). Power is relative and contextual and can be abused by any moral agent, even the marginalized self.

What does it mean to view and experience the world as a marginalized person? Drawing on Du Bois's depiction of "double consciousness," Trimiew asserted the existence of considerations prior to the question posed by the empowered self, situated with a comfortably "free and sustainable" perspective: "[T]he truly marginalized person" must reframe the question: "'Besides my ongoing experience of being oppressed, in a marginalized community, what else is going on?'" (10–11). Thus, members of marginalized communities rightly prioritize their own dignity and basic human needs before responsibly considering how to respond to God's action elsewhere. This moral imperative is rooted in God as liberator, with a preferential option for the poor—an understanding that should compel all responsible selves "to oppose the oppression of a neighbor" (15). Trimiew offered the above as a corrective to the inadequate understanding of responsibility that allowed Niebuhr to do "nothing" (except repent) in the face of oppression.[41] The repentance advocated by Niebuhr required a moment of reinterpreting the past and his own complicity; for Trimiew, such reinterpretation required solidarity with the oppressed to see rightly a fitting response (4, 12).

Trimiew's differentiation between the oppressed and the empowered serves the larger goal of repairing the covenanted community that we all share—I am reminded of Martin Luther King Jr.'s metaphor of "the world house."[42] According to Trimiew,

> one of the primary ways of restoring community is for the oppressed to engage in the fitting act of demanding recognition of their humanity and ... to fight to meet their own basic human needs. An appropriate response from oppressors would be to hear them and subsequently to recognize their humanity.[43]

Recognizing the human dignity of marginalized selves, though, is only a precursor to responsible, fitting action on the part of empowered selves. Trimiew acknowledged, "we have an obligation to intervene, if necessary, in the struggle of others to survive if they cannot meet their own basic human needs" (87). Thus, moral responsibility differs based on which side of an oppressive social structure one finds oneself.

Trimiew offered a material context for applying Niebuhr's ethic of appropriate response. The interpretative stage of moral discernment must be grounded in the prerequisites of mutual dignity and availability of basic goods—commitments Trimiew found "manifested in creation and human community" as well as the biblical narrative (89). Through recognition of human dignity and attention to material needs,

> All people become more fully human ... Oppressors are able to become more fully human by listening and hearing the cries of the oppressed, and ... can then begin the process of repentance and reparative justice that allows them to reclaim the humanity from which their acts of oppression had alienated them ...

---

[41]To be sure, Niebuhr's idea of "doing nothing" involved a profound process of introspection and repentance. H. Richard Niebuhr, "The Grace of Doing Nothing," in *An Eerdmans Reader in Contemporary Political Theology*, ed. William T. Cavanaugh, Jeffrey W. Bailey, and Craig Hovey, 254–8 (Eerdmans, 2012).

[42]Martin Luther King Jr., "Where Do We Go from Here: Chaos or Community?" in *A Testament of Hope: The Essential Writings and Speeches of Martin Luther King, Jr.*, ed. James Melvin Washington (HarperSanFrancisco, 1986), 617.

[43]Trimiew, *Voices of the Silenced*, 18.

> Marginalized selves realize their fullest humanity in resisting oppression and in meeting their own basic needs and those of others ... as fully competent moral agents.[44]

Recognition of dignity, attentive listening, repentance, and justice—each is integral to the healing and repair of individuals and moral community. Trimiew asserted, "forming solidarity with the truly disadvantaged must be a part of any viable responsibilist ethics" (99). Ultimately, Trimiew viewed the responsibilities of oppressor and oppressed as stemming from the same ultimate value (God) joining us in one covenant community.

Solidarity with the marginalized benefits both the oppressor and the oppressed— and is necessary for the oppressed to interpret rightly what is going on in the world. This is a step that Niebuhr did not take. Trimiew claimed, "Niebuhr could not hear the cries of the oppressed of his generation, except as cries of suffering, but not as calls for dialogue. His social location made him socially deaf" (90, see also 5). Consistent with other liberation theologies, Trimiew understood the perspective of the marginalized to have an epistemological advantage over the empowered location and suggested, "the oppressed are probably the group best suited to make moral judgments with regard to the issues of justice and sustainability" (xii, 11, 19). Thus, solidarity with marginalized selves and communities aids relatively empowered selves and communities to interpret anew social relationships, human response, and even God in Christ (12).

Oppression comes in many forms. Trauma, regardless of its causes, is its own form of oppression. The way in which the moral community responds to trauma determines the extent to which victim-survivors are marginalized and further traumatized. In the context of trauma, victim-survivors and those who bear witness to them need each other. Both must ask what is going on, interpret their situations faithfully, and discern the fitting course of action. A trauma-informed approach to Christian ethics offers those who bear witness to trauma survivors the tools for becoming responsible selves in community.

Discussion Questions

1 Make a list of basic human needs. Compare your list to well-known lists, such as Abraham Maslow's hierarchy of needs, Martha Nussbaum's list of central human capabilities, or the Human Development Index used by the United Nations. What commonalities do you find? What are the differences?

2 What does your church or faith community say about basic human needs? If your faith tradition does not have an official statement, consult Roman Catholic Social Teaching, the World Council of Churches, the Lutheran World Federation, the National Association of Evangelicals' "For the Health of the Nation" publication, the United Methodist Social Principles, or a social statement from another denomination or faith-based institution.

---

[44]Trimiew, 100.

3 The experiences of empowerment or marginalization are context-dependent. When have you experienced marginalization or disempowerment? When have you experienced empowerment? How did these experiences shape your perception of "what is going on" and what your fitting response would be?

4 Who are the "truly disadvantaged" in your community? What would your solidarity with them look like?

1.2
Trauma-Informed Response

Michael, an undergraduate, is taking a course on Christian ethics. His classmates see that he is passionate about the subject. Michael always has an opinion, no matter the moral issue under discussion. However, he acts differently during the current unit on Christian approaches to war. Michael has been absent or extremely tardy several times lately. During the most recent class, he became angry about a Bible passage and left the room, prompting another student to remark, "What's wrong with him?"

Life Church experiences turmoil every autumn during their financial pledge drive. The treasurer expresses anxiety about the next year's budget; the church council chair does not want to talk about money in church; and long-time members show distrust about the budgetary process. Noticing the congregation's extreme responses, Pastor Linda vents to a colleague: "What's wrong with these people?"

LaToya is a nursing student in Philadelphia taking classes and working as a resident at the main hospital downtown. On Thursday, September 1, 2022, she saw a national news report about the killing of an unarmed Black man shot in bed by an Ohio police officer. The body-camera footage showed the officer pushing open a bedroom door and immediately firing at twenty-year-old Donovan Lewis. LaToya is in her apartment alone, planning to spend the evening working on her homework, but she cannot concentrate. "What's wrong with me?" she wonders.

"What's wrong with you?" When a person is habitually distracted, inattentive, or disruptive, I might wonder what is wrong with them. If vocalized, this question about their unwelcome behavior, at best, might suppress outward disruption so that social interactions can continue as "normal." Yet, my response would likely perpetuate a cycle of shame and blame, exacerbating the underlying issues and contributing to an ongoing public health crisis. Beginning in the 1980s and accelerating through the early 2000s, increased understanding of the psychological and physiological effects of trauma has offered a different way to address these presenting issues. Instead of confrontation, community leaders and service providers are advised to focus on care. Now, I know to ask instead, "What has happened to you?"[1] This shift from confrontation to care is the crux of a new paradigm in public services, a trauma-informed approach.

---

[1] Susan Salasin, "Sine Qua Non for Public Health," *National Council Magazine*, no. 2 (2011): 18.

This chapter introduces the basics of trauma and trauma-informed response as a basis for Christian ethics and responsible love of neighbor. Drawing on recent insights from psychology, neuroscience, and public health studies, this chapter presents a basic definition and description of trauma, introduces the features of a trauma-informed community approach, and discusses care for religious leaders and others who deal with their own traumatic pasts, as well as the secondary effects of encountering and supporting traumatized individuals in their communities.

Trauma Basics

Modern trauma studies are a relatively recent development. The term "post-traumatic stress syndrome" entered the American Psychiatric Association's Diagnostic and Statistical Manual of Mental Disorders (DSM-III) in 1980. Coincidently, this is the same year that the US Equal Employment Opportunity Commission defined workplace "sexual harassment" and identified it as a violation of civil rights. Both warfare and workplace were recognized as sites of trauma and violation. These parallel developments are not unrelated. Collectively, sexual harassment, abuse, and assault are among the most common forms of trauma experienced in the United States. The interdisciplinary study of trauma gained momentum with Judith Herman's influential book, *Trauma and Recovery*, first published in 1992, and the Adverse Childhood Experiences (ACE) Study, published in 1998.[2] As awareness of trauma has risen among communities and service organizations, many religious leaders have scrambled to understand trauma and its effects.

Simply put, trauma is the result of an experience that is too much to handle. Trauma begins with an event that overwhelms one's sense of safety and agency. Herman stated that "traumatic events … overwhelm the ordinary human adaptations to life."[3] Trauma engages psychic, physiological, and neurological survival mechanisms when a person encounters a grave threat. A person experiences an event as traumatic when their very existence is threatened and autonomic impulses of fight, flight, freeze, or fawn govern their response.[4] Trauma can be experienced as a loss of agency—a profound sense of powerlessness. Yet, a trauma victim is also a survivor, having coped with overwhelming danger in ways too deep to fathom.[5] However, trauma does not end when the danger has subsided.

A central feature of trauma is that it disrupts one's personal narrative, interfering with one's integrated experience of the world. Traumatic memories interrupt the

---

[2]Vincent J. Felitti et al., "Relationship of Childhood Abuse and Household Dysfunction to Many of the Leading Causes of Death in Adults: The Adverse Childhood Experiences (ACE) Study," *American Journal of Preventive Medicine* 14, no. 4 (1998): 245–58; Judith Lewis Herman, *Trauma and Recovery: The Aftermath of Violence, from Domestic Abuse to Political Terror* (Basic Books, [1992]2015).

[3]Herman, *Trauma and Recovery*, 33.

[4]For a brief introduction, see PTSD UK, "Trauma: It's More Than Just 'Fight or Flight,'" https://www.ptsduk.org/its-so-much-more-than-just-fight-or-flight/.

[5]Foregrounding the language of "survivor" over "victim" is an intentional aspect of a trauma-informed response. See glossary of terms in: SAMHSA, "Trauma-Informed Care in Behavioral Health Services," Treatment Improvement Protocol (TIP) Series 57. HHS Publication No. (SMA) 13-4801 (SAMHSA, 2014), xvi–xix.

present in ways unbounded by chronology. A traumatic memory can be neither coherently articulated nor forgotten. It is an unspeakable response to horror, a response that refuses to be integrated into the past even as it haunts the present. Herman called this "the dialectic of trauma": being "caught between the extremes of amnesia or of reliving the trauma."[6] Besser van der Kolk, another pioneering researcher in the field, described it this way: "trauma is not just an event that took place sometime in the past; it is also the imprint left by that experience on mind, brain, and body."[7] A traumatized person relives their terror again and again, triggered involuntarily by sensory reminders.

Trauma resides deep in the body, altering one's physiology.[8] Because trauma overwhelms the normal coping mechanisms, the experience is fragmented rather than integrated into a person's experience. Effects are most noticeable when a trauma survivor is triggered by external stimuli. During a flashback, the trauma survivor's autonomous systems respond as if the original threat were present, for example, when a war veteran with post-traumatic stress disorder (PTSD) responds viscerally to the sound of a car backfiring, as if the noise presented a mortal danger. For a person with PTSD, the trigger brings the past trauma into the present moment, and they relive the original experience, engaging in survival response to the stimulus. Traumatic memories can be triggered by emotions, sights, smells, noises, and many other reminders of the original traumatic experience. However, such misplaced survival responses are maladaptive and disruptive, further alienating the person from their immediate environment, relationships, community, and even their sense of self.

Trauma is a wound with complex roots. In 2014, the Substance Abuse and Mental Health Services Administration (SAMHSA) provided the following definition of individual trauma to serve as a common reference point among various sectors of public service provision:

> Individual trauma results from an event, series of **events,** or set of circumstances that is **experienced** by an individual as physically or emotionally harmful or life threatening and that has lasting adverse **effects** on the individual's functioning and mental, physical, social, emotional, or spiritual well-being. [original emphasis][9]

This definition focuses on individuals and highlights what SAMHSA referred to as "the three E's of trauma": events, experiences, and effects.[10] Trauma can result from a single horrifying event as well as a series of events or set of circumstances experienced by an individual as traumatic. Furthermore, "Traumatic experiences have features that are both temporal (occurring in a certain moment of a traumatic event) and structural (occurring as a result of ongoing systemic social and economic

---

[6] Herman, *Trauma and Recovery*, 47. Shelly Rambo explored the narrative disruption of trauma as a site for theological exploration and meaning in *Spirit and Trauma: A Theology of Remaining* (Westminster John Knox, 2010).

[7] Bessel van der Kolk, *The Body Keeps the Score: Brain, Mind, and Body in the Healing of Trauma* (Penguin, 2014), 21.

[8] van der Kolk, 21.

[9] SAMHSA, "SAMHSA's Concept of Trauma and Guidance for a Trauma-Informed Approach," HHS Publication No. (SMA) 14–4884 (SAMHSA, 2014), 7.

[10] SAMHSA, 8.

inequalities)."[11] Trauma is a wound of the entire person, and its effects can be felt throughout a community and across generations.[12]

The experience of trauma varies from person to person and is compounded by previous social, psychological, developmental, and cultural factors. Researchers use the term "potentially traumatic event," since the experience of the event (as traumatizing or not) will vary from person to person.[13] Traumatic life events include military combat, natural disaster, life-threatening accident, sexual assault, abandonment, death of a loved one, and many other psychologically overwhelming situations. Trauma can also result from multiple events creating prolonged exposure to threat, including domestic violence, bullying, poverty, abuse, and racism.[14] Not every adverse experience is traumatic, yet the same event(s) might be traumatic for one person and not for another, depending on how the event is experienced by the individual within their community. Thus, the event of trauma cannot be isolated from the way it is experienced. Personality, social support network, developmental health, previous experiences, and other complex factors shape whether an event is experienced as traumatic. These factors contribute to a person's degree of resilience.

Resilience allows a person to heal from trauma or recover from a potentially traumatic event without being traumatized. Resilience is "the capacity to bounce back from adversity."[15] Researchers in the late 1990s examined the relationship between "childhood abuse and neglect and household challenges and later-life health and well-being."[16] The landmark ACEs study clearly showed that "adverse childhood experiences are common and they have strong long-term associations with adult health risk behaviors, health status, and diseases."[17] Furthermore, "early exposure to ACEs is associated with traumatic stress reactions and subsequent exposure to trauma in adult years."[18] Thus, persons with a history of adverse experiences and who lack strong social or familial support are statistically less resilient than the general population and more likely to experience subsequent adverse events as traumatic.

Trauma is a complicated and multifaceted concept: it can be collective (community-wide), epigenetic (inherited or intergenerational), social-cultural (e.g., racism), complex (involving a series of events), vicarious, or participatory. Participatory

---

[11]L. Callid Keefe-Perry and Zachary Moon, "Courage in Chaos: The Importance of Trauma-Informed Adult Religious Education," *Religious Education* 114, no. 1 (2019): 31, https://doi.org/10.1080/003440 87.2018.1435989.

[12]Resmaa Menakem, *My Grandmother's Hands: Racialized Trauma and the Pathways to Mending Our Hearts and Bodies* (Central Recovery, 2017), 45.

[13]Isaac R. Galatzer-Levy, Charles L. Burton, and George A. Bonanno, "Coping Flexibility, Potentially Traumatic Life Events, and Resilience: A Prospective Study of College Student Adjustment," *Journal of Social and Clinical Psychology* 31, no. 6 (2012): 542–67, https://doi.org/10.1521/jscp.2012.31.6.542.

[14]Shannon Davidson, "Trauma-Informed Practices for Postsecondary Education: A Guide," (Education Northwest, 2017), 4, https://educationnorthwest.org/sites/default/files/resources/trauma-informed-practices-postsecondary-508.pdf.

[15]van der Kolk, *The Body Keeps the Score*, 163.

[16]Centers for Disease Control and Prevention, "About the CDC-Kaiser ACE Study," https://www.cdc.gov/violenceprevention/aces/about.html.

[17]Felitti et al., "The Adverse Childhood Experiences (ACE) Study," 254.

[18]SAMHSA, "Trauma-Informed Care," 47.

trauma, in which the victim is also an offender, can result in moral injury in addition to PTSD.[19] According to Jonathan Shay, "moral injury is present when (1) there has been a betrayal of what's right (2) by someone who holds legitimate authority (3) in a high-stakes situation."[20] For example, the psychological effects of killing during times of war may cause a combatant to suffer moral injury, going against their well-formed conscience. Moral injury can also occur in other institutional contexts in which people experience betrayal by an authority figure.[21] Not all war combatants suffer moral injury, not all people who experience trauma develop diagnosable disorders, and many people suffer debilitating experiences without reaching the clinical threshold of trauma. However, a trauma-informed approach renders these distinctions irrelevant. It is not the purpose of trauma-informed Christian ethics to diagnose moral injury, PTSD, or various forms of trauma. We can promote healing and integration back into community regardless of our knowledge of an individual's past moral injury or trauma.

Discussion Questions

1 How does trauma differ from other experiences of pain, harm, or loss?

2 Consider an occasion that was likely traumatic for someone you know. Can you identify the event, experience, and effects of the trauma?

3 What roles do friends, family, and community play in strengthening one's resilience?

Trauma-Informed Response

Trauma-informed response is a community-wide effort involving social work, public health, policing, law, education, ministry, and other sectors of public service. Analogous to the way compliance with the American Disabilities Act (ADA) guides organizations in how to be welcoming and accommodating of persons with physical challenges—without knowing ahead of time who might benefit from these accommodations, trauma-informed response guides the wider community in how to be supportive of persons healing and recovering from trauma. Most sectors are neither trained nor equipped to provide acute medical care or trauma-specific services or interventions—and are not expected to do so. First responders and medical emergency rooms are needed for this work. Psychiatrists and counselors assist in longer-term healing, much like nurses and physical therapists do for physical wounds. Thus, trauma-informed response is not about expert trauma care. Rather,

---

[19]Sarah Travis, *Unspeakable: Preaching and Trauma-Informed Theology* (Cascade, 2021), 18.

[20]Jonathan Shay, "Casualties," *Daedalus* 140, no. 3 (Summer 2011): 183.

[21]Karen V. Guth, *The Ethics of Tainted Legacies: Human Flourishing after Traumatic Pasts* (Cambridge University Press, 2022), 46–54. For a Christian analysis of moral injury, see Warren Kinghorn, "Combat Trauma and Moral Fragmentation: A Theological Account of Moral Injury," *Journal of the Society of Christian Ethics* 32, no. 2 (2012): 67–71, https://doi.org/10.1353/sce.2012.0041.

trauma-informed response is about participating in a community-wide network of support.

Religious organizations, faith leaders, and secular helping professionals can partner with mental health and other service providers to become part of a trauma-informed community. "SAMHSA defines any setting as 'trauma-informed' if the people there *realize* how widespread trauma is, *recognize* signs and symptoms, *respond* by integrating knowledge into practice, and *resist* doing further harm."[22] This fourfold description (realize, recognize, respond, and resist) provides guidance for secular leaders and organizations to contribute to a community of care for survivors of trauma. For religious leaders and faith communities, *reconnect* serves as a fifth "R" of trauma-informed response.[23]

Realizing the widespread impact of trauma is essential. Trauma is not an unusual experience, and many people bear the effects of trauma in their everyday lives. The ACEs study revealed that adverse childhood experiences are disturbingly prevalent in US society.[24] ACEs, such as parental divorce, an alcoholic or incarcerated family member, and child abuse and neglect, remain prevalent. In a national survey of adults during 2011–20, "approximately two thirds reported at least one ACE; one in six reported four or more ACEs."[25] In 2024, the Centers for Disease Control and Prevention (CDC) estimated, "At least one in four girls and one in 20 boys in the United States experience child sexual abuse."[26] Thus, a trauma-informed approach does not view a trauma survivor as the exception. Rather, "trauma-informed care is initiated by [the] assumption that every person seeking services is a trauma survivor"[27] A trauma-informed approach is for the benefit of every member of the community, including people seeking to participate in communities of faith.

Recognizing the signs and symptoms of trauma requires an understanding of the common external indications of trauma. The effects of trauma on persons and relationships are real and noticeable, such as

- Difficulty focusing, attending, retaining, and recalling
- Tendency to miss appointments or other obligations
- Challenges with emotional regulation
- Fear of taking risks
- Anxiety about deadlines, social interactions, or public speaking
- Anger, helplessness, or dissociation when stressed

---

[22]SAMHSA, "Spotlight: Building Resilient and Trauma-Informed Communities—Introduction," SMA17-5014, February 2017, 9, https://store.samhsa.gov/product/Spotlight-Building-Resilient-and-Trauma-Informed-Communities-Introduction/SMA17-5014.

[23]Karen A. McClintock, *Trauma-Informed Pastoral Care: How to Respond When Things Fall Apart* (Fortress, 2022), 22.

[24]SAMHSA cited the ACEs report as one of two studies significantly influencing the development of the trauma-informed care model. SAMHSA, "Trauma-Informed Care," 8.

[25]CDC, "Prevalence of Adverse Childhood Experiences among U.S. Adults—Behavioral Risk Factor Surveillance System, 2011–2020," https://www.cdc.gov/mmwr/volumes/72/wr/mm7226a2.htm.

[26]CDC, "About Child Sexual Abuse," 2024, https://www.cdc.gov/child-abuse-neglect/about/about-child-sexual-abuse.html.

[27]Salasin, "Sine Qua Non for Public Health," 18.

- Withdrawal and isolation
- Involvement in unhealthy relationships[28]

Any one of these behaviors might not be an indication of trauma. However, multiple or abrupt changes in behavior might be indicative of someone struggling with past trauma, and we can learn to recognize the deleterious effects.

The effects of trauma became readily apparent during the spring of 2020, the first months of societal response to Covid-19. People suffered from distraction, inability to concentrate, and short attention spans, exhibiting the effects of trauma (though most were unaware of this connection). Furthermore, persons of color were the most affected. The long-term trauma of racism compounded the effects of ACEs and other potentially traumatic events, contributing, for example, to the well-documented disproportionate impact of Covid-19 on Black and Latinx communities in the United States.[29] Furthermore, the resurgence of the Black Lives Matter movement, sparked by the murder of George Floyd on May 25, 2020, compounded trauma upon trauma for many persons, families, and communities of color.

Responding as a trauma-informed organization or leader involves more than strategies for immediate intervention. A trauma-informed institution "responds by fully integrating knowledge about trauma into policies, procedures, practices."[30] Thus, trauma-informed crisis intervention is but one part of an overall, organizational response, the purpose of which is to "promote a culture based on beliefs about resilience, recovery, and healing from trauma."[31] In faith communities, it is just as important for church secretaries, lay leaders, and volunteers to become trauma-informed as it is for clergy and professional ministerial staff. Furthermore, faith communities are partners with all service sectors when responding to the effects of trauma in our communities.

When we learn to recognize the signs of prior trauma, we can then learn to respond in appropriate and helpful ways to the people we serve. Trauma overwhelms a person's normal stress-response and elicits a survival-based alarm system. Trauma triggers behaviors that were essential to survival during the original traumatic event. However, when traumatic memories are triggered (often with no conscious awareness by the survivor), the body responds as if the original threat were still present. The very behaviors that ensured survival in the first instance become ineffective and inappropriate when triggered at other times and places: "maladaptive behaviors are really misapplied survival skills."[32] Responding with understanding and compassion

---

[28] Adapted from A. Hoch et al. in Davidson, "Trauma-Informed Practices," 8.

[29] SAMHSA, "Double Jeopardy: COVID-19 and Behavioral Health Disparities for Black and Latino Communities in the U.S," (Submitted by OBHE), https://www.samhsa.gov/sites/default/files/covid19-behavioral-health-disparities-black-latino-communities.pdf. For an example analysis of a specific geographic area, see Matt Nowlin, Jeramy Townsley, Jay Colbert, and Sharon Kandris, "The Inequalities behind COVID-19 Disparities for African Americans in Indianapolis," *SAVI*, May 15, 2020, https://www.savi.org/the-inequalities-behind-covid-19-disparities-for-african-americans-in-indianapolis/.

[30] SAMHSA, "Concept of Trauma," 9.

[31] SAMHSA, 10.

[32] Davidson, "Trauma-Informed Practices," 13.

will help reduce anxiety, contributing to the health and resiliency of individuals and the entire community.

Resisting doing further harm is the fourth aspect of a trauma-informed approach. Failing to realize, recognize, and respond appropriately to a survivor of trauma can do harm. Re-victimization can easily occur when we fail to shift from an attitude of blame, "What's wrong with you?" to a stance of care, "What has happened to you?" This shift in perspective, to a trauma-informed approach, allows religious leaders and others to become partners in healing for survivors of trauma. The work of recovery involves practices of mind and body designed to empower a person to integrate their traumatic memories into their sense of self, reducing the past's hold on their present reality.

Leaders of communities of faith have an additional opportunity to exercise trauma-informed care. The tools and practices of ministry can address relational ruptures in addition to the physiological effects of trauma. Thus, Karen McClintock, a psychologist and pastor, added **reconnect** to SAMHSA's four Rs. Prayer, ritual, accompaniment, community—these are just a few of the ways that ministerial leaders are trained and equipped to "reconnect victims to loved ones, caring communities, and faith."[33] Since ministry is a relational endeavor, persons called to and affirmed in ministerial vocations can be of great value in providing opportunities for victim-survivors to recover, repair, and renew relationships.

Discussion Questions

Re-read the three vignettes at the beginning of this chapter to answer these questions.

1   Can you **recognize** the signs of trauma in each case? How do Michael, Life Church, and LaToya exhibit signs of trauma?

2   Each case takes place in a different context: a college classroom, a congregation, and an urban apartment. Do some quick internet searching to help you **realize** the widespread occurrence of trauma histories carried by persons in each context. For example, how common is it for undergraduate students to have trauma histories? What kinds of trauma might congregations experience? How common is violence in your community, and how do specific features (e.g., guns, police, race) heighten the traumatic features of violence for individuals and their communities?

3   What relational ruptures are implied in each case? What might **reconnection** look like for Michael, Life Church, and LaToya?

Principles of Trauma-Informed Care

Trauma-informed response is guided by six key principles: safety; trustworthiness and transparency; peer support; collaboration and mutuality; empowerment, voice,

---

[33]McClintock, *Trauma-Informed Pastoral Care*, 22.

and choice; and cultural, historical, and gender issues.[34] Each of these principles guides trauma-informed practices, allowing every sector of society to contribute to a community of trauma-informed care, including religious organizations.

Safety is the first priority—not only physical but also psychological. A person dealing with the effects of trauma must feel safe to de-escalate their physiological survival-response, allowing them to be fully present in their surroundings. In a congregational setting, safety may involve clearly marked exits, nearby restrooms, and the ability to leave the sanctuary or classroom at any time. As an organization endeavors to become a safer place, it is important to ask victim-survivors how they define safety, rather than assume. What changes to the environment will make them feel emotionally safer? The level of commitment to and awareness of safety is revealed at the first contact. How are the organization's efforts to create a safer space communicated?

Trustworthiness and transparency comprise the second principle of a trauma-informed approach. Many traumatic experiences occur within relationships that should have been characterized by love and trust. When a family member or person in authority abuses their power over someone more vulnerable, trust is betrayed. Furthermore, the survivor may feel betrayed by bystanders or others who failed to protect them. Re-establishing trust is therefore an important part of healing for survivors. To lessen perceived threats and to provide a conducive environment for recovery, congregations must be clear and transparent about policies, roles, and professional boundaries in ministry. For example, how does the congregation communicate about its safe church protocols for ministry with children and youth? What is the nature of confidentiality expected when talking with a staff person or minister? How are sensitive prayer requests handled?

Peer support is another key principle. Victim-survivors need opportunities to seek out and support each other. Hearing the experiences of others can create a sense of connection among victim-survivors. Conversely, being heard by someone who understands the complexity of the experience of trauma first-hand can help normalize the difficult path of healing and recovery. Congregations can create opportunities for peer support through prayer partners, bible study groups, and recovery ministries, for example. Each of these forms of peer ministry must carefully attend to issues of safety and transparency, such as confidentiality and information sharing.

Collaboration and mutuality are essential to becoming a trauma-informed community. The event of trauma is something that happens *to* a person, overwhelming them; healing and recovery is a process that happens *with* a person, inclusive of them. Partnering with survivors is a hallmark of healthy collaboration. Furthermore, a commitment to mutuality requires the leveling of power differences throughout an organization. Mutuality refers not only to relationships between client and service provider, parishioner and pastor, but also to relationships among employees; all can contribute to "meaningful sharing of power and decision-making."[35] In a congregational setting, power differentials exist between clergy and cleaning staff, part-time and full-time employees, and staff and volunteers, to name only a few relationships.

---

[34]SAMHSA, "Concept of Trauma," 10–11.
[35]SAMHSA, 11.

Empowerment, voice, and choice are principles underlying all others. Empowerment means helping the victim-survivor discover and develop their own capacities. Because trauma is an experience of disempowerment, healing must promote avenues of empowerment. Voice and choice are important aspects of regaining power for survivors of trauma. Trauma impairs a person's ability to make choices about their own well-being and evokes a deep sense of helplessness. To restore a sense of agency, trauma survivors need to voice their preferences and to make choices about the way they want to be treated. For example, in a trauma-informed classroom setting, students have choices of assignments or readings and may even have some control over deadlines, to be worked out with the instructor. In a religious setting, people may pray or participate as is comfortable to them rather than feel coerced into activities or rituals. Even a ritual designed to welcome visitors can be disempowering if there is no choice to opt out. Not least, trigger warnings about sensitive or potentially disturbing content can empower participants to choose whether or how they would like to participate.

Finally, all trauma has a social context. Attention to cultural, historical, and gender issues is integral to trauma-informed care. Recognition of historical trauma, being "responsive to the racial, ethnic and cultural needs of individuals," addressing stereotypes, providing gender-sensitive services, and valuing "traditional culture connections" are all part of a trauma-informed response.[36] Especially for faith communities, it is important not to impose one's own cultural assumptions and values onto victim-survivors of trauma.

Discussion Questions

1 Which of the key principles of a trauma-informed setting is most important to you right now? What difference would it make to you were this principle enhanced in your current setting?

2 Consider a specific community setting that you are part of, such as a school, congregation, or workplace. Which key principles of a trauma-informed organization are already present? Which key principles are most evidently lacking?

Care for the Caregivers

Trauma is remarkably prevalent in society. Helping professionals, diaconal workers, and faith leaders potentially encounter many victim-survivors of trauma. The more we practice trauma-informed care, the more attuned we become to the survivors of trauma who surround us daily. Furthermore, the more reliably we uphold the core values of trauma-informed response, the more the people around us will perceive us to be safe, trustworthy, and empowering, thus prompting more frequent divulging of their trauma histories and experiences. An increased awareness of and proximity

---

[36]SAMHSA, 11.

to trauma can manifest symptomatically as we bear witness to victim-survivors of trauma.

Repeated exposure to other people's traumas can negatively impact our physical, emotional, and spiritual health. Burnout, compassion fatigue, secondary traumatic stress, and vicarious traumatization are real and present dangers.[37] Secondary traumatic stress is a result of knowing about someone else's trauma and helping or desiring to help them; vicarious traumatization refers to the physiological, emotional, and spiritual effects of being exposed to the primary trauma of another person, either as a primary witness to the traumatic event itself or bearing witness to effects of trauma on survivors. Compassion without adequate rest and self-care takes a toll. Listening can hurt![38]

Caregivers and others who bear witness to victim-survivors must take time to debrief with colleagues, pastors, counselors, and other professionals about the emotional, spiritual, and physical toll that such work demands.[39] Being aware of trauma helps us through this journey, but the vicarious effects are no less intense and no less real just because we have some knowledge about it. Furthermore, practicing trauma-informed care may also prompt a more conscious awareness of our own unhealed traumatic wounds. Thus, I must offer a word of warning to persons entering ministry as a profession. Many people enter ministry with the intention of helping others but do so before adequately attending to their own healing. Somehow, it seems more socially and spiritually acceptable to love others than to love ourselves. Yet, it is an ethical duty to love and care for ourselves.[40] We cannot be effective in ministry when the gaping wounds of our own unaddressed, past traumas still fester.[41] Victim-survivors of trauma can be effective healers—after they have traveled the journey of healing themselves.

Finally, it is important to remember that a trauma-informed approach is the work of an entire community. This book is designed for community members and leaders, not trauma specialists. Professionals whose responsibility includes direct trauma intervention, triage, or healing must utilize the resources of their profession. In

---

[37]The dangers are recognized in disciplines as diverse as nursing, social science fieldwork, and pastoral care. See, for example, Vicki D. Lachman, "Compassion Fatigue as a Threat to Ethical Practice: Identification, Personal and Workplace Prevention/Management Strategies," *MEDSURG Nursing* 25, no. 4 (2016): 275–8, https://www.nursingworld.org/globalassets/docs/ana/ethics/compassionfatigue.pdf; Nena Močnik, "Re-Thinking Exposure to Trauma and Self-Care in Fieldwork-Based Social Research: Introduction to the Special Issue," *Social Epistemology* 34, no. 1 (2020): 1–11, https://doi.org/10.1080/02691728.2019.1681559; and Frederick Streets, "Social Work and a Trauma-Informed Ministry and Pastoral Care: A Collaborative Agenda," *Social Work & Christianity* 42, no. 4 (2015): 470–87. https://nacsw.org/Publications/SWC/SWC42_4WEB.pdf.

[38]Tzvi Michelson and Avraham Kluger, "Can Listening Hurt You? A Meta-Analysis of the Effects of Exposure to Trauma on Listener's Stress," *International Journal of Listening* 37, no. 1 (2021): 1–11, https://doi.org/10.1080/10904018.2021.1927734.

[39]For a helpful discussion of self-care practices, see Sharon Browning, Donna Duffey, Fred Magondu, John A. Moore, and Patricia A. Way, *The Little Book of Listening: Listening as a Radical Act of Love, Justice, Healing, and Transformation* (Good Books, 2024), 73–84.

[40]For example, the Code of Ethics for Nurses explicitly states, "The nurse owes the same duties to self as to others, including the responsibility to promote health and safety …." Lachman, "Compassion Fatigue," 276. See also Matthew 22:39 and Mark 12:31.

[41]Henri J. M. Nouwen, *The Wounded Healer: Ministry in Contemporary Society* (Doubleday, 1972), 90.

contrast, the role of religious professionals is to promote trauma-informed practices in communities of support, complementing but not supplanting the role of trauma specialists.

Leadership and Ministry

The importance of bringing a trauma-informed approach to religious leadership cannot be overestimated. The degree to which religious leaders understand trauma (or not) significantly impacts their missional effectiveness and ability to respond to persons seeking to participate in churches, synagogues, mosques, and other religious communities. Trauma affects mind, body, and soul, causing the survivor to reassess who they are and who God is. It changes the way we think about God, sin, and salvation. Previously held theologies of atonement and redemption may prove unhelpful or even false. We enter ministry ignorant about trauma at our own peril—and to our congregants' detriment.

The work of ministry involves and attends to the whole person, the embodied self in community, and trauma is part of that social, personal reality for many persons. "Knowing something about trauma should change the shape of Christian ministry," claimed Shelly Rambo, who is well-known for her groundbreaking theological work in trauma; "Insights from trauma," she observed, provide "a new starting point in caring for others."[42] Trauma-informed response is essential to core activities of faith communities, such as hospitality and invitation, the care of souls, preaching and teaching, loving our neighbors, and working toward justice in the wider community. The lens of trauma changes the way we do ministry. In the words of Serene Jones, "understanding trauma is not just a kind of secondary issue—it is rather the most central event of our faith."[43] When Paul declared that he knew nothing but "Jesus Christ, and him crucified," he bore witness to a traumatic experience at the core of the gospel (1 Cor. 2:2).

Knowledge of trauma and trauma-informed response is not optional for Christian ethics and ministerial care. Trauma-informed practices are now a community standard among secular social service organizations, including public schools and law enforcement, and should become so for faith communities and their leaders. How are religious leaders to care for the souls of persons if they are not attuned to traumatic suffering? How are we to avoid doing harm in teaching and preaching if we are not aware of the unintended effects on persons with trauma histories? Religious leaders, diaconal workers, and secular service providers must all learn how to bear witness to victim-survivors of trauma in our communities.

---

[42]Shelly Rambo, "How Christian Theology and Practice Are Being Shaped by Trauma Studies," *The Christian Century*, November 1, 2019, https://www.christiancentury.org/article/critical-essay/how-christian-theology-and-practice-are-being-shaped-trauma-studies.

[43]Serene Jones, *Trauma + Grace: Theology in a Ruptured World*, 2nd ed. (Westminster John Knox, 2019), xii.

Discussion Questions

1 Ask someone in a helping profession or role of caregiving (paid or volunteer) what vicarious effects they have noticed when working with traumatized individuals. What self-care practices help them remain healthy in this work?

2 How might experiences of trauma change the way people think about God, faith, and community?

3 Consider how the principles of trauma-informed response might be implemented in the three vignettes at the beginning of this chapter. How might a trauma-informed faith leader or community make a difference?

1.3
Bearing Witness

"I'm just not sure I can believe in God anymore after the accident," said Jaemyoung. "My parents assured me that 'everything happens for a reason' and that it is 'all part of God's plan'. But if God is love, why did God allow this tragedy? It seems so random and meaningless."

Trauma affects the whole person, including our spiritual or religious dimensions. According to the Substance Abuse and Mental Health Services Administration (SAMHSA), psychological trauma is characterized, in part, by "lasting adverse effects on the individual's functioning and mental, physical, social, emotional, or spiritual well-being"[1] In the example above, Jaemyoung expresses a deep spiritual loss in the aftermath of a traumatic accident. What tools are available to address such a loss? A person's spiritual well-being is difficult to identify and define within a broad, secular context without the expertise of religious professionals. This chapter engages religious ethics for the purpose of better equipping trauma-informed institutions and individuals to understand their work in relation to spiritual well-being and transcendent values.

The framework of bearing witness draws attention to the spiritual well-being of both the trauma survivor and the one responding to the survivor. Bearing witness to the trauma survivor is an ethical response to suffering involving the responder in specific practices of social action. It is a spiritually informed, moral response to suffering, characterized by distinct moral themes, modes of transcendence, and relational practices. It has resonance in fields as diverse as literature, holocaust studies, health care, philosophy, theatre, and theology. Bearing witness to trauma survivors is a set of liberating practices with transcendent dimensions, a social action of radical solidarity with those who have suffered.

Bearing witness consists of four identifiable practices—grounded being, attentive presence, historical clarity, and meaningful participation—correlating to distinct perspectival moments, modes of transcendence, moral themes, and stages of recovery and response. I begin with a broad understanding of spirituality, transcendence, and

---

[1]SAMHSA, "SAMHSA's Concept of Trauma and Guidance for a Trauma-Informed Approach | SAMHSA Publications and Digital Products," 2014, 7, https://store.samhsa.gov/product/SAMHSA-s-Concept-of-Trauma-and-Guidance-for-a-Trauma-Informed-Approach/SMA14-4884.

faith as these concepts relate to trauma and the transformative work of healing and recovery. Then, I present religious ethics as a resource for this work of transformation, aligning distinct modes of transcendence and moral themes in four perspectival moments—existence, present, past, and future. Mapping these modes and themes onto Judith Herman's stages of recovery and SAMHSA's four-fold description of trauma-informed care allows the work of trauma response and recovery to be interpreted in transcendent terms. I conclude by recognizing the social action of bearing witness as a political effort with spiritual implications, for which an understanding of religious ethics is a helpful ally.

Spirituality, Transcendence, and Faith

A trauma-informed approach to Christian ethics requires knowledge of the spiritual dimensions of trauma. Herman named the dialectic of trauma as being at once unspeakable and yet demanding to be told. From a spiritual standpoint, the experience of trauma is doubly unspeakable, involving both the transcendent and the atrocious. Thus, for trauma-informed responders, it is vital to gain familiarity with concepts, categories, and vocabulary often employed to speak of the unspeakable—whether spiritual or traumatic. Trauma recovery and trauma-informed response require consideration of spiritual well-being and a sense of the transcendent, which many people express through religious categories and traditions. Understanding trauma's effects on spiritual well-being is essential for a holistic response to trauma. Caregivers, service sectors, and communities seeking to attend to the trauma survivor's holistic well-being must become not only trauma-informed but also spiritually informed.

Aspects of religion and spirituality pertain to all parties involved in a trauma-informed community. For example, in her groundbreaking book *Trauma and Recovery*, Herman noted that some survivors find renewed purpose through their recovery:

> [A] significant minority, as a result of the trauma feel called to engage in a wider world. These survivors recognize a political or religious dimension to their misfortune and discover that they can transform the meaning of their personal tragedy by making it the basis for social action. While there is no way to compensate for an atrocity, there is a way to transcend it, by making it a gift to others. The trauma is redeemed only when it becomes the source of a survivor mission.[2]

The activities and themes of which Herman wrote—transformation, redemption, transcendence, mission, meaning-making, and social action—invite reflection on the spiritual and religious dimensions of trauma and recovery. Here the term *recovery* does not mean a destination or endpoint but rather the ongoing work of integrating

---

[2]Judith Lewis Herman, *Trauma and Recovery: The Aftermath of Violence, from Domestic Abuse to Political Terror* (Basic Books, [1992] 2015), 207.

traumatic histories into one's life narrative and journey of healing. A spiritually informed response to trauma allows survivors and responders alike to find renewed purpose through their collaborative work of healing and recovery. Yet, secular and religious service providers need guidance to recognize how trauma-informed response and recovery relate to notions of value rooted in spirituality or religion.

There are many parallels between traumatic and spiritual experiences. Both kinds of experience fall outside of "normal" perception and coping, both involve the holistic body (even an "out of body experience" has meaning only in reference to the body), both are inadequately communicated through words yet demand to be shared (evidencing Herman's dialectic of trauma), and both are politically disruptive, changing and challenging existing relationships, one's sense of justice, and one's self-perceived place in the world. Both trauma and spirituality shake up and reshape how one makes meaning and how one contributes meaningfully to the world. If healing from trauma involves reconstruction of one's personal narrative, narrating the transcendent in spiritual terms must be included in the stages of recovery and tools of trauma-informed response.

The deleterious effects of trauma on spiritual well-being are widely recognized. Much literature already exists related to spirituality, trauma, and resilience.[3] Effects of trauma include loss of meaning, difficulty recovering intimacy, guilt, shame, and a myriad of physiological manifestations. Each of these effects negatively impacts spiritual well-being. For example, Besser van der Kolk observed, "Survivors of trauma often begin to fear that they are damaged to the core and beyond redemption."[4] Trauma undermines one's sense of self, self-worth, and humanity. Van der Kolk also wrote of "the inner void—the holes in the soul" resulting from previous, adverse experiences of alienation from self and others.[5] Resmaa Menakem described intergenerational trauma as "a soul wound."[6] The relational ruptures of trauma undermine the survivor's sense of basic trust necessary to human flourishing. According to Herman, "Basic trust, acquired in the primary intimate relationship, is the foundation of faith"; traumatic events shatter this basic trust, "creating a crisis of faith" (54–5). Because of the spiritual aspects of trauma, the effects are compounded when God is implicated as a perpetrator, such as cases of spiritual abuse in churches or sexual abuse by clergy (see Chapter 3.3 for discussion). Fundamental self-worth, human connection, and basic trust are deeply spiritual issues.

---

[3]See, for example, Christine A. Courtois, "First, Do No More Harm: Ethics of Attending to Spiritual Issues in Trauma Treatment," in *Spiritually Oriented Psychotherapy for Trauma*, ed. Donald F. Walker, Christine A. Courtois, and Jamie D. Aten, 55–75 (American Psychological Association, 2015), https://doi.org/10.1037/14500-004; Kimberly Matheson, Ajani Asokumar, and Hymie Anisman, "Resilience: Safety in the Aftermath of Traumatic Stressor Experiences," *Frontiers in Behavioral Neuroscience* 14 (2020): 9–10, https://doi.org/10.3389/fnbeh.2020.596919; Crystal L. Park, Joseph M. Currier, J. Irene Harris, and Jeanne M. Slattery, *Trauma, Meaning, and Spirituality: Translating Research into Clinical Practice* (American Psychological Association, 2017); and Frederick Streets, "Social Work and a Trauma-Informed Ministry and Pastoral Care: A Collaborative Agenda," *Social Work & Christianity* 42, no. 4 (2015): 470–87, https://nacsw.org/Publications/SWC/SWC42_4WEB.pdf.

[4]Bessel A. van der Kolk, *The Body Keeps the Score: Brain, Mind, and Body in the Healing of Trauma* (Penguin, 2014), 2.

[5]van der Kolk, 298.

[6]Resmaa Menakem, *My Grandmother's Hands: Racialized Trauma and the Pathway to Mending Our Hearts and Bodies* (Central Recovery, 2017), 10.

Spirituality encompasses all human experience of the transcendent, expressed through many different words and concepts. Rita Nakashima Brock and Gabriella Lettini named their work with veterans recovering from PTSD as "soul repair."[7] Emphasizing the holistic, embodied nature of trauma, Menakem described the *vagus nerve* as the "soul nerve"; his therapeutic work helps others find calm through contact with his "settled, regulated nervous system."[8] Healing and recovery from trauma clearly have a spiritual component for Menakem. Trauma disrupts one's relationships, autobiographical narrative, and connection to the transcendent—adversely affecting spiritual well-being. Trauma ruptures relationships to self, loved ones, community, and even God. Yet, Menakem asserted that teaching his clients "to access a settledness that is always and already present ... the Infinite Source ... doesn't require a name, or an explanation, or a belief."[9] One does not have to speak about God to name the spiritual impact of trauma or to find healing.

The transcendent can go by many names. The transcendent is the universal, Infinite Source to which each person has a connection. It is that ever-present reality beyond our capacity to understand—what is known as Truth or Reality in Hinduism[10]; what enables the I-Thou relationship depicted by Martin Buber[11]; and what Howard Thurman called "the sound of the genuine."[12] When developing his well-known theory of faith development, James Fowler embraced a theory (story) of the self, based on a triadic structure of relational engagement: self, others, and what he termed "the ultimate Other, or the center(s) of value and power in one's life structure."[13] This highest or ultimate center of value in one's life represents the locus of faith—God, "the ultimate Other," "the Infinite Source," the Holy, and so on. Rebecca Chopp, a feminist theologian, identified "God as the term of the transcendent" in the Christian tradition.[14] Transcendence is often used to describe that which is wholly other to human experience; however, transcendence can only be expressed immanently, in this-worldly terms.

Many cultures make sense of the transcendent through traditions of faith. Fowler described faith development theory as "the journey of the faithful or religious self, with its companions and life challenges, toward increasingly reflective and responsible relation to and grounding in the Holy."[15] Fowler's operational definition of faith included at least seven aspects, such as perspective taking, moral judgment, social awareness, and form of world coherence.[16] Traumatic experiences disrupt all of these features of faith, often requiring the victim-survivor to reassess what

---

[7] Rita Nakashima Brock and Gabriella Lettini, *Soul Repair: Recovering from Moral Injury after War* (Beacon, 2013).
[8] Menakem, *My Grandmother's Hands*, 138, 152.
[9] Menakem, 152.
[10] S. Cromwell Crawford, "Ethical Foundations for Hindu Bioethics," *Dialogue & Alliance* 17, no. 2 (2003): 84.
[11] Martin Buber, *I and Thou*, 2nd ed. (Scribner, 1958).
[12] Howard Thurman, "The Sound of the Genuine," *The Spelman Messenger* 96, no. 4 (1980): 14–15, https://radar.auctr.edu/islandora/object/sc.001.messenger%3A1980.03/.
[13] James W. Fowler, "Faith Development Theory and the Postmodern Challenges," *The International Journal for the Psychology of Religion* 11, no. 3 (2001): 163, https://doi.org/10.1207/S15327582IJPR1103_03.
[14] Rebecca S. Chopp, "Theology and the Poetics of Testimony," *Criterion* 37, no. 1 (1998): 10.
[15] Fowler, "Faith Development Theory and the Postmodern Challenges," 165.
[16] Fowler, 161.

they previously believed and had been taught about themselves, others, and God. Transcendence is the path through this traumatic wilderness. Chopp described transcendence as "the power and spirit of transfiguration."[17] Transcendence can refer to that which empowers humans to think beyond themselves, imagine possibilities, and join in collective action. It can be enfleshed, as a relational term, suggesting awe and wonder.[18] In Christian feminist theology, "transcendence is expressed in the hope that the memories of suffering will be told and not go unredeemed, in the hope that personal and social existence can and will be transformed."[19] Thus, transcendence is very much part of the human experience, pertaining to memories, suffering, redemption, social relationships, hope, and transformation.

Discussion Questions

1   What does the word *transcendent* mean to you? What words does your faith tradition or culture use to name experiences of the transcendent?

2   The author wrote, "the experience of trauma is doubly unspeakable, involving both the transcendent and the atrocious." In what ways does language fail to communicate both wondrous and horrifying experiences?

3   Consider Jaemyoung's response to a traumatic accident. What aspects of his faith and spirituality have been disrupted?

Religious Ethics and Transformation

Trauma recovery and trauma-informed response take place, albeit in radically different ways, through shared moments of transcendence and transformation. Healing and recovery benefit from attention to the transcendent, helping repair ruptured relationships with self, others, community, and God. Bearing witness to trauma survivors can also be transformative—and risky. To be involved—and no bystander can avoid being involved, even when choosing not to act—is to experience something of trauma and its effects. The experience can be difficult to communicate: "witnesses as well as victims are subject to the dialectic of trauma" (Herman, 2). Survivor and responder are intertwined. Furthermore, the human capacity for transcendence is what enables a moral response to trauma in the first place. Thus, religious ethics provides helpful tools for naming the spiritual aspects of trauma.

To transform tragedy and trauma into meaningful social action, we need to identify specific modes of transcendence. One way to speak about the transcendent and morality while considering the social nature of humanity and the interconnectedness of the natural world is through process theology, which helpfully bridges science

---

[17]Chopp, "Theology and the Poetics of Testimony," 10.

[18]Mayra Rivera, *The Touch of Transcendence: A Postcolonial Theology of God* (Westminster John Knox, 2007); Shelly Rambo, "Trauma, Transformation, and Transcendence," in *Conflict Transformation and Religion: Essays on Faith, Power, and Relationship*, ed. Ellen Ott Marshall, 155–71 (Palgrave Macmillan, 2016).

[19]Chopp, "Theology and the Poetics of Testimony," 10.

and Christian faith. In her book *The Fall to Violence: Original Sin in Relational Theology*, Marjorie Suchocki, a process theologian, named the ability to transcend oneself and circumstances as the defining feature of humanity in contrast to other hominids.[20] To be human is to have the capacity to recognize the self in relation to others and others as subjects equal to oneself.

Suchocki's relational theology provides tools for humanity's unique ability to conceptualize and transcend violence. She defined sin as "the unnecessary violation of the well-being of any aspect of creation" (48). Humanity is uniquely capable of sinning because of "the ability to transcend our violent tendency" (94). Thus, she claimed, "sin is a salvific word" implying "the possibility of ... transformation" (164). She identified three modes of transcendence—memory, empathy, and imagination—corresponding to past, present, and future perspectival moments, respectively (36). I also identify her recognition of humanity as a mode of transcendence, rooted in existence as a perspectival moment.

These modes of transcendence correspond temporally and spatially to the social nature of humanity within creation. We need memory to name patterns of violence rooted in our past, empathy to recognize violence mediated through the interrelatedness of humanity in the present, and imagination to see "violence perpetuated through social structures" and to construct a future free of this violence (36). These modes of transcendence address ruptures of time and space, suggesting a framework for bearing witness to the neighbor's trauma.

Taken together, these four modes of understanding oneself in relation to others allow for the possibility of morality by providing meaningful choice in relation to violence. In Suchocki's Christian parlance, evil is not "sin" if there is no ability to transcend one's violent tendencies (94). The reverse is also true. The ability to recognize, remember, empathize, and imagine implicates one in an interconnected world of sin and allows for a moral response. In other words, these four modes of transcendence enable human moral agency. Trauma due to human atrocities can be named sinful, unjust, and immoral because of the human ability to recognize the victim-survivor as equally human, empathize with their suffering, remember the wider circumstances that enabled the violation, and imagine more just relationships. Thus, the ability to transcend oneself supplies both a moral possibility and a moral imperative.

Each perspectival moment and mode of transcendence correlates to a moral theme essential to trauma response and recovery: dignity, love, justice, and solidarity, respectively. Persons bearing witness to trauma survivors need this language to address concerns about individual worth, regard for others, a sense of right and wrong, and community life. These universal concepts and commitments surface in many religions and philosophies, traditions and institutions as diverse as the Roman Catholic Church,[21] the World Council of Churches,[22]

---

[20]Marjorie Hewitt Suchocki, *The Fall to Violence: Original Sin in Relational Theology* (Continuum, 1994), 94.

[21]USCCB, "Seven Themes of Catholic Social Teaching," 2005, https://www.usccb.org/resources/seven-themes-catholic-social-teaching.

[22]Myriam Wijlens and Vladimir Shmaliy, eds., *Churches and Moral Discernment: Volume 1: Learning from Traditions*, Faith and Order Paper No. 228 (WCC, 2021), 160.

TABLE 1.3.1 *Four Modes of Transcendence and Moral Themes*

Perspectival Moment	Mode of Transcendence	Moral Theme
I. Existence	recognition	dignity
II. Present	empathy	love
III. Past	memory	justice
IV. Future	imagination	solidarity

Islam,[23] Judaism,[24] Sikhism,[25] Buddhism,[26] the American Humanist Association,[27] and diverse forms of Protestantism.[28] Table 1.3.1 shows the correlations between these moral themes, four modes of transcendence, and distinct and overlapping existential and temporal perspectival moments.

The Declaration of a Global Ethic by the Parliament of the World's Religions provides a helpful entry point for the moral themes of dignity, love, justice, and solidarity. This document identifies commonalities in religious ethics and humanist thought for addressing unnecessary suffering and other worldwide problems. According to one of its initiators, "The 'Global Ethic' is the articulation of the basic principles of right and wrong, which in fact are found to be affirmed by all major—and not so major—religions and ethical systems of the world, past and present."[29] The Global Ethic was designed to connect rights and religion, politics and morality. The declaration begins with a call to solidarity in light of the interdependence of humanity and the natural environment.[30] An appeal to the "Golden Rule" provided a common starting place for ethical behavior, "We must treat others as we wish others

---

[23]"A Common Word between Us and You," October 13, 2007, https://www.acommonword.com/downloads-and-translations/; Pope Francis and Sheikh Ahmad Muhammad Al-tayyeb, "Document on Human Fraternity for World Peace and Living Together," February 4, 2019, http://www.vatican.va/content/francesco/en/travels/2019/outside/documents/papa-francesco_20190204_documento-fratellanza-umana.html.

[24]Central Conference of American Rabbis, "The Guiding Principles of Reform Judaism," https://www.ccarnet.org/rabbinic-voice/platforms/article-guiding-principles-reform-judaism/.

[25]Simran Jeet Singh, "On the Anniversary of His Birth, a Reflection on the Life of Guru Nanak," *Religion News Service*, November 30, 2020, https://religionnews.com/2020/11/30/550-years-after-his-birth-a-reflection-on-the-life-of-sikhisms-founder-guru-nanak/.

[26]Bstan-'dzinrgya-mtsho, Dalai Lama XIV, *Ethics for the New Millenium* (Riverhead, 1999).

[27]American Humanist Association, "Humanism and Its Aspirations: Humanist Manifesto III, a Successor to the Humanist Manifesto of 1933," https://americanhumanist.org/what-is-humanism/manifesto3/.

[28]National Association of Evangelicals, "For the Health of the Nation: An Evangelical Call to Civic Responsibility," National Association of Evangelicals, 2024, https://www.nae.org/for-the-health-of-the-nation/; National Council of Churches of Christ in the USA, "A 21st Century Social Creed," 2007, https://nationalcouncilofchurches.us/christian-unity/a-21st-century-social-creed/; *The Book of Discipline of the United Methodist Church 2016* (UMPH, 2016), ¶¶ 160–6.

[29]Leonard J. Swidler, "The Movement for a Global Ethic," *Journal of Ecumenical Studies* 53, no. 1 (2018): 1, https://doi.org/10.1353/ecu.2018.0005.

[30]Parliament of the World's Religions, "Towards a Global Ethic: An Initial Declaration of the Parliament of the World's Religions," *Council for a Parliament of the World's Religions*, 2018, 4, https://web.archive.org/web/20210817123530/https://www.global-ethic.org/wp-content/uploads/2020/12/WEE_2018.pdf.

to treat us."[31] This appeal leads directly to a recognition of "the full realization of the intrinsic dignity of the human person."[32] The declaration includes commitments to human rights, justice, and "a spirit of compassion with those who suffer."[33] The authors intended to create a shared foundation of ethics to function alongside the Universal Declaration of Human Rights, drawn from religious and philosophical traditions based on a recognition of "an Ultimate Reality."[34] In this Declaration, the transcendent meets human rights, religious ethics enters into political discourse, and imagination is engaged to allow humans of all faith traditions to work together, in solidarity, for a better world.

An examination of dignity, love, justice, and solidarity in specific religious and philosophical traditions provides a fuller picture of the resources of religious ethics.

Dignity

Trauma can upend one's sense of value as a human person; thus, recognition of the inherent dignity of the survivor is a necessary starting place for recovery and healing. When bearing witness, we reckon with existence by recognizing the individual dignity of the human being, establishing grounds for equality and human rights.

The Abrahamic traditions include a creation story in which God created humans in the image of the divine, endowing each person with inestimable worth. For example, "the dignity of the human person … is the foundation of all the principles" of Roman Catholic Social Teaching.[35] When Muslim and Christian leaders engage in interfaith dialogue, shared human dignity provides a common starting point. For example, a document co-written by Pope Francis and Sheikh Ahmad Muhammad al-Tayyeb begins, "In the name of God who has created all human beings equal in rights, duties and dignity …."[36] Likewise, the World Council of Churches expressed, as its first methodological assumption about moral discernment in the churches, "human persons are created in the image of God" and "each human person has a unique dignity,"[37] and Protestants across the theological spectrum ground their social ethics and political engagement in the dignity of humans as made in the image of God.[38]

Dignity is also a fundamental belief of the humanist tradition. The Humanist Manifesto III declares its commitment to the "inherent worth and dignity" of every person.[39] The US Declaration of Independence states, "all men are created equal, that

---

[31]Parliament of the World's Religions, 4, 10; Swidler, "Movement for a Global Ethic," 5.

[32]Parliament of the World's Religions, "Declaration towards a Global Ethic," 4, 8, 10.

[33]Parliament of the World's Religions, 7, 14.

[34]Swidler, "Movement for a Global Ethic," 5.

[35]USCCB, "Seven Themes of Catholic Social Teaching."

[36]Francis and al-Tayyeb, "Human Fraternity."

[37]Wijlens and Shmaliy, *Churches and Moral Discernment*, 160.

[38]National Association of Evangelicals, "For the Health of the Nation"; National Council of Churches of Christ in the USA, "A 21st Century Social Creed"; *The Book of Discipline of the United Methodist Church 2016*, ¶ 161.

[39]American Humanist Association, "Humanism and Its Aspirations."

they are endowed by their Creator with certain unalienable Rights."[40] The Preamble to the Universal Declaration of Human Rights begins with a recognition of "the inherent dignity and of the equal and inalienable rights of all members of the human family" and its first article declares, "All human beings are born free and equal in dignity and rights."[41]

These commitments to dignity and equality correspond to fundamental beliefs in many religious traditions. The first teaching in the Sikh tradition, the concept of *ik oankar*, meaning "the oneness of the divinity," provides a foundational commitment to equal treatment and rights for all persons.[42] The Dalai Lama, the leader of Tibetan Buddhism, asserted "the fundamental oneness of the human family" as a basis for ethical thought and action.[43] Among the Bantu people and many cultures across Africa, the term *Muntu* refers to fundamental dignity of the human being, based on "the moral character, the essence of genuine humanity, the essence of a deeply humane being."[44]

Love

Since trauma recovery centers on healing relationships, the moral theme of love is an essential resource for the work of bearing witness to the trauma survivor. Love refers to a relational ideal promoted within many religious traditions, enacting human dignity on an interpersonal level in the present. In the Sikh tradition, oneness is practiced through the pursuit of a "deep connection of love."[45] The Dalai Lama observed, "human nature is basically disposed toward love and compassion," and asserted "that the capacity for empathy which underlies it is of crucial importance when it comes to ethics."[46] Thus, love as an expression of empathy is rooted deeply in Buddhist ethics. As noted above, the "Golden Rule," expressing love for fellow humans, is so common among various religious traditions and philosophies that it provided a starting point for the Declaration of a Global Ethic.[47]

The concept is central to the Abrahamic traditions: Judaism, Islam, and Christianity all elevate love as one of if not the highest expression of faithful living. For example, a group of prominent Muslim scholars seeking to establish peaceful relations with Christian leaders asserted, "The basis for this peace and understanding already exists. It is part of the very foundational principles of both faiths: love of the

---

[40]"Declaration of Independence: A Transcription," *National Archives*, https://www.archives.gov/founding-docs/declaration-transcript.

[41]United Nations, "Universal Declaration of Human Rights," https://www.un.org/en/about-us/universal-declaration-of-human-rights.

[42]Singh, "On the Anniversary of His Birth."

[43]Bstan-'dzinrgya-mtsho, Dalai Lama XIV, *Ethics for the New Millenium*, 163.

[44]Mutombo Nkulu-N'Sengha, "Bumuntu Memory and Authentic Personhood: An African Art of Becoming Humane," in *Memory and the Narrative Imagination in the African and Diaspora Experience*, ed. Tom Spencer-Walters, 306–7 (Bedford, 2011).

[45]Singh, "On the Anniversary of His Birth."

[46]Bstan-'dzinrgya-mtsho. Dalai Lama XIV, *Ethics for the New Millenium*, 72.

[47]Swidler, "The Movement for a Global Ethic," 5.

One God, and love of the neighbour."[48] When discussing human fraternity, Sheikh Ahmad Muhammad al-Tayyeb and Pope Francis together affirmed, "Faith leads a believer to see in the other a brother or sister to be supported and loved."[49] Love of God and neighbor are central to Jewish law (Torah) and provide a common moral starting point with Christian traditions: "love your neighbor as yourself" (Lev. 19:18; Mt. 19:19).

Justice

Justice refers to a sense of right relationship, both interpersonally and systemically, involving memory to redress past injustices. For example, in the Sikh tradition, oneness and love naturally lead to a commitment to service and justice, the third central teaching of founder Guru Nanak.[50] Among the many different conceptions of justice,[51] justice in relation to oppression and suffering is most relevant to bearing witness to survivors of trauma. Justice is often expressed in terms of special consideration for the vulnerable. Muslim and Christian "believers are called to express this human fraternity by safeguarding creation and the entire universe and supporting all persons, especially the poorest and those most in need."[52] One of the primary themes of Roman Catholic Social Teaching is "to put the needs of the poor and vulnerable first."[53] In Judaism, God is depicted as siding with the oppressed and giving special protections to the vulnerable; justice in the Hebrew scriptures is expressed as *mishpat* and *tzadeqah*, attending to rights, responsibilities, and right relationships. Protestants often focus on justice in terms of protecting human rights and addressing systemic injustices, as illustrated by the social creed tradition.[54] Supporting the most vulnerable is the essence of justice in the work of trauma response.

Solidarity

Solidarity brings dignity, love, and justice into social action, based on the interrelatedness of humanity as well as the natural world, and is shaped by imagining a better future. In the Sikh tradition, love and justice naturally lead to collective efforts to serve one another: "If we truly love, we will be driven to engage politically and make the world a better place for all."[55] One of the seven themes of Catholic Social Teaching, solidarity is based on the idea of humanity as "one human family."[56]

---

[48]"A Common Word."
[49]Francis and al-Tayyeb, "Human Fraternity."
[50]Singh, "On the Anniversary of His Birth."
[51]Karen Lebacqz, *Six Theories of Justice: Perspectives from Philosophical and Theological Ethics* (Augsburg, 1986); Vic McCracken, ed., *Christian Faith and Social Justice: Five Views* (Bloomsbury, 2014).
[52]Francis and al-Tayyeb, "Human Fraternity."
[53]USCCB, "Seven Themes of Catholic Social Teaching."
[54]See discussion in Darryl W. Stephens, *Methodist Morals: Social Principles in the Public Church's Witness* (University of Tennessee Press, 2016), 82–92.
[55]Singh, "On the Anniversary of His Birth."
[56]USCCB, "Seven Themes of Catholic Social Teaching."

Solidarity is a key concept in Christian liberation theology, in which the oppressed find common cause in the struggle to be liberated from suffering. In many cultures across Africa, the term *Bumuntu* (or, more familiarly to Western ears, *Ubuntu*), refers to "hospitality and solidarity: 'I am because we are, and because we are therefore I am.'"[57] In Jewish tradition, *tikkun olam*, or "repairing the world," provides motivation for social justice.[58] In ecumenical Protestantism, solidarity generally refers to the intersection of hope and community. A visible example of Protestant solidarity was manifest in the effort toward "justice, peace and the integrity of creation," in which members of the World Council of Churches sought to address human and ecological suffering.[59] Solidarity is also expressed in the Global Ethic of the Parliament of the World's Religions, which opens with a preamble, "The world is in agony … But this agony need not be."[60] The document proceeds to seek cooperation among the world's religions to imagine participating in building a better world by addressing suffering. Thus, solidarity points to the interrelatedness of survivor and responder, imagining the possibilities of working together for recovery and healing from trauma.

Discussion Questions

1 When we speak of modes of transcendence, we are talking about ways in which humans can connect with a reality beyond themselves. How do recognition, memory, empathy, and imagination help you find meaning and purpose beyond yourself?

2 Which of the four moral themes (dignity, love, justice, or solidarity) is emphasized most by your faith community or culture? Which is emphasized least, and why?

3 Do you think that religion can contribute to healing a traumatized world? Why or why not?

Trauma-Informed Response and Recovery

Models of healing and recovery from trauma, as well as trauma-informed response, are designed to address the reality of traumatic suffering and empower the survivor to flourish within new and renewed relationships. Herman's stages of recovery and SAMHSA's fourfold description of trauma-informed care correlate to the distinct perspectival moments, modes of transcendence, and moral themes introduced above. In this section, I map the transcendent dimensions of trauma-informed response and recovery onto four perspectival moments, setting the stage for a fully developed depiction of bearing witness in the next section.

---

[57]Nkulu-N'Sengha, "Bumuntu Memory and Authentic Personhood," 306.

[58]Jill Jacobs, "The History of 'Tikkun Olam,'" *Zeek: A Jewish Journal of Thought and Culture*, June 2007, http://www.zeek.net/706tohu/.

[59]Heino Falcke, "The Ecumenical Assembly for Justice, Peace and the Integrity of Creation," *The Ecumenical Review* 56, no. 2 (2004): 184–91.

[60]Parliament of the World's Religions, "Declaration Towards a Global Ethic," 3.

TABLE 1.3.2 *Four Stages of Trauma-Informed Response and Recovery*

Perspectival Moment	Mode of Transcendence	Moral Theme	Trauma-Informed Response (SAMHSA)	Stage of Trauma Recovery (Judith Herman)
I. Existence	recognition	dignity	realize	overcoming relational barriers
II. Present	empathy	love	recognize (identify and name)	safety
III. Past	memory	justice	respond	reconstruction of narrative
IV. Future	imagination	solidarity	resist	reconnection and restoration

Herman identified three stages preceded by the necessary step of establishing a healing support relationship. I interpret this preliminary step as the first of four stages of the healing process—overcoming relational barriers, safety, reconstruction of narrative, and reconnection and restoration (Herman, 3, 156, 267, 276). Similarly, trauma-informed response consists of four "key assumptions"—realize, recognize, respond, and resist.[61] "SAMHSA defines any setting as 'trauma-informed' if the people there realize how widespread trauma is, recognize signs and symptoms, respond by integrating knowledge into practice, and resist doing further harm."[62] These stages and assumptions correlate to the four modes of transcendence previously identified: recognition, empathy, memory, and imagination (see Table 1.3.2).

Existence

The first moment of trauma-informed response and recovery is grounded existentially. Trauma-informed response begins with realizing the widespread occurrence of trauma.[63] Trauma is a fact of existence in this world. Realizing the ubiquity of trauma also entails an awareness of what trauma is and what is required to recover from trauma. The experience of trauma includes loss of meaning, guilt, shame, and a myriad of other disruptions to healthy living and relationships. Trauma is, simply put, an experience that is too much to handle with the body's normal coping mechanisms. Trauma impacts one's very existence.

Recognition enables the responder to realize the widespread occurrence of trauma and the survivor to overcome relational barriers, thus addressing existence as a perspectival moment of trauma-informed response and recovery. Recognition of the

---

[61]SAMHSA, "SAMHSA's Concept of Trauma," 9–10.

[62]SAMHSA, "Spotlight: Building Resilient and Trauma-Informed Communities—Introduction | SAMHSA Publications and Digital Products," 2017, https://store.samhsa.gov/product/Spotlight-Building-Resilient-and-Trauma-Informed-Communities-Introduction/SMA17-5014.

[63]SAMHSA, "Spotlight."

survivor's humanity is essential for the survivor to (re)claim their agency. Employing imagery from Buber, recognition allows the responder-survivor relationship to become I-You instead of I-It.[64] According to Herman, "the first principle of recovery is the empowerment of the survivor" (133). Empowerment occurs through healing relationships, which give the survivor a sense of being recognized as an agent of their own healing. Thus, overcoming "barriers of shame and secrecy" through existential recognition is a prerequisite to all stages of healing and recovery (Herman, 276). Pamela Birrell indicated that effective listening in the healing relationship must "reach below the surface to the level of experience and being"; the responder must consider the survivor "an individual with a unique and deep subjectivity."[65] Realizing the reality of trauma in the world helps remove the stigma of shame and denies trauma the power of secrecy.

Present

The second moment of trauma-informed response and recovery is focused on the present. According to SAMHSA, trauma-informed response proceeds by identifying and naming the signs and symptoms of trauma.[66] Trauma reveals itself in social withdrawal, irritability, dissociation, difficulty recovering intimacy, PTSD, and an inability to remain fully attentive in the present moment, to list only a few common symptoms. Since trauma is a whole-body response to an overwhelming experience due to life-threat or social betrayal,[67] a sense of safety is paramount for healing and recovery.

Empathy enables the responder to identify and name the signs and symptoms of trauma and to establish a safe environment for the survivor of trauma. Herman named "attending to safety in the present" as the first of three stages of recovery once a healing relationship is established (269, see also 156). Safety is an immediate concern for the trauma survivor. Safety addresses the needs of the survivor in the here and now, "making intolerable feelings bearable through connection with others" (276). To establish such a relationship requires empathy on the part of the responder. Empathetic presence allows one to re-establish safe human connection, thus addressing the present as a perspectival moment of trauma-informed response and recovery.

Past

The third moment of trauma-informed response and recovery is rooted in the past. According to SAMHSA, an appropriate response to the trauma survivor involves integrating knowledge into practice.[68] Everything one has learned about trauma becomes relevant to trauma-informed response. To respond appropriately to

---

[64] Buber, *I and Thou*, 16–17.
[65] Pamela J. Birrell and Jennifer J. Freyd, "Betrayal Trauma: Relational Models of Harm and Healing," *Journal of Trauma Practice* 5, no. 1 (2006): 55, https://doi.org/10.1300/J189v05n01_04.
[66] SAMHSA, "Spotlight."
[67] Birrell and Freyd, "Betrayal Trauma," 50.
[68] SAMHSA, "Building Resilient and Trauma-Informed Communities."

trauma requires action intentionally informed by one's past training and experience. The past is also the focus of Herman's stage of recovery, reconstruction of narrative through remembrance and mourning (156). Reconstructing the trauma narrative allows the survivor to grieve the past so that it can become part of the past rather than remain an ever-present, recurring nightmare. Memory, then, serves both survivor and responder, integrating knowledge into practice and assisting in reconstructing the trauma narrative. Reckoning with the past is thus a crucial perspectival moment of trauma-informed response and recovery.

Future

The fourth moment of trauma-informed response and recovery finds meaning in the future. According to SAMHSA, to resist doing further harm is the fourth feature of trauma-informed response.[69] One can lower the likelihood of re-traumatization by avoiding triggering stimuli, being aware of the dynamics of revictimization, and becoming an ally and advocate for the survivor's healing and future well-being. This work requires imagining a future for the survivor that is free of the shackles of traumatic physiological response.

Imagination enables one to resist re-traumatization and to empower reconnection. Herman identified the final stage of recovery as "reconnection": "Having come to terms with the traumatic past, the survivor faces the task of creating a future" (196). This task requires imagination and hope. The work of reconnection is accomplished through reconciling relationships with self, others, and community, thereby allowing for deepening of intimacy and concern for the next generation (Herman, 206). Resisting re-traumatization involves responders, as well as survivors working to create organizational cultures conducive to the well-being of all. Thus, imagination addresses the future as a perspectival moment of trauma-informed response and recovery.

Discussion Questions

1 Most wounds can be healed with medicines, bandages, and time. However, traumatic wounds cannot be isolated; they affect one's entire self, making them more difficult to treat. What do you think happens to untreated traumatic wounds?

2 Trauma healing and recovery often requires the assistance of licensed counselors, psychiatrists, and support groups. What mental health supports are available in your community? Which ones have been helpful to you? What services or supports did you find lacking or difficult to access?

3 Consider yourself a friend of Jaemyoung, quoted at the beginning of this chapter. Isolate one "moment" of bearing witness (i.e., one row on Table 1.3.2) and consider how these concepts might shape your understanding and interpretation of his situation as well as your response.

---

[69]SAMHSA.

Bearing Witness as Social Action

The framework of bearing witness provides a bridge between religious ethics and trauma-informed response and recovery. This multifaceted moral activity finds resonance with relational models of healing, such as that espoused by Birrell and Jennifer Freyd. Birrell expressed concern that, in non-relational medical approaches, "trauma becomes a medical pathology rather than a religious, moral, or ethical happening."[70] I, too, seek to offer "an ethic of compassion and mutuality" in response to trauma.[71] Where Birrell offered three aspects to a relational model of psychiatric treatment—listening, mutual empathy, and compassion—I employ a similar and more detailed framework for persons who do not specialize in psychiatry.[72] To correlate concepts central to religious ethics (as well as humanist constructs of human rights) to trauma-informed response and recovery, I present bearing witness as a social action with implied if not explicit religious dimensions.

Bearing witness, as I have developed the concept in relation to Christian ethics and trauma studies, is a spiritually informed model of trauma-informed response. Presented in four perspectival moments, this model draws on multiple disciplines, combining trauma recovery and trauma-informed response and attending to embodied existence and transcendent reality. The model correlates SAMHSA's definition of trauma-informed response,[73] Herman's stages of recovery (v, 3, 276), and distinct modes of transcendence with prominent moral themes drawn from religious ethics. Bearing witness reckons with human existence, present, past, and future through recognition, empathy, memory, and imagination and engages the moral themes of dignity, love, justice, and solidarity, respectively. The work of bearing witness involves four identifiable practices of social action: grounded being, attentive presence, historical clarity, and meaningful participation (see Table 1.3.3).

Bearing witness is a guide to moral action connecting survivor and responder and attending to the spiritual well-being of both. As a trauma-informed response, responder and survivor are interrelated: "To study psychological trauma means bearing witness to horrible events" (Herman, 7). Bearing witness is, therefore, a risk-laden and purposeful action of moral engagement, putting the responder at risk of indirect or vicarious traumatization.[74] To bear witness is to attest to the truth of another person's story—and to act upon it.

Bearing witness involves both personal and political relations, finding overlap between the sacred and the secular and demanding moral engagement. Kelly Oliver, a professor of philosophy specializing in politics and gender, proposed bearing witness as a way of bringing ethical concerns into politics, noting, "witnessing has both the juridical connotations of seeing with one's own eyes and the religious connotations

---

[70]Birrell and Freyd, "Betrayal Trauma," 59.

[71]Birrell and Freyd, 60.

[72]Birrell and Freyd, 54–9.

[73]SAMHSA, "Building Resilient and Trauma-Informed Communities"; SAMHSA, "SAMHSA's Concept of Trauma," 9.

[74]I. Lisa McCann and Laurie Anne Pearlman, "Vicarious Traumatization: A Framework for Understanding the Psychological Effects of Working with Victims," *Journal of Traumatic Stress* 3, no. 1 (1990): 131–49, https://doi.org/10.1002/jts.2490030110.

TABLE 1.3.3 *Bearing Witness in Four Perspectival Moments*

Perspectival Moment	Mode of Transcendence	Moral Theme	Practice of Social Action	Trauma-Informed Response (SAMHSA)	Stage of Trauma Recovery (Judith Herman)
I. Existence	recognition	dignity	grounded being	realize	overcoming relational barriers
II. Present	empathy	love	attentive presence	recognize (identify and name)	safety
III. Past	memory	justice	historical clarity	respond	reconstruction of narrative
IV. Future	imagination	solidarity	meaningful participation	resist	reconnection and restoration

of testifying to that which cannot be seen."[75] The concept of bearing witness is also familiar to the profession of nursing.

> Bearing witness is [a way of] being with and relating to others that is based on values and beliefs that give rise to a commitment to attend to, honour, and stay with persons' truths, perspectives, priorities, hopes, and dreams; that is, their lived experience … [it] is a distinct way of being and relating with persons because of the ontological view about human beings and health that underlines it.[76]

Rooted in ethics (values and beliefs) and attuned to the victim-survivor's spiritual life (truths, perspectives, priorities, hopes, and dreams), bearing witness lends itself to religious mapping. Bearing witness allows us to respond and relate to victim-survivors as their whole, embodied selves through four distinct practices of moral action.

Grounded Being

Bearing witness recognizes human dignity through the practice of grounded being. Bearing witness requires, first and foremost, recognition of the survivor as a

[75]Kelly Oliver, "Witnessing, Recognition, and Response Ethics," *Philosophy & Rhetoric* 48, no. 4 (2015): 483, http://muse.jhu.edu/article/602490.
[76]Rahel Naef, "Bearing Witness: A Moral Way of Engaging in the Nurse-Person Relationship," *Nursing Philosophy* 7, no. 3 (2006): 149, https://doi.org/10.1111/j.1466-769X.2006.00271.x.

person, grounding the relationship in mutual being-ness. In nursing, for example, recognition of the survivor's shared human dignity is a fundamental part of bearing witness:

> we can only bear witness when we acknowledge the other's irreducibility and infinity ... Bearing witness is enacting the moral responsibility arising from the encounter with the other, and it is a form of ethical resistance because when we bear witness, we acknowledge the other as other and turn towards him or her.[77]

This activity of "ethical resistance" can include both identifying the initial cause of trauma as essentially unjust as well as avoiding doing further harm. Bearing witness is a means of "enacting one's moral agency in nursing"[78]—and not only in nursing. Tamsin Jones, a political theologian, described bearing witness as "a spiritual exercise" that presupposes and enacts hope by attending to "the truth of resistance in the face of dehumanization."[79] The trauma survivor's existence is itself a testament to this truth of resistance. Drawing on Oliver's philosophical work, Jones identified three characteristics of bearing witness: a relational view of human subjectivity, an encounter with radical otherness, and a way of seeking truth that is pluralistic and dynamic.[80] Bearing witness involves recognizing common humanity, encountering that which cannot be adequately described or understood, and acting on that knowledge. In this way, the responder becomes a partner with the survivor to find and declare unspeakable truths.

Attentive Presence

Bearing witness reckons with the present moment through the practice of attentive presence, exercising empathy as an expression of love. Umair Haque, a writer in leadership studies and economics, described bearing witness as "our first and truest responsibility" as humans during troubled times.[81] The process, according to Haque, seeks to transform injustices, allowing the one bearing witness to "reclaim a sense of ourselves as fully human." He named three aspects of bearing witness: seeing through the eyes of those harmed, seeing through the eyes of history, and seeing through the eyes of humanity. These aspects correspond to present, past, and future, respectively.

The humanity of responder and survivor are intertwined by bearing witness in the present. Anne Bogart, a theatre professor, described this dynamic in terms of audience and actor: to bear witness is to "develop a point of view in relation to what one has seen." Bearing witness is a moral activity requiring not only attentive

---

[77]Naef, 149.

[78]Naef, 152.

[79]Tamsin Jones, "Bearing Witness: Hope for the Unseen," *Political Theology* 17, no. 2 (2016): 139, 141, https://doi.org/10.1080/1462317X.2016.1161300.

[80]Jones, 141–3.

[81]Umair Haque, "Why Our First Responsibility Is Bearing Witness," *Medium*, May 26, 2018, https://medium.com/on-eudaimonia/why-our-first-responsibility-is-bearing-witness-2e493c4d3fd.

presence but also participation. Bogart traced increased levels of moral response through the stages of seeing, witnessing, and bearing witness:

> The steps from seeing to witnessing to bearing witness travel from inaction to conscious action. First we see others. Seeing does not require the responsibility of consciousness. In order to shift from seeing to witnessing, we must attempt connection, understanding and interpretation. Finally, to bear witness requires the courage to show up fully and take responsibility for one's own anxiety and to "be with" fully and compassionately. To bear witness asks for what ministers, therapists and peacemakers call a "non-anxious presence."[82]

Bogart clearly understood bearing witness as a moral activity pertaining not only to theatre and the arts but also to helping professionals and service providers, religious and secular.

In Bogart's depiction, bearing witness involves connection, attentiveness, interpretation, and responsibility. The responsibility "to 'be with' fully and compassionately" is what I name "attentive presence," exercised through empathy. "Empathetic listening occurs when we recognize the deep humanity of another and enter into their felt experience without judgment or manipulation."[83] This kind of attentiveness, or attention, is an expression of love, a connection explored by Simone Weil, Iris Murdoch, and others.[84] Recovery from trauma is based, in part, on "the hope that restorative love may still be found in the world" (Herman, 211). Trauma-informed response through attentive presence reassures the victim-survivor that such love exists.

Historical Clarity

Bearing witness reckons with the past through the practice of historical clarity, exercising memory in the work of justice. For example, bearing witness is a fundamental principle of Doctors Without Borders, an organization committed to speaking out publicly about the trauma and suffering encountered during disaster relief work: "we are duty-bound to raise our voices and speak out on behalf of our patients. Our decision to do so is always guided by our mission to do no harm, preserve respect and dignity, and protect life and health."[85] There is no morally neutral way to care for a victim of trauma.

---

[82]Anne Bogart, "Bearing Witness," *SITI Company*, February 18, 2016, https://web.archive.org/web/20160228005129/http://siti.org/content/bearing-witness.

[83]Sharon Browning, Donna Duffey, Fred Magondu, John A. Moore, and Patricia A. Way, *The Little Book of Listening: Listening as a Radical Act of Love, Justice, Healing, and Transformation* (Good Books, 2024), 24.

[84]Christopher Cordner, "What Did Iris Murdoch Mean by 'Attention'?," *ABC Religion & Ethics*, Australian Broadcasting Corporation, July 11, 2019, https://www.abc.net.au/religion/iris-murdoch-and-the-meaning-of-attention/11301690.

[85]MSF, "What Guides Us," https://www.doctorswithoutborders.org/who-we-are/principles/bearing-witness.

Responding to and caring for survivors of trauma requires bearing witness to emotionally difficult and potentially traumatizing truths and naming the injustices. In *Trauma and Recovery*, Herman wrote that to insist on "neutrality" is to side with the perpetrator (7). Some helping professionals may be uncomfortable with this admission of bias. However, Herman made a clear distinction between "the technical neutrality of the therapist" and "moral neutrality":

> Working with victimized people requires a committed moral stance. The therapist is called upon to bear witness to a crime. She must affirm a position of solidarity with the victim ... it involves an understanding of the fundamental injustice of the traumatic experience and the need for a resolution that restores some sense of justice.

(135)

Thus, trauma-informed responders must engage in the work of justice, which can only be done through the practice of historical clarity.

Historical clarity has different demands for survivors and responders. For the survivor, it involves integrating one's memories of the trauma into one's life story, "remembrance and mourning" (Herman, 242). Herman asserted the power and centrality of this aspect of bearing witness within her therapeutic context: "The consulting room is a privileged space dedicated to memory" (246). For the responder, the work of memory involves cultural and institutional memory, reconstructing the narrative of complicity in the unjust social structures that enable and perpetuate traumatic violence, such as institutional betrayal,[86] racism, rape culture, war crimes, forced migration, genocide, and other forms of social and political oppression. Reckoning with the past through a lens of justice requires, in religious terms, some form of collective repentance and lament, acknowledging that this trauma should not have happened and resolving, "Never more!"

Meaningful Participation

Ultimately, persons bearing witness must reckon with the future through the practice of meaningful participation, exercising imagination in the work of solidarity. In nursing, "bearing witness ... is attentive presence, involving relationship with others, standing in solidarity with others, being in community."[87] Herman affirmed these aspects of the work recovery, for both survivor and responder by asserting the importance of community and relational connections, "the solidarity of a group," as essential to recovery; thus, she declared, "bearing witness ... is an act of solidarity" (247). Working together in solidarity requires meaningful participation.

---

[86]Carly Parnitzke Smith and Jennifer J. Freyd, "Dangerous Safe Havens: Institutional Betrayal Exacerbates Sexual Trauma," *Journal of Traumatic Stress* 26, no. 1 (2013): 119–24, https://doi.org/10.1002/jts.21778.
[87]Naef, "Bearing Witness," 150.

Meaningful participation occurs when survivor and responder meet in imagining and crafting a better future, culminating in the work of bearing witness. For Oliver, invoking imagination is an ethical responsibility:

> The tension between eyewitness testimony and bearing witness, between subject position and subjectivity, is the dynamic operator that moves us beyond the melancholic choice between either dead historical facts or traumatic repetition of violence. It is the tension between our social-political contexts and our ethical responsibility to imagine life otherwise.[88]

Oliver's description recapitulates the practices of bearing witness. Grounded in being, the responder, enacts subjectivity, becoming part of the action. Attentive presence enters the tension between bystanding ("eyewitness testimony") and social action (bearing witness), allowing for the possibility of transcending the "traumatic repetition." Historical clarity places the fact of this trauma in the past while also making room for the possibility that the future can be different. Meaningful participation not only imagines "life otherwise" but also takes responsibility for bringing it about in solidarity with the survivor. Bearing witness thus integrates the practices of grounded being, attentive presence, historical clarity, and meaningful participation.

Unlike traumatic repetition, in which the past disrupts the present, the cycle of bearing witness constantly integrates the past into the present as it looks to the future. This work is done in solidarity. Where Herman declared, "only an ongoing connection with a global political movement for human rights could ultimately sustain our ability to speak about unspeakable things" (237). I assert that such a global political movement is enhanced through interreligious understanding and the resources of religious ethics.

The role of the trauma-informed responder is to bear witness to the survivor through recognition, love, justice, and solidarity, enabling the survivor to realize their ability to live out these moral themes themself. The survivor may even develop a sense of mission. A survivor's mission typically consists of public action involving various forms of participation: truth-telling, pursuing justice, strategic alliances, and giving to others (Herman, 207–11). Responders can support survivors by joining their demand for specific elements of justice-making and accompanying them through the journey.[89] Additionally, Herman noted, "In taking care of others, survivors feel recognized, loved, and cared for themselves" (209), reinforcing a positive, supportive cycle by bearing witness to others. Choosing sides with the survivor, in solidarity and with the intent to shape a better future, renders bearing witness a political endeavor. Bearing witness to trauma requires, as Herman asserted, "the context of a political movement" (32). Bearing witness to the survivor is, therefore, a politically engaged form of social action.

---

[88]Oliver, "Witnessing, Recognition, and Response Ethics," 483.

[89]Marie M. Fortune, *Is Nothing Sacred?: When Sex Invades the Pastoral Relationship* (Harper & Row, 1989), 112–18.

Discussion Questions

1 Which practice of social action comes most naturally to you? Which do you find most challenging?

2 In what ways is bearing witness not morally neutral? Whose interests are prioritized?

3 Can you effectively bear witness to someone who you think is at fault or who you do not believe? How does the practice of bearing witness respond to questions of guilt, fault, or truth?

A Religious Journey

The process of regaining spiritual well-being is, for many victim-survivors, a religious journey. Persons like Jaemyoung, introduced at the beginning of this chapter, need to address the spiritual impact of their trauma to heal. Religious ethics is a valuable resource and partner in addressing the personal, systemic, and political aspects of trauma. A basic understanding of religious ethics facilitates solidarity with persons of many religious traditions or no religious tradition. Likewise, service providers, helping professionals, and other responders may find the work of trauma-informed response to be a spiritually demanding journey. Religious ethics offers significant support for the social action of bearing witness through dignity, love, justice, and solidarity, concepts that resonate within the wide diversity of religious traditions and philosophies around the world. Responders must become spiritually informed to bear witness effectively to survivors of trauma.

When one works toward liberation in solidarity with others, the effort is inevitably political and spiritual, with all the risk that such action entails. "To speak publicly about one's knowledge of atrocities is to invite the stigma that attaches to victims" (Herman, 2). The act of bearing witness to trauma brings unjust structures to light, exposing violence for what it is. To bear witness to the trauma survivor is to become involved, to stake moral ground, and to engage in the struggle. Herman argued, "these attacks … remind us that creating a protected space where survivors can speak their truth is an act of liberation. They remind us that bearing witness … is an act of solidarity" (247). Suffering is both a political[90] and a theological problem.[91] Likewise, bearing witness to suffering is both a political and spiritual form of social action. A religious perspective is not necessary; however, many people draw on their faith for the strength necessary to engage in this difficult spiritual work.

---

[90]Cynthia Halpern, *Suffering, Politics, Power: A Genealogy in Modern Political Theory* (State University of New York Press, 2002).

[91]M. Shawn Copeland, "'Wading through Many Sorrows': Toward a Theology of Suffering in Womanist Perspective," in *A Troubling in My Soul: Womanist Perspectives on Evil and Suffering*, ed. Emilie M. Townes, 109–29 (Orbis, 1993).

Responders desiring to attend to a victim-survivor's spiritual well-being must themselves be attuned to the spiritual aspects of their work. When informed by and grounded in spirituality, responders can realize the full power of bearing witness to victim-survivors to aid in healing, recovery, and liberation after trauma. Diaconal actors are particularly well-situated to do so.

1.4

Diakonia

With advances in trauma studies over the past thirty years, we now know that trauma is one of the most pervasive and widespread causes of broken relationships and estrangement from community. Furthermore, Christians are called to bear witness to this reality. If, as Paul claimed, "God ... has given us the ministry [*diakonīan*] of reconciliation" (2 Cor. 5:18), reconciliation and repair among individuals and within communities broken by trauma are central to the diaconal vocation of all Christians.

In this chapter, I explore points of connection between trauma-informed ethics and diakonia, both of which imply a stance of liberating service to others. Diaconal praxis and methodology ground trauma-informed response in Christian vocation. Conversely, trauma studies inform diaconal ministries with a clinical understanding of suffering. Through an interdisciplinary approach, trauma-informed Christian ethics joins responsible interfaith collaboration (*diapraxis*) and community-building (*conviviality*) as a tool to empower ecumenical diakonia in seeing, reflecting, and acting.[1] Where conviviality normally begins with the question, "How can we live together?" a trauma-informed approach begins with the question, "How can we live together in the aftermath of trauma?" Combining these perspectives, trauma-informed Christian ethics provides guidance for diaconal workers bearing witness to individual victim-survivors and traumatized communities, equipping all of us to participate in social change movements for justice, healing, and possible reconciliation.

Service as Liberative Praxis

Diakonia is an embodied and lived theology of service to others in the name of Christ. The Greek word is often translated as servant or servanthood, for example, in the words of Jesus: "The greatest among you will be your servant [*diakonos*]"

---

[1]My methodology is inductive, analytical, interdisciplinary, and liberation-focused. Thus, my critical reflection on the praxis of diakonia finds common cause with Kjell Nordstokke's development of "the science of *diakonia*." Kjell Nordstokke, *Liberating Diakonia* (Tapir Akademisk, 2011), 29–37, 60–2.

(Mt. 23:11). Jesus called his followers to diakonia by washing their feet. Thus, the basin and towel are signs of diaconal ministry for the whole church. Diakonia is often defined simply as Christian-motivated social service—but it is much more than just a desire to live out one's faith by helping others.

The work of diakonia takes many forms within and beyond the church. Diaconal workers are persons motivated by Christian faith to serve in helping professions. Nurses, social workers, teachers, police officers, administrators, and many others who find Christian vocational fulfillment through helping others may identify their work as a form of diakonia. Diakonia is also about being sent to communicate or serve on behalf of Christ and his church. Diakonia is the work of an emissary, a messenger or mediator sent by a person in a position of power.[2] Christians are sent by Christ to serve their neighbors. The church sends members of the diaconate— deacons, deaconesses, and other consecrated, commissioned, and ordained leaders— to serve communities on behalf of the church. Deacons are sometimes sent by their bishops as emissaries on behalf of the episcopate.

Ecumenical diakonia claims a history, methodology, and distinctive missional form of discipleship. Contemporary ecumenical diakonia builds on an older tradition of deaconesses representing institutionalized piety and service and, more recently, deacons (both men and women) representing a renewed understanding of the church's ministry through liturgy and ordination.[3] Currently, ecumenical diakonia is a specific expression of "the diaconate of all believers."[4] As a missional enterprise, it is also provocative, "calling into being ... new ways of seeing, judging and acting."[5] This three-fold formula (see-judge-act) provides a basic methodology for contemporary ecumenical diakonia, which is focused on liberation and empowerment of the poor, suffering, and oppressed.

Diakonia becomes liberative when compassion is wedded to social analysis and empowerment. Diaconal workers strive to join in solidarity with persons who are suffering, enhancing their moral agency and the flourishing of each member of the community. Furthermore, the image of the suffering servant must be de-subjugated to become liberative for those serving in diaconal roles.[6] Since ecumenical diakonia is relational and focused particularly on the needs of the oppressed and marginalized, it requires a community-based, liberative ethic. Liberation theology, centered on the

---

[2]John N. Collins, *Diakonia Studies: Critical Issues in Ministry* (Oxford University Press, 2014), 3–36. See also Benjamin L. Hartley, "The Problem and Promise of the Diaconate," in *Diaconal Studies: Lived Theology for the Church in North America*, ed. Nessan and Stephens, 51–62 (Regnum Books International, 2024).

[3]Nordstokke, *Liberating Diakonia*, 18.

[4]WCC and ACT Alliance, *Called to Transformation: Ecumenical Diakonia* (WCC, 2022), 16, https:// www.oikoumene.org/resources/publications/ecumenical-diakonia.

[5]WCC and ACT Alliance, 15. This trifold schema arises from Latin American liberation theology and is influential in Roman Catholic and ecumenical documents. Carlos E. Ham, "Seeing-Judging-Acting: A Learning Method for Empowerment in Diaconia from a Latin American Perspective," in *International Handbook on Ecumenical Diakonia*, ed. Ampony et al., 631–8 (Regnum Books International, 2021); and Nordstokke, *Liberating Diakonia*, 35.

[6]Man-Hei Yip, "De-Subjugating the Servant Image as a Theo-Diaconal Intervention," in *Diaconal Studies: Lived Theology for the Church in North America*, ed. Nessan and Stephens, 123–32 (Regnum Books International, 2024).

perspective and needs of the poor, provides an essential framework. However, most North American diaconal actors are not poor, and attempts at solidarity are laden with power differentials. Thus, we must consider the question: How can persons of privilege participate in a praxis of liberation?

An ethic of bearing witness to victim-survivors of trauma can assist diaconal workers attempting to serve as ambassadors of God's reconciliation in the world (2 Cor. 5:18-20). A trauma-informed praxis of diakonia aims to see, judge, and act in ways that contribute to human flourishing—for the good of victim-survivors, the human community, and all of creation. Thus, the theology and practice of diakonia must not only become trauma-informed but also contribute to the shaping of individual and community responses to trauma.

Aid and Agency

Healing from trauma is a lengthy and arduous process requiring community support. According to Judith Herman, trauma traps the survivor in a continual, traumatic moment in which the survivor may feel helpless in the face of existential threat.[7] To aid recovery, the individual trauma survivor can be assisted by a trained therapist and a community of support, including diaconal workers and other individuals bearing witness to their humanity and suffering.

Herman's depiction of the helpless victim presents a problem of agency, though. If a trauma victim is considered helpless, what is the victim's role in her own survival and recovery? And how do well-meaning supporters, such as diaconal workers, avoid reinforcing victimhood, both in the lives of individuals and in the ways we characterize them? Traci West, a Black feminist Christian ethicist, brought attention to this problem in her research on sexual violence against Black women. As a corrective, West developed *resistance ethics* to recognize the inner resources women bring to their own survival.[8] To recognize and empower Black women and others, West coined the term *victim-survivor*, symbolizing the moral agency of those harmed by violence and sexual abuse.[9] While the victim-survivor's moral agency can be enhanced through supportive relationships, her agency must not be supplanted by those desiring to help. Equipped with Herman's feminist approach and West's Black feminist liberationist corrective, we can now turn to the practice of response to trauma.

Trauma-informed response is not a substitute for the trained expertise of trauma specialists attending to acute needs. Rather, trauma-informed response is a tool for all sectors endeavoring to make their community a safer and more welcoming place, conducive to healing. Becoming trauma-informed requires significant study, training, and practice—and, I argue, it is intimately related to diaconal methodology.

---

[7]Judith Lewis Herman, *Trauma and Recovery: The Aftermath of Violence—From Domestic Abuse to Political Terror*, 2nd ed. (Basic Books, 2015), 47–50.

[8]Traci C. West, *Wounds of the Spirit: Black Women, Violence, and Resistance Ethics* (New York University Press, 1999), 55. For my development of West's resistance ethics through a trauma-informed lens, see Chapter 3.1.

[9]West, *Wounds of the Spirit*, 1, also 57–67, 152.

Discussion Questions

1 What is a diaconal worker? Give examples and explain how faith motivates and informs diaconal workers in helping professions.

2 What does it mean to be helpless? How does the term *victim-survivor* reject a presumption of helplessness to draw attention to a person's agency in surviving trauma?

Methodology for Diaconal Praxis

Care for those who are suffering is rooted in the Levitical edict to love one's neighbor as oneself.[10] Emphasized throughout the Hebrew scriptures in special protections for widows, orphans, immigrants, and the poor and reinforced through Jesus's ministry and teaching, this call to compassion found organizational structure in the early church (Acts 6:1-7). Through the intervening centuries, Christians have provided care for others in myriad ways, including hospitals, schools, and direct assistance to individuals in need. Care and compassion for the suffering have become synonymous with diakonia, defined in some contexts as Christian-motivated social service. However, diakonia is currently undergoing an ecumenical rebirth with a more sophisticated sense of responsibility to respond to oppressive social structures. It is *liberating* service. Contemporary diaconal methodology provides the connective tissue between compassion, social justice, and reconciliation.

Ecumenical diaconal praxis goes well beyond individual acts of mercy. The holistic and prophetic nature of ecumenical diakonia is rooted in justice: "We cannot understand or practice diakonia apart from justice and peace. Service cannot be separated from prophetic witness or the ministry of reconciliation. Mission must include transformative diakonia."[11] Thus, scholars note a paradigm shift toward a more ecclesial, holistic, and prophetic practice of diakonia, moving from "humble service" to solidarity with the oppressed.[12] Contemporary diakonia is contextual; it aims to alleviate suffering and involves an analysis of power structures; and, ultimately, it is action-oriented.[13] This evolving understanding of ecumenical diakonia exposes social sin and is committed to social justice, human rights, and enhancing the capabilities and participation of everyone in the community. Thus, diaconal actors support others in being the subjects of their own liberation.

The question of agency again becomes problematic due to power differentials between victim-survivors and persons attempting to serve them. Diaconal workers are in a position of relative privilege when engaging in acts of mercy. Working with

---

[10]See, for example, Johannes Eurich, "Ethics of Diaconia: The Relevance of Good Life, Common Good and Global Justice in Diaconia," in *International Handbook on Ecumenical Diakonia*, ed. Ampony et al., 542 (Regnum Books International, 2021).

[11]WCC and ACT Alliance, *Called to Transformation*, 33.

[12]Stephanie Dietrich, Kari Karsrud Korslein, Kjell Nordstokke, and Knud Jøregensen, "Introduction: Diakonia as Christian Social Practice," in *Diakonia as Christian Social Practice: An Introduction*, ed. Dietrich et al., 2 (Regnum Books International, 2014).

[13]WCC and ACT Alliance, *Called to Transformation*, 16–17, 32.

the poor on mission is a power-laden endeavor, necessitating careful attention to the ethics of these encounters. For example, in 2011, the World Council of Churches (WCC), Pontifical Council for Interreligious Dialogue of the Roman Catholic Church, and the World Evangelical Alliance issued a joint statement on recommendations for missional conduct, warning against exploitation, allurements, and abuse of power.[14] The document also voiced commitments to mutual respect and solidarity, religious freedom, interreligious cooperation, and the common good. Likewise, the Addis Ababa Consultation on Diakonia created guidelines for a diaconal code of conduct in 2008.[15] These guidelines name the central obligations and responsibilities of diaconal work: healing and reconciliation, integrity of creation, peace and justice, service, mutual transformation, respect, and accountability, as well as solidarity, participation, and building alliances.

When the diaconal worker bears witness to suffering, she must be careful not to usurp the agency of the persons she intends to help. An ethic of solidarity is necessary for allies to enhance rather than override the agency of victim-survivors. Privileged actors often prioritize reconciliation over attending to the causes of injustice and suffering. This is an acute problem when white people attempt to address systemic racism, for example.[16] The desire of the privileged to reconcile prematurely is due to differences in perspective and experience with oppression—but reconciliation cannot be separated from justice. Ecumenical diaconal methodology provides tools for the difficult journey from compassion to justice to reconciliation.

The prophetic dimension of ecumenical diakonia relies on a contextual methodology. For example, a joint document of the WCC and ACT Alliance, *Called to Transformation*, asserts: "diaconal intervention reflects social reality and seeks in its performance to alleviate human suffering and promote justice, peace and human dignity."[17] As a contextual theology rooted in action, "diakonia therefore includes an analysis of the social and political environment."[18] This contextual analysis is essential to the "see–reflect–act" methodology of ecumenical diakonia—a process that privileges the perspective of the poor and marginalized, employs a hermeneutics of suspicion about power and privilege, and promotes wide participation and empowerment.[19] Thus, ecumenical diakonia is not simply service or loving action; rather, ecumenical diakonia necessitates social analysis and an evaluation of power structures.

---

[14]World Council of Churches, Pontifical Council for Interreligious Dialogue of the Roman Catholic Church, and the World Evangelical Alliance, "Christian Witness in a Multi-Religious World: Recommendations for Conduct," (2011), https://www.oikoumene.org/resources/documents/christian-witness-in-a-multi-religious-world.

[15]Kjell Nordstokke, ed., *Diakonia in Context: Transformation, Reconciliation, Empowerment: An LWF Contribution to the Understanding and Practice of Diakonia* (Lutheran World Federation, 2009), 91–2, https://lutheranworld.org/resources/document-diakonia-context-transformation-reconciliation-empowerment. See also WCC and ACT Alliance, *Called to Transformation*, 113–14.

[16]For an analysis and discussion of this problematic tendency among white Christians, see Jennifer Harvey, *Dear White Christians: For Those Still Longing for Racial Reconciliation*, 2nd ed. (Eerdmans, 2020).

[17]WCC and ACT Alliance, *Called to Transformation*, 16.

[18]WCC and ACT Alliance, 17.

[19]Nordstokke, *Diakonia in Context*, 59–60.

Ecumenical diakonia claims a responsibility to respond to oppressive social structures through solidarity and empowerment. Diaconal actors build alliances with these values in mind. As Christians, they partner with persons of many faiths (or of no faith tradition) to achieve common goals through dialogue and action—a process called *diapraxis*.[20] Thus, the Lutheran World Federation described an example of diapraxis in India as "action together in solidarity that engages in the promotion of justice, a better quality of life, and the alleviation of human suffering."[21] The practice of dialogue combined with collaborative work toward shared material goals resonates with insights from intercultural missional theology, pragmatic ethics, and critical community research.[22] Ecumenical diaconal action is rights-based and focuses on building citizenship, community, and alliances for the betterment of persons and society.[23]

When contextual sophistication prioritizes the voices and needs of the oppressed, diakonia becomes a powerful, liberative praxis rooted in discipleship.[24] Diakonia advocates for dignity, love, justice, and solidarity in cooperation with all who hold those values. According to *Called to Transformation*, "Diaconal action thus includes care for creation and commitment to promote human dignity and justice, in solidarity with the poor and excluded, working with all people of good will."[25] Methodologically, ecumenical diakonia involves an intentional cycle of action, theory, and reflection, mutually reinforcing and deepening our understanding of ourselves and our actions in light of God's continuing action in the world. Diakonia is therefore political in the most profound sense, motivating and theorizing the work of discipleship with a contextual awareness of social structures and a sense of justice to transform and reshape power.

The concept of *conviviality* provides support for this kind of liberative diaconal methodology. Conviviality is a political and economic vision for recentering relationships of trust within cultures overrun by the divisions and individualism created by neo-liberal, globalized market economies. "Conviviality refers to the art and practice of living together" and is based on relationality, respect of difference

---

[20]Nordstokke, 88, citing Lissi Rasmussen, "From Diapraxis to Dialogue. Christian- Muslim Relations," in *Dialogue in Action: Essays in Honour of Johannes Aagaard*, ed. Lars Thunberg, Moti Lal Pandit, and Carl V. F. Hansen, 282 (Prajna 1988). See also WCC and ACT Alliance, *Called to Transformation*, 84–5.

[21]Lutheran World Federation, *Mission in Context: Transformation, Reconciliation, Empowerment: An LWF Contribution to the Understanding and Practice of Mission* (Lutheran World Federation, 2004), 52, https://lutheranworld.org/resources/publication-mission-context-transformation-reconciliation-empowerment.

[22]Respectively, see, for example: Darryl W. Stephens, *Reckoning Methodism: Mission and Division in the Public Church* (Cascade, 2024), 106–7; Willis Jenkins, *The Future of Ethics: Sustainability, Social Justice, and Religious Creativity* (Georgetown University Press, 2013), 9, 18; and Tony Addy, "Community Practice and Critical Community Research: Perspectives from Conviviality and the CABLE Approach," Diaconia 10, no. 2 (2020): 161–79, https://doi.org/10.13109/diac.2019.10.2.161.

[23]Nordstokke, *Diakonia in Context*, 61–6.

[24]On the connections between liberation theology and diaconal methodology, see Craig L. Nessan, "Liberation Theology and Diaconia: Methods of Learning," in *International Handbook on Ecumenical Diakonia*, ed. Ampony et al., 591–6 (Regnum Books International, 2021); and Dionata Rodrigues de Oliveira, "Liberating *Diakonia* in a Brazilian Perspective,"*Diaconal Studies: Lived Theology for the Church in North America*, ed. Nessan and Stephens, 89–99 (Regnum Books International, 2024).

[25]WCC and ACT Alliance, *Called to Transformation*, 46.

among persons and communities, and "reciprocal relationships ... as a foundation for life together."[26] It offers a liberative, relational corrective to the development model of diakonia and other forms of Christian mission.[27] When combined with diaconal commitments, the vision of conviviality helps the church move away from a service provision mentality, in which we provide *for* others, to a more liberative mentality, in which we work *with* others in shared community.[28] Conviviality equips the diaconal church to "move ... toward sharing life, based on empathy, reciprocity and presence."[29] These commitments of contemporary ecumenical diakonia resonate deeply with trauma-informed ethics.

Discussion Questions

1 Describe the methodology of diakonia. What does solidarity have to do with serving others?

2 Define diapraxis and conviviality. How are these terms related to diaconal practice?

3 Consider a time when you served persons in your community. Perhaps you have volunteered in a voting precinct, served meals at a food kitchen, or done some other kind of service work. In that situation, were there clear divisions between who was serving and who was being served? How were power differentials acknowledged and addressed?

Bearing Witness through Diakonia

Diaconal praxis brings a missional understanding to the universal moral themes of dignity, love justice, and solidarity that animate this book's model of bearing witness. These connections arose organically from my research with deaconesses and others in ministry on the margins. Through personal interviews, I heard stories of bearing witness to suffering persons in many contexts, grounded in shared human dignity. For example, United Methodist deaconesses are mandated to alleviate suffering, eradicate causes of injustice, and develop full human potential and build a global community. Respectively, I interpreted these mandates as love, justice, and solidarity, and I could see clear evidence of these moral themes in the day-to-day ministries of persons in a variety of ministries, past and present.[30] I discovered that a trauma-informed approach equips relatively privileged diaconal workers to bear witness to victim-survivors of trauma and other persons who may be suffering.

---

[26]Tony Addy, ed., *Seeking Conviviality: Reforming Community Diakonia in Europe* (Lutheran World Federation, 2014), 18.

[27]WCC and ACT Alliance, *Called to Transformation*, 29–30.

[28]Tony Addy, "Seeking Conviviality: A New Core Concept for the Diaconal Church," in *The Diaconal Church*, ed. Dietrich et al., 168 (Regnum Books International, 2019).

[29]Addy, 168.

[30]See Part Two of this volume for examples.

TABLE 1.4.1 *Bearing Witness through Diakonia*

Perspectival Moment	Mode of Transcendence	Moral Theme	Practice of Social Action	Liberating Service (diakonia)
I. Existence	recognition	dignity	grounded being	equality, reciprocity, human rights
II. Present	empathy	love	attentive presence	seeing, listening, ensuring basic goods
III. Past	memory	justice	historical clarity	reflecting/judging, restitution
IV. Future	imagination	solidarity	meaningful participation	acting, collaboration, reconciliation

The ethical model of bearing witness supports the methodology and commitments of ecumenical diakonia (Table 1.4.1). This trauma-informed model mirrors the methodology of diakonia (seeing-reflecting/judging-acting) in its reckoning with present, past, and future, respectively. However, it bears repeating that a trauma-informed response does not enter these moments in a neat, linear fashion. Diaconal method and bearing witness both require holistic integration of these heuristic steps. Thus, the diaconal tools of responsible interfaith collaboration (diapraxis) and community building (conviviality) are not confined to a specific moment of bearing witness, instead permeating the whole.

Bearing witness is particularly appropriate when working across differences of culture and religion. Suffering knows no creed. The spatial and temporal perspectival moments and corresponding modes of transcendence are rooted in the human experience as such, even though they may be interpreted differently by various faith traditions. For example, *recognition* is the ability of humanity to see dignity in each person, transcending oneself to realize the widespread occurrence of trauma as part of the common human existence. Three other modes of transcendence—empathy, memory, and imagination—describe how humans connect with each other, God, and all of creation. Thus, this model treats spirituality and transcendence as a point of common connection for all of humanity, to which individuals and communities may bring their own faith commitments.

Dignity in Reciprocity

Recognizing human dignity is the existential ground for rights-based advocacy and the first objective of diaconal work.[31] The concept of dignity, expressed theologically in the image of God, is central to a convivial approach to diaconal praxis.[32] Dignity honors each person as a bearer of rights with their own subjectivity.[33] The importance

---

[31]Nordstokke, *Diakonia in Context*, 91. See also WCC and ACT Alliance, *Called to Transformation*, 42.
[32]Addy, *Seeking Conviviality*, 13, 21–3.
[33]Eurich, "Ethics of Diaconia," 544.

of grounding ministry in reciprocal human dignity is evident, for example, when pioneering white women insisted on meeting with Black women as equals in the racially segregated Methodist Episcopal Church, South in the 1930s. Recognized dignity and equality is also a prerequisite to community for LGBTQIA+ persons, many of whom have suffered trauma because of their sexual or gender identity. From a trauma-informed perspective, dignity honors the agency of the victim, recognizing that "traumatised people are survivors."[34] Thus, upholding the reciprocal dignity of victim-survivors is preliminary to any diaconal work to overcome relational barriers imposed by trauma.

Reciprocity also entails recognizing one's own dignity as a diaconal worker. A diaconal worker should not bear witness to someone else's trauma at the expense of their own dignity or well-being. God loves and bestows worth on each of us, including those of us in ministry. We should love ourselves as well as our neighbor. Even voluntary "diaconal suffering" has necessary limits.[35] For diaconal workers to be fully present and attentive, to bear witness to others, we must attend to our own trauma histories, seek reconciliation in our own lives, and welcome the healing presence of God's grace within ourselves. We are not only wounded healers but also healers in the process of healing, seeking to accompany others in their own process of healing.

Love—Seeing

Having established a grounding in shared existence, diaconal workers seeking to love their neighbors can exercise empathy in a trauma-informed way through attentive presence. Diaconal methodology begins with "seeing" the other person fully in the moment. This awareness necessitates empathetic listening, the first step in liberative methodology for diakonia.[36] According to the Lutheran World Federation, *diaconal* means "to focus on listening to and accompanying the 'marginalised other'."[37] Thus, the Addis Ababa consultation asked for "a culture of listening" in diaconal work.[38] The vision of conviviality also names our listening presence as the first step in developing community.[39] When trauma-informed, attentive presence creates a sense of safety for victim-survivors and is a profound form of love.

Listening with empathy allows us to transcend ourselves to be fully present with another person, attending to their expressed needs. A diaconal practice of empathy insists on ensuring that every person, especially the most vulnerable persons in our communities, has access to basic goods. For example, empathy can motivate a deaconess to provide food and medication to refugee families waiting to cross the Mexican border into the United States. Empathy can also motivate a volunteer to provide water to someone waiting in line for hours to vote or to offer a haven for a

---

[34]Christine Gühne, "Diaconia in Contexts of Traumatisation—An Introduction," in *The Diaconal Church*, ed. Dietrich et al., 454 (Regnum Books International, 2019).

[35]Nessan, "Liberation Theology and Diaconia," 593.

[36]Nessan, 594.

[37]Addy, *Seeking Conviviality*, 12.

[38]Nordstokke, *Diakonia in Context*, 71.

[39]Addy, *Seeking Conviviality*, 32.

woman suffering abuse by her husband. Ministry presence of this kind is essential to diaconal service. Empathy also emphasizes reciprocity and equality. Empathy means encountering our neighbor on their own terms, as an equal with distinct identity and experiences from ourselves.[40] We must be attentive to hear from the person we are serving about their needs, rather than assume that we already know what is best for them.

Justice—Reflecting/Judging

Bearing witness proceeds by seeking historical clarity about issues of justice and oppression, both for the victim-survivor and the one bearing witness to them. Diaconal methodology describes this step as reflecting/judging, involving data-gathering, introspection, and discernment. Reconstruction of memory is a necessary part of healing and recovery from trauma. At its core, bearing witness is honoring the truth of someone else's story, that is, how they narrate their past. Thus, for traumatized communities, "truth-telling is an essential element of the reconciliation process and trauma healing."[41] Such truth-telling requires reckoning with the past.

The church in mission can facilitate healing through diaconal action that engages the past through social and political analysis—essential components of conviviality. By interrogating power structures and our own complicity, individually and collectively, we can expose the root causes of suffering and oppression.[42] For example, we can ask: How are non-white, non-heterosexual, and non-cisgender persons put at risk by laws, policies, and other forms of discrimination? Why are so many immigrants attempting to enter the United States from Mexico? Why are voter lines so long in certain precincts? Why are rates of intimate partner abuse so high?

Social analysis leads to historical clarity and is a prerequisite to the work of reconciliation and healing. According to Robert Schreiter, memory work is "acknowledging the truth of what has happened, seeking justice to redress the wrongdoing that has occurred, and creating the social space for a different relationship" to the past and those involved in past harms.[43] Historical reckoning is central to the see-reflect-act methodology of diakonia, illuminating why "no diaconal action can be seen in isolation from its societal and political context."[44] Reflecting on the past may reveal a need for restitution to right past wrongs. The focus on justice as part of the prophetic dimension of ecumenical diakonia prepares us for meaningful participation in God's transformation of the world.

---

[40]Addy, 16.

[41]Nagaju Muke, "Diaconia in Traumatised Societies: Learning from the Rwandan Context," in *The Diaconal Church*, ed. Dietrich et al., 461 (Regnum Books International, 2019).

[42]The perspectival moment of reckoning with the past encompasses the middle three elements of the liberative, action-reflection (praxis-oriented) methodology described in Nessan, "Liberation Theology and Diaconia," 593–4.

[43]Robert J. Schreiter, "Reconciliation and Healing as a Paradigm for Mission," *International Review of Mission* 94, no. 372 (2005): 81, https://doi.org/10.1111/j.1758-6631.2005.tb00487.x.

[44]Nordstokke, *Diakonia in Context*, 62.

Solidarity—Acting

Bearing witness strives for solidarity with victim-survivors of trauma, collaboratively imagining a more just future conducive to the flourishing of all creation. From a trauma-informed perspective, this moment emphasizes nurturing connection and restoration among victim-survivors and resisting re-traumatization. From a diaconal perspective, empowerment and transformation enable meaningful participation in community with persons who are suffering. Diaconal methodology describes this step as "acting." To work convivially is to establish relationships of trust, building up community so that those persons most affected by trauma and suffering may find the means to flourish through their own initiatives. Exercising a preferential option for the marginalized, diaconal workers bear witness in solidarity with the persons they serve by helping them to imagine and create their own future.

Diaconal workers are called to be allies, not substitute agents, in the work of healing and reconciliation. The work of meaningful participation is illustrated by the Addis Ababa consultation's priority of "local expertise and commitment ... open for mutual empowerment."[45] We learn to ask questions such as: What kind of future does this refugee family want for themselves? What kind of voting experience do the citizens in this precinct prefer? What kinds of supports and legal protections do LGBTQIA+ persons in my community say they need? What do my neighbors say they need our community to do as we strive to become antiracist? The agency of those we intend to serve must be supported and enhanced.

Discussion Questions

1   Why is recognition of human dignity a starting point for bearing witness? How would your ability to bear witness to someone else's experience of trauma be hindered if you did not first see them as a child of God, equal to yourself?

2   What is the importance of listening in the practice of attentive presence?

3   Why does the practice of historical clarity require social analysis?

4   When attempting solidarity through the practice of meaningful participation, whose vision and needs are primary—the victim-survivor of trauma or the person bearing witness to them?

Role and Power

Combining diaconal methodology with a trauma-informed approach, several issues need continual attention: self-care; role, power, and agency; and the goal of reconciliation. Vicarious trauma is an ever-present risk. As diaconal workers encountering persons with trauma histories and entering spaces fraught with trauma, we must be attentive to our own health and flourishing, at times removing ourselves

---

[45]Nordstokke, 71.

from the situation to attend to our own care. Furthermore, we must be far enough along in our own healing and recovery from past trauma histories to be able to focus on the needs of our neighbors. Too many well-intentioned people enter ministry and other helping professions to avoid dealing with their own issues, attempting to heal others instead of tending to their own woundedness. Self-care is not selfish. It is part of the greatest commandment of God (Mt. 22:39).

We must know our role. To participate in the diaconate of all Christians is to occupy a particular role in relation to those we serve. As an ethical bystander, sometimes called *upstander*, our role is to bear witness to persons and communities who have suffered and are suffering from past trauma. Faith-based helping professionals, or diaconal workers, are part of a community of support. Social workers, police officers, medical professionals, counselors, psychologists, teachers, and directors of not-for-profit agencies each have different supportive roles. A trauma-informed community needs people in many different sectors whose roles complement each other as we seek to empower victim-survivors.

Diaconal work is unavoidably encumbered by power differentials. As diaconal workers, we must recognize and prioritize the moral agency of those persons and communities we seek to serve, resisting the urge to substitute our own expertise and capabilities for theirs. In the language of professional ethics, religious leaders have a fiduciary duty to act in the best interests of others. We must act in solidarity and support. Answers and solutions must arise within the community. Our role is that of an ally, not a patron.

Finally, diaconal workers should resist the temptation to seek reconciliation without the necessary work of grounded being, attentive presence, historical clarity, and meaningful participation. As a privileged actor, my goal might be reconciliation, but I must ask myself if this goal is self-serving. Am I seeking a sense of closure because I am tired of dealing with a particular issue? What are the priorities and goals of the people I intend to serve? Liberative solidarity prioritizes the agency of the most vulnerable among us.

Discussion Questions

1   What is your role? If you are currently employed in helping professional or volunteer with a community organization (such as a church, YWCA, and so on), write down that role. If you are studying for or preparing to enter such a role, write down your anticipated role.

2   How does your organization, employer, or ministry context handle issues of self-care, power differentials, and empowerment? What policies and practices keep you focused on staying healthy and serving the best interests of others?

From Theory to Action

Desire and intent for a world without trauma are insufficient if we do not bear witness to survivors. The ministry (*diakonīan*) of reconciliation requires bearing witness with dignity, love, justice, and solidarity as we see, reflect, and act in collaboration with traumatized persons and communities. Sensitivity to past and current trauma is necessary for diaconal work in today's world.

This chapter has explored a deep resonance between the methodology of ecumenical diakonia and bearing witness. A trauma-informed approach to Christian ethics is consistent with the values and commitments of diakonia as a praxis of liberating service and complements existing tools, such as diapraxis and conviviality. A liberative, trauma-informed response is a necessary partner to diaconal theology and praxis, underscoring the complexities of moral agency that arise as we attempt to work with people on the margins without causing harm. The model of bearing witness provides an ethical and trauma-informed approach to diakonia. Furthermore, diaconal theology provides a point of spiritual connection for diaconal workers on the front lines of trauma response, providing theological framing for its spiritual and transcendent dimensions. For diaconal workers and other Christians, bearing witness to our neighbors takes the form of concrete action—practices of discipleship in communities of faith.

PART TWO

Practices of Discipleship

2.1

Grounded Being

Christians who are passionate about bettering their lives and the lives of others engage in moral witness. They do this through individual example as well as collective action—what John Wesley called personal and social holiness. The process of bearing witness guides us in this ethical task in the context of trauma. This chapter is the first of four illustrating and discussing a specific moment of bearing witness.

Bearing witness begins with created existence, our grounded being. "Then the Lord God formed a human (*adam*) from the dust of the ground (*adamah*) and breathed into its nostrils the breath of life, and the human became a living being" (Gen. 2:7, translation by author). From dust we were made, and to dust we shall return. Yet, we are animated dust, empowered by divine breath, *ruach*, the Holy Spirit. The pinnacle of this holy activity was the creation of community, separating woman (*ishshah*) and man (*ish*) for them to dwell with each other and with God (Gen. 2:23). More inclusively, in the first creation story, "Then God said, 'Let us make humans [*adam*] in our image, according to our likeness … '" (Gen. 1:26). We are community reflecting the divine image.

In the first moment of bearing witness, we find ourselves within the natural world as part of God's good creation. We recognize our equality with all of humanity as siblings in the kin-dom of God. This kinship includes friends, family, strangers, and enemies. We are in relationship not because we like each other, not because we are always in agreement, and not because one of us controls the other but because we are equally loved by God. God's kin-dom extends beyond family, beyond the church, and beyond Christianity. Each person is bestowed worth and dignity by God's love. God's prevenient grace enables our recognition of the image of God in each other before we are ever aware of it. Aware of the possibilities and limitations, a faithful moral witness requires recognition of basic human rights and reverence for nature. Profoundly, the experience of bearing witness challenges us to reckon with all created existence in light of faith.

This chapter begins with the dilemma of the church's moral witness and places ethics in a spectrum including morals and etiquette. Theologically, this moment is informed by prevenient grace and the image of God. Through the mode of recognition, we can recognize human dignity in our neighbors, providing a basis for political human rights. This moral witness is both risky and necessary, requiring ethical discernment and prophetic insight.

A Moral Dilemma

When I was growing up, I learned that there are two topics to avoid in polite conversation: politics and religion. My family, which included democrats and republicans and perhaps a few libertarians and socialists, did not shy away from talking about important political issues of the day. Passions ran deep; convictions were strong; and respect was paramount. And there was certainly plenty to talk about. During my childhood, the United States experienced the first Apollo moon landing, the first Earth Day, the resignation of President Richard Nixon, and the US military withdrawal from Vietnam. It was a tumultuous time not unlike our own.

In my family, religion was less discussed than practiced (or not). My grandmother was a lifelong Methodist. My mother continued this adherence, so my brother and I grew up cradle Methodists. My grandfather, a devout humanist, had no patience for the mythology of the Bible and the way he saw Christianity practiced in the Deep South. On Sunday mornings, he religiously attended to his various hobbies of woodworking and winemaking while my grandmother went to church. My mother's four siblings each found their place somewhere within this wide spectrum of parental religiosity. My father, for his part, left Methodism for a more welcoming faith community after he and my mother separated and subsequently divorced. In that day and age, United Methodists did not look kindly on the man who divorced his wife. It was his family more so than my mother's that helped me hone the skills of polite conversation. The weather was always a safe topic.

How times have changed! In recent years, the topic of weather has become a political lightning rod and a test of religious fealty in some circles. We can thank anthropogenic climate change and the resultant global warming for that loss: even the weather is no longer a safe topic in polite conversation.

The witness of the church has never been confined to polite conversation, though. The moral witness of the church often requires disruption.[1] It is not about avoiding contentious topics to keep the peace. Moral witness may involve overturning social norms or transgressing niceties. It is not about turning the other way when confronted with injustice.[2] Moral witness involves speaking out against what is wrong. It is not about condoning oppression for the sake of maintaining current relationships and institutional structures. Moral witness often requires upsetting the way things are now to realize a more just treatment of the most vulnerable in society. Instead of silence and complicity, the moral witness of the church demands that we speak up for justice and change. Christian moral witness is about noticing that all is not well in the world, including the weather, and bearing witness to the will of God for a more just world.

Moral witness involves risk. When we reexamine inherited morals, when we question social structures, and when we attempt to make things right, we risk being wrong. Nevertheless, we must attempt a moral witness. The church's moral witness involves coming together as a community full of differing opinions, theologies, and

---

[1] Traci C. West, *Disruptive Christian Ethics: When Racism and Women's Lives Matter* (Westminster John Knox, 2006).

[2] Walter Wink, *Jesus and Nonviolence: A Third Way*, Facets Series (Fortress, 2003), 12.

experiences to discern the will of God. If the church's moral witness is characterized by faithful disruption, we must begin by recognizing a dilemma: the church has not always proclaimed a just witness. "We have failed to be an obedient church," as the Holy Communion liturgy so frankly admits. How do we live out a faithful moral witness when we might be wrong?

Discussion Questions

1 Which topics do you avoid in polite conversation, such as a family gathering? Why?

2 Consider a time when you spoke out about a moral wrong, even when it required you to be disruptive. How did your faith inform your witness?

3 With a conversation partner, share a time when you or your faith community took a stance on a moral issue and later changed your mind, realizing you had been mistaken (or at least not completely correct—perhaps the situation turned out to be more complicated than anticipated). What did you learn about the risk of moral witness from this experience?

Etiquette, Morals, and Ethics

We can see evidence of past successes and failures as we explore the church's moral witness through several levels—etiquette, morals, and ethics. Each level of moral witness offers opportunity for both justice and injustice. We fail to offer a credible and faithful moral witness when our regard for etiquette leads to apathy and indifference to suffering, when our moral codes are motivated more by social respectability than love of God, and when our ethical justifications become self-serving rationalizations. It is a messy business. Drawing on examples from my own tradition, Methodism, I present etiquette in terms of guidelines for civility, morals in terms of rules for holy living, and ethics in terms of public policy advocacy. While it is helpful to distinguish between etiquette, morals, and ethics, these levels overlap in practice. We are constantly navigating all at once.

Etiquette and Civility

We cannot get along in society—or with anyone else—without some practice of etiquette or civility. Words, attire, social customs, and body language are all aspects of etiquette. When we follow proper etiquette, we conform to the social expectations of our culture, context, role, and relationship to other persons. There is usually no moral discernment required when observing proper etiquette; we simply conform to what is expected of us. For example, in the United States, it is typically expected that I shake hands when meeting someone—each of us using our right hand. The ritual does not work if one of us uses the left hand. However, in some organizations, such as Scouts BSA (which my daughter joined the first year they began allowing girls to participate), members will greet each other with a left-handed shake. Neither is wrong; it is only a matter of being appropriate to the circumstance. There is no transcendent or higher law associated with rules of etiquette, which vary tremendously from culture to culture. This is not to say, however, that etiquette is morally neutral. It typically supports the status quo, just and unjust alike, and provides little traction for imagining a more just world. While adhering to proper etiquette may not require moral discernment, refusal to observe etiquette often does. Etiquette, or civility, can serve both as a guide to healthy relationships and as a means of reinforcing unjust social structures.

The practice of civility can be a vital part of the church's moral witness. In fact, political discourse in the United States has become so divisive and polarized that achieving civility is considered progress in many contexts.[3] This is not a newfound need. I remember attending a forum on the church and homosexuality in Dallas, Texas, in 2000. I expected to hear arguments for or against the acceptance of homosexuality in the UMC. I am sure that most of the speakers fulfilled this expectation, though I do not remember these arguments. What I remember is a statement by one of my professors at Perkins School of Theology. He said that perhaps the most important feature of the church's discussion was not our stance on homosexuality but rather how we treat each other through disagreement. Civility in public discourse—and at the family dinner table—is vital to our ability to get along with one another in community. During the intervening years, I have wondered if this professor's response was morally sufficient. Too many people mistakenly believe that civility is an adequate substitute for recognizing the inherent and equal dignity of all humanity. When certain classes of people are excluded from the conversation, the fitting response may be civil disobedience rather than polite conversation. Appeals to etiquette are not always helpful to the church's moral witness and can even be harmful without a context of justice.

Sometimes, etiquette is leveraged to silence debate or stall efforts toward justice. For example, in 1963, white leaders of Birmingham, Alabama, believed that African American citizens were not behaving properly as they protested the city's racial segregation. Proper "racial etiquette" for African Americans in Alabama at that time (often enforced by law) required deference to white persons in all aspects of social interaction.[4] Eight white clergymen of Alabama—including four bishops, an auxiliary bishop, and a rabbi—made an "appeal to both our white and Negro citizenry to observe the principles of law and order and common sense" on April 12, 1963.[5] The "common sense" part of this appeal could simply refer to white folks' sense of etiquette. Their request belied the unjust power structures at the time: the laws of

---

[3] On the importance of actively engaging those with whom we disagree, see Layton E. Williams, *Holy Disunity: How What Separates Us Can Save Us* (Westminster John Knox, 2019).

[4] The existence of "racial etiquette"—"a set of interpretive codes and racial meanings which operate in the interactions of daily life"—serves as a means of reinforcing racial divisions and discrimination. Michael Omi and Howard Winant, "Racial Formations," in *Race, Class, and Gender in the United States: An Integrated Study*, 9th ed., ed. Paula S. Rothenberg with Kelly S. Mayhew, 16 (Worth, 2014).

[5] C.C.J. Carpenter, Joseph A. Durick, Hilton J. Grafman, Paul Hardin, Nolan B. Harmon, George M. Murray, Edward V. Ramsage, and Earl Stallings, "Alabama Clergymen's Letter to Dr. Martin Luther King, Jr.," April 12, 1963, https://teachingamericanhistory.org/document/letter-to-martin-luther-king/.

Birmingham did not recognize the "Negro citizenry" as full and equal citizens. The white clergy leaders said that the nonviolent resistance efforts of Martin Luther King, Jr. were "unwise and untimely." Whose timetable and whose interests were they prioritizing?

Etiquette can enable respectful ways of interacting with each other when understood in the context of Christian conferencing. Christian conferencing is a structured way of nurturing the holy life, advocated by John Wesley as a means of grace. It is a practice of nurture and accountability within a faith community to help church members understand each other and show respect for each other amid disagreement. Common guidelines include "Listen before speaking ... Speak about issues, do not defame persons ... Strive to accurately reflect the views of others."[6] Such principles often begin with a theological assertion rooted in our shared existence, "Every person is a child of God," and include an admonition to "strive to understand from another's point of view."[7] Principles of etiquette train us to treat each other with civility and respect. However necessary, etiquette is insufficient for the church's moral witness. We also need morals.

Morals and Holy Living

Morals, in contrast to etiquette, involve a recognition of what is right and good. Often, morals are ingrained from an early age. When a parent tells a child, "Behave yourself!" the child is expected to act in a way she has been taught is right. This admonition only works with a rightly formed conscience within the context of specific relationships. We learn morals by rote and through practice. Good character, formed over time through practices conducive to right behavior, will strengthen our ability to act morally. This is the basis of virtues in Christian morality. Morals are handed down through traditions, taught in school, and upheld in law. However, most morals are contextual: they are culturally conditioned and change over time.[8] Thus, appeals to morals in the church's witness must be open to testing.

Many Christian traditions consider personal morality a vital part of the life of faith. However, what was considered immoral for one generation at one point in history might be considered morally neutral or even good at another point in time. For example, Methodists of my grandparents' generation learned that playing cards and billiards were immoral diversions. Remember the song, "Ya' Got Trouble," from the Music Man? "Right here in River City / Trouble with a capital 'T' / And that rhymes with 'P' and that stands for pool!" This musical, set in 1912, depicted the cultural values into which my grandmother was born. The difference in morals across two generations explains why she was puzzled and amazed that our United Methodist congregation in the 1980s installed a pool table in the youth lounge.

---

[6]UNY Communications, "The Principles of Holy Conferencing," July 8, 2016, http://www.unyumc.org/news/article/the-principles-of-holy-conferencing.

[7]Sally Dyck, "Eight Principles of Holy Conferencing: A Study Guide for Churches and Groups," 2012, http://mnumc-email.brtapp.com/files/eefiles/documents/holy_conferencing_study_guide_2012.pdf.

[8]Ellen Ott Marshall, therefore, urged "a hermeneutic of suspicion toward the classification of certain behaviors as virtuous or not." Ellen Ott Marshall, *Introduction to Christian Ethics: Conflict, Faith, and Human Life* (Westminster John Knox, 2018), 120.

A long-standing tradition of Methodist moral witness involves rules for holy living. In 1739, a small group asked John Wesley to guide them in faith. The only precondition to join the United Societies was a desire for salvation. To remain a part of the group, though, required adherence to three rules: do no harm, do good, and "attending upon all the ordinances of God."[9] These General Rules still inform the ethos of many Wesleyan and holiness denominations today. Wesley was specific. Doing no harm included abstaining from liquor, slaveholding, and "taking such diversions as cannot be used in the name of the Lord Jesus." Methodists are still known for their distaste for alcohol. Disagreement over the rule against slaveholding led to the largest schism in US Methodism: Northern and Southern Methodists split in 1844, prior to the US Civil War.

Small group nurture and accountability provided a context for these moral rules, which sometimes became codified into church law. For Wesley, it was not enough to avoid indecent amusements. The use of leisure time should be positively uplifting to the soul. Methodists were taught to avoid "singing those songs, or reading those books, which do not tend to the knowledge and love of God." There was no neutral entertainment when it came to growth in the life of faith. Later generations warned each other about "pernicious" diversions "antagonistic to vital piety," such as novels, dancing, gambling, and the theatre. The rule against unholy diversions may seem quaint to modern ears but still flows through the blood of Methodists. In addition to appropriate amusements, churchgoers learned about modest jewelry and attire, observing the Christian Sabbath, honoring marriage, and avoiding divorce. The history of Methodist teachings against divorce and remarriage after divorce exposes the limitations of putting morals into law. Methodism's rules against divorce were in full force in the 1920s as US society grappled with increasing divorce rates amidst rapid social change. One hundred years later, The United Methodist Church no longer considers divorce a sin or an obstacle to remarriage.

While specific examples of immoral behavior have changed over the years, most Christian churches have consistently taught that individual behavior matters—not only for the individual's sake but also as a moral witness of the church. Because morals can change over time, rules against certain behaviors are often contested in the church. This is especially so for rules about clergy behavior. Clergy are expected to model the morality expected of all Christians and are more closely accountable under church law than the layperson. When enforcement becomes particularly legalistic, this is an indication that morals are in flux. Situations of contested morals can serve both to reinforce the church's moral witness and to expose it as insufficient. We need to remain attuned to the faithful reasons behind these moral rules. Ethical discernment is crucial precisely at such times.

Ethics and Public Policy Advocacy

A third level of moral witness is ethics, the intentional practice of examining our morals. Ethical reflection is needed especially when morals change or become contested. Ethics provides tools for seeking validation, explaining reasons, and

---

[9] *The Book of Discipline of The United Methodist Church 2020/2024* (UMPH, 2024), 78–80.

connecting with logic. This is the task of ethics. Ethics is self-critical reflection on what is right, good, and virtuous. When we try to make sense of what we have been taught about morals, we are engaged in ethics. Ethics requires not only acting in a right or good manner but also for the right reasons. Intent matters. Ethics also involves a consideration of consequences. Ethical behavior is responsible. We can learn to be polite and to act morally without questioning what we have been taught, but we can only claim to act ethically when we have determined its validity for ourselves.[10] The church's public policy advocacy illustrates intentional efforts of ethical engagement.

Many Christian organizations engage in public policy advocacy and encourage their members to do so as well. The United States Conference of Catholic Bishops (USCCB), for example, publishes a booklet every four years, *Forming Consciences for Faithful Citizenship*. This "call to political responsibility" promotes a non-partisan engagement with relevant social issues, grounding its discussion in the principles of Catholic Social Teaching: "the infinite worth and dignity of every human life, the common good, solidarity, and subsidiarity."[11] Likewise, the National Association of Evangelicals promotes civic responsibility through a similar booklet, which begins, "Our responsibility to society is grounded in the truth that all people are made in the image of God."[12] Presbyterian, Lutheran, Methodist, and other churches also promote faithful engagement in the issues and politics of public life.[13]

The quintessential example of Christian public policy engagement is the Prohibition movement. One significant leader of this national effort to rid society of beverage alcohol was Frances Willard. She worked through the Women's Christian Temperance Movement from its founding in 1874 to her death in 1898, serving as its president for twenty years.[14] Willard was an effective organizer and spokesperson. She recognized alcohol and drunkenness as the underlying sources of many social ills, "the determinate factors in crime, abuse, poverty, unemployment, and corruption."[15] Many Christian women and men agreed with her. By the turn of the twentieth century, temperance among Methodists and others meant total abstinence from alcohol. Herbert Welch, a Methodist bishop, created unfermented grape juice as a communion element. Church members signed temperance pledge cards annually. The Methodist Episcopal Church established a political lobby in the nation's capital in 1912 and named it the Board of Temperance, Prohibition and Public Morals—the

---

[10]Robin W. Lovin, *Christian Ethics: An Essential Guide* (Abingdon, 2000).

[11]USCCB, *Forming Consciences for Faithful Citizenship: A Call to Political Responsibility from the Catholic Bishops of the United States, with New Introductory Note* (USCCB, 2024), vii, https://www.usccb.org/sjp/forming-consciences-faithful-citizenship.

[12]National Association of Evangelicals, *For the Health of the Nation: An Evangelical Call to Civic Responsibility* (National Association of Evangelicals, 2024), https://www.nae.org/for-the-health-of-the-nation/.

[13]See, for example, Christian Iosso, Darryl W. Stephens, and Roger A. Willer, "Prospects for Ecumenical Ethical Witness: Confronting Climate Degradation," *Ecumenical Review* 70, no. 4 (2018): 772–87, https://doi.org/10.1111/erev.12400.

[14]Russell E. Richey, Kenneth E. Rowe, and Jean Miller Schmidt, *The Methodist Experience in America: A History, Volume I* (Abingdon, 2010), 240–1.

[15]Richey, Rowe, and Schmidt, 240.

building, which sits next to the Supreme Court and across from the US Capital, still houses religious advocacy organizations.[16]

Such advocacy does not always go as planned. The United States adopted a constitutional amendment prohibiting the manufacture and sale of alcoholic beverages in 1919. It was repealed in 1933. Prohibition was a short-lived success and a long-lived caution for Christian moral witness through public policy advocacy.

An Ambiguous and Necessary Task

If Prohibition taught us anything, it taught us that the church's moral witness is more complex and demanding than supporting any single policy proposal. Moral witness is an ambiguous but necessary undertaking. We must be cautious in claiming that God is on our side on any issue. Yet, we must also take action motivated by faith even when we cannot have complete certainty. The church's moral witness is always in process, unfinished, incomplete, and uncertain.

Public policy advocacy requires ethical and theological discernment. Differing opinions in public policy debates generally do not strike at the root of Christianity. The core of the gospel is not at stake in most public policy decisions. At stake is our witness as Christians—how we treat each other and our neighbors. Too many public debates motivated by religious principles devolve into demonization of those who think, believe, or act differently. We must retain humility and respect common human dignity even as we advocate for what we believe is right and good.

There are times when churches have proclaimed a witness—but too timidly. For example, in the 1780s, Methodists adopted a strict rule against slaveholding and buying and selling slaves. However, this church quickly backtracked as exceptions multiplied and enforcement grew lax. The early Methodist witness against slavery faltered.

My ancestors were likely to blame, at least in part, for this failure of witness. My family tree has roots in the Deep South of the United States. Generations ago, my parents' parents' parents' parents owned farms in Georgia and Alabama. I have no reason to believe they did not own slaves. I know they went to church and lived in racially segregated neighborhoods—both were considered proper etiquette at the time. I do not know whether they witnessed against the evil of slavery or used the Bible to justify enslavement of African Americans. Protestant moral witness went both ways.

This example from my past hardly instills confidence in the church and its moral witness. It took many decades for most white-majority churches to declare unequivocally and consistently that slavery is an evil. Why was there moral ambiguity about this form of evil for so many white Christians for such a long period of time?

Determining a moral witness on the tough issues facing church and society today is a courageous task. There is risk involved, whether we are bold, timid, or silent. We cannot escape the fact that what we do or do not do and what we say or do not say constitutes a witness to our faith—or exposes our lack of faith. This is a daunting and necessary task. However, we are not left morally adrift. Christian moral witness is securely grounded in our beliefs about God.

---

[16]Richey, Rowe, and Schmidt, 336.

Discussion Questions

1   Consider the ambiguity and necessity of civility. When have you experienced insistence on "good manners" or proper etiquette as a barrier to justice? When have you prayed for civility to repair a broken relationship?

2   Consider the ambiguity and necessity of moral codes. Name an obsolete moral expectation you were taught as a child. Name an enduring moral expectation you continue to uphold.

3   Consider the ambiguity and necessity of public policy advocacy. How have you gotten involved in supporting community efforts to address social problems? This might include letter writing, voting, participating in a community forum, contacting your political representatives, and so on. How did your faith inform these actions?

Prevenient Grace and the Image of God

The church's moral witness begins with each person's fundamental identity in relation to God and each other. This identity is premised on God's love for all of humanity. God's love for us bestows worth; we are important because God loves us; and we are equal because God loves each of us perfectly. Wesleyan beliefs in prevenient grace, the image of God, and unlimited (universal) atonement provide a context for understanding bestowed worth as the ground of our commitment to equality and human rights.

Prevenient grace is the power and presence of the Holy Spirit acting in our lives before we are even aware of God. By the time we recognize God's gracious action, we realize that God has been with us every step of the way. It is not God's presence but our awareness of God's presence that needs awakening. Recognizing the image of God in ourselves and our neighbors is somewhat like this. Every human bears the image of God. "Then God said, 'Let us make humans in our image, according to our likeness ...' So God created humans in his image, in the image of God he created them; male and female he created them" (Gen. 1:26-27). Not only are you and I created in the image of God but also every other person in this world bears the image of the divine. Each one of us reflects the Creator. And God declared us "very good." And after the Fall, Christ renewed our relationship with God, restoring the image of God within us. Nothing, not even the power of sin or death, can separate us from the love of God (Rom. 8:38-39). When it comes to guidelines for etiquette or civility, this means we must begin with the assumption that "Every person is a child of God."[17] This reminder is helpful for interpersonal interactions.

A theological recognition of bestowed worth is also the foundation for human rights.

---

[17]Dyck, "Eight Principles of Holy Conferencing." Several biblical passages indicate that right belief and action are requisite to the claim "child of God" (Jn 1:12; Rom. 8:16; 1 Jn 3:1). The moral posture of bearing witness, however, does not require me to know the status of my neighbor's faith before treating them as an equal before God.

> Our Judaic and Christian heritage ... declares that all of us have great and equal worth: the worth of being made in the image of God and of being loved redemptively by God. It adds that God holds us accountable for how we treat each other—and for how we treat God. It is this framework of conviction that gave rise to [natural human] rights.[18]

To have a right is to lay a claim on others, to assert one's inherent and equal worth, in relationship.[19] The concepts of bestowed worth and inherent dignity support claims to basic human rights, such as those stated in the *Universal Declaration of Human Rights*. Thus, Christian support and advocacy for political human rights emerged from God's bestowed worth on all of humanity.

A person's basic humanity is not something that can be negotiated or compromised with Christian integrity. We are all equal in the sight of God. Period. "There is no longer Jew or Greek, ... slave or free, ... male and female, for all of you are one in Christ Jesus" (Gal. 3:28). Kindred in Christ can disagree over theological opinions. However, to deny another person's full participation in the discussion and equal standing in the community is to deny their equal status as a human being. Thus, there is a false symmetry in debates that pit one group's desire to regulate another group against the latter's insistence upon being recognized as fully human, as having inherent dignity—an inestimable worth bestowed by God.[20] It is precisely because the church has not consistently upheld each person's inherent dignity and worth in policy and practice that we need to bear witness, recognizing the image of God in each other.

Bearing witness through recognition of our created existence thus reveals certain theological emphases. Each moment of bearing witness correlates to Wesleyan theological themes, identified through specific activities of God and moral emphases (Table 2.1.1). We will explore these divine activities and theological themes throughout Part Two of this book.

Returning to the first moment of bearing witness, a theological commitment to inherent dignity can motivate prophetic moral witness. In 1937, the (white) Women's Missionary Council of the Methodist Episcopal Church, South advocated for a racially integrated church—thirty years before Methodism officially desegregated. Members of the Council worked together with Black women leaders of the Colored Methodist Episcopal Church "in Leadership Schools for colored women."[21] Ten years of working cooperatively as missionary women across racial lines opened their eyes to "new visions of God and of his love for all men"—that is, for all men and women regardless of race.[22]

---

[18]Nicholas Wolterstorff, *Justice: Rights and Wrongs* (Princeton University Press, 2008), 393.

[19]Ellen Ott Marshall also emphasized a relational view of rights. Marshall, *Introduction to Christian Ethics*, 56–7. She supported rights through a theological reference to *imago Dei*. Wolterstorff differed slightly by rooting rights primarily in bestowed worth. Wolterstorff, *Justice*, 360, 393.

[20]This is an example of distorting "the practices of honoring and claiming rights." Wolterstorff, *Justice*, 7.

[21]Alice G. Knotts, *Fellowship of Love: Methodist Women Changing American Racial Attitudes, 1920–1968* (Kingswood, 1996), 265, citing "Report of the Study Group on Unification of the Women's Missionary Council, 1937."

[22]Knotts, *Fellowship of Love*, 266, citing "Report of the Study Group on Unification."

TABLE 2.1.1 *Wesleyan Theological Themes of Bearing Witness*

			Wesleyan Theological Themes		
Perspectival Moment	Mode of Transcendence	Moral Theme	Activity of God	Moral Emphases	Practice of Social Action
I. Existence	recognition	dignity	creation, bestowed worth, prevenient grace	image of God, equality, human rights	grounded being
II. Present	empathy	love	convicting grace, redemption	humility, care for vulnerable	attentive presence
III. Past	memory	justice	justifying grace, forgiveness	repentance, reparation, restitution	historical clarity
IV. Future	imagination	solidarity	sanctifying grace, renewal of creation	holiness, reconciliation, *shalom*	meaningful participation

This experience inspired the white women's Council to speak against plans for continued racial segregation in the soon-to-be-formed Methodist Church:

> We believe that such a Methodist connectionalism transcending race and nation and economic class will be better able to create in us the mind which was in Christ Jesus who taught us of one God who is the Father of all and in whom we are all brothers one of another.[23]

Prophetically, they spoke for racial integration in the church based on their understanding of the mind of Christ. Behind this statement stood several affirmations, including: "the supreme worth of the individual," "human brotherhood," and "Divine fatherhood."[24] Alice Knotts summarized well the impact of these affirmations: "The divine fatherhood of God implied the claim that all people equally were children of God regardless of race."[25] This basic affirmation took courage and entailed risk.

Methodist women continued their moral witness for equality of race even as their church increased its structures of segregation. In 1948, they promoted civil rights education by widely distributing *To Secure These Rights: The Report of the President's Commission on Civil Rights* and by publishing and distributing a study

---

[23]Knotts, 266, citing "Report of the Study Group on Unification."
[24]"Twenty-seventh Annual Report of the Women's Missionary Council, 1937," 157, quoted in Knotts, *Fellowship of Love*, 87. The Council focused on intra-Christian relationships.
[25]Knotts, *Fellowship of Love*, 87.

guide to accompany it.[26] In 1950, the Women's Division published a comprehensive legal study of segregation laws across the United States and, in 1952, produced the first Charter of Racial Policies within the Methodist Church.[27] Equality in the kin-dom of God was their first affirmation: "We believe that God is the Father of all people of all races and we are His children in one family."[28] These historical examples of integration and the work of racial justice show how the potential power of grounding the church's moral witness on prevenient grace and the image of God.

Discussion Questions

1   What does "created in the image of God" mean to you? How does this affirmation help you understand your inherent dignity, value, and equality in church and society? How does this affirmation help you see each person around you in the same light?

2   When have you experienced being treated as less than equal because of some attribute of the way God made you (e.g., skin color, sex, height, left-handedness, range of ability, etc.)?

3   Read portions of the *Universal Declaration of Human Rights* with a group and discuss how your faith leads you to uphold the basic political rights affirmed in this document.

The Risk of Moral Witness

Moral witness entails risk. It often requires us to take a stand in the face of disagreement and uncertainty. An action by Phil Wogaman shows the need for discernment, or prophetic insight, and illustrates the differences between etiquette, morals, and ethics. Wogaman is a retired pastor and retired seminary professor. He taught Christian ethics and served as dean at Wesley Theological Seminary. On May 31, 2017, he publicly surrendered his clergy credentials in protest of the treatment of LGBTQ persons seeking ordination in the Baltimore-Washington Annual Conference of the UMC.[29] Proper etiquette did not call for contesting the conference Board of Ordained Ministry's decision to defer the candidacy of T.C. Morrow, who is a married lesbian. A polite response might have included bowing to the authority of the Board

---

[26]Knotts, 170.

[27]Knotts, 196–7. In 1978, the Women's Division created a new "Charter for Racial Justice," which was adopted by General Conference in 1980 and has been repeatedly readopted. United Women in Faith, "Charter for Racial Justice in an Interdependent Global Community," https://uwfaith.org/what-we-do/serve-and-advocate/racial-justice/.

[28]Knotts, *Fellowship of Love*, 197.

[29]"In Protest of LGBTQ Treatment in UMC, Phil Wogaman Surrenders Clergy Credentials," *UM-Insight*, May 31, 2017, http://um-insight.net/in-the-church/ordained-ministry/in-protest-of-lgbtq-treatment-in-umc-phil-wogaman-surrenders/. For his first-person account, see J. Philip Wogaman, *Surrendering My Ordination: Standing Up for Gay and Lesbian Inclusivity in The United Methodist Church* (Westminster John Knox, 2018).

through silence or "agreeing to disagree"; however, Wogaman chose disruption. He recognized an obstacle to full human flourishing and spoke up about it.

Contesting Morality

Wogaman is an ethicist. He has spent a career critically examining morals. Just because church law declared homosexuality immoral did not resolve the ethical dilemma for him. His denomination's Social Principles taught as much—at least when it came to secular laws. "Governmental laws and regulations do not provide all the guidance required by the informed Christian conscience."[30] Law alone does not adjudicate contested morals. We must discern for ourselves. In relation to civil disobedience, the UMC asserted, "we recognize the right of individuals to dissent when acting under the constraint of conscience and, after having exhausted all legal recourse, to resist or disobey laws that they deem to be unjust or that are discriminately enforced."[31] Would the church advise the same degree of conscientious decision-making regarding its own law? Wogaman apparently believed so. Determining the continued validity of inherited morals requires ethical reflection.

Reflecting on the past is one way to gain perspective on the present. The year Wogaman was born, Methodist clergy were expected to model high moral standards just as they are today. Debt, drugs, and divorce defined the boundaries of clergy morality in 1933. Methodists were taught to avoid incurring large debts. Methodists abstained from alcohol. Methodists did not condone divorce, except for the one scriptural cause taught by Jesus himself (Mt. 5:32). If a member violated these rules, it was a transgression; if a pastor violated these rules, it was a scandal. Methodist pastors were expected to pay their debts, abstain from alcohol and tobacco and avoid the sin of divorce. These were the morals of the tradition in which Wogaman grew up. However, Methodist morals changed during Wogaman's lifetime.

In 2017, church law in The UMC said little about debt, drugs, and divorce of clergy.[32] Clergy were still expected to answer "no" to the "historic" question, "Are you in debt so as to embarrass you in your work?"[33] However, the reality of large student debt from seminary education often made a mockery of this denial. Methodism no longer supported Prohibition. Abstinence from alcohol was no longer a litmus test of clergy ethics. United Methodism no longer considered divorce a sin or a disqualification for ordained ministry. Instead, the part of church law that had prohibited divorced clergy had been changed to prohibit the ordination of "self-avowed, practicing homosexuals." This was the morality that Wogaman contested. His action challenged his church to re-examine its moral witness.

---

[30] *The Book of Discipline of The United Methodist Church 2016* (UMPH, 2016), ¶ 161.K.

[31] *The Book of Discipline of The United Methodist Church 2016*, ¶ 164.F.

[32] The lengthy footnote on "moral and social responsibility of ordained ministers" notwithstanding. *The Book of Discipline of The United Methodist Church 2016*, ¶ 310.2d. For discussion, see Darryl W. Stephens, *Methodist Morals: Social Principles in the Public Church's Witness* (University of Tennessee Press, 2016), 44.

[33] *The Book of Discipline of The United Methodist Church 2016*, ¶ 336.

Ethical Discernment

The church's moral witness changes and evolves. We know this from the history of Methodist morals over Wogaman's lifetime. The Methodism of 1933 was fractured. What is now The United Methodist Church was then five different denominations. Some ordained women; some did not. Some segregated African Americans from white persons; some did not. All of them believed themselves to be acting morally.

In the nineteenth century, US Methodists, like their Baptist and Presbyterian counterparts, separated over slavery and issues of authority and power in the church. When southern and northern Methodists reunited in 1939, women and African Americans bore the burden of political compromise. The united church was racially segregated, and women in the Methodist Protestant Church lost the right to be ordained. In each case, a power-wielding majority claimed scriptural support to enact laws pertaining not to themselves but to others: men making decisions about women; white people making decisions about Black people; cis-hetero persons making decisions about LGBTQ persons (1 Cor. 14:34-35; Gen. 9:22-27; Rom. 1:26-27, respectively). Methodism's previous focus on the personal morality of debt, drugs, and divorce proved insufficient moral guidance for addressing the systemic challenges of gender justice, racial equality, and LGBTQ rights.

A moral witness requires more than conformity to social norms or legislating restrictions on the behavior of clergy. It requires discerning the difference between God's justice and human hubris, between righteousness and sin. Moral witness involves ongoing ethical reflection. The ethical challenge is to discern when we are being conformed to the world and when we are being transformed: "Do not be conformed to this age, but be transformed by the renewing of the mind, so that you may discern what is the will of God—what is good and acceptable and perfect" (Rom. 12:2). However, it is much easier to identify justice in hindsight. Discerning the will of God in the present moment requires prophetic insight.

By prophetic, I do not mean predicting the future. Rather, prophecy in the modern sense is the ability to interpret the present in light of God's future kin-dom. Prophetic insight discerns the more faithful path in a world of ambiguity and uncertainty. "For we know only in part, and we prophesy only in part" (1 Cor. 13:9). Prophetic insight keeps us focused on God's way when our tendency is to want to go our own way. Prophetic means advocating for the future God intends for us.

There are many examples of prophetic leadership prompting moral change in the Christian tradition. Teressa Hoover, Martin Luther King Jr., Daniel Berrigan SJ, Oscar Romero, Walter Rauschenbusch, Dorothy Day—each found a way, through God's power, to resist injustice and oppression. They risked overstepping the bounds of etiquette, challenging existing morals to lead the church to a more faithful witness.

Bearing Witness

Grounded in God's creation and sparked by prevenient grace, the process of bearing witness provides guidance for the church's moral witness. Bearing witness helps us navigate the risk inherent in this endeavor. In the example above, Wogaman recognized kinship with another human being, a common dignity under God. His attentive presence showed love for this neighbor, prompting empathy. Seeking historical clarity, he discerned a pattern of injustice and sought to make amends. His participation derived meaning from the will of God for the church as he understood it, and he acted in solidarity for the sake of reconciliation in community. These are the four moments of bearing witness.

Bearing witness is not an individualistic, solitary endeavor—Wogaman is not a lone ranger. Rather, his witness emerges from relationships and is rooted in community. Bearing witness may start within Christian community through small group accountability. Christian conferencing provides a context for discernment within the Christian community. Through this means of grace, we nurture and hold each other accountable within the family of faith. Yet sometimes the church still gets it wrong. Sometimes we become too insulated within our congregations, and we lose touch with our neighbors with whom we may have less in common. Thus, we also need to be held accountable by those outside of our congregations, beyond our denominational structures, and throughout the world. From a standpoint of equal dignity, we need to act in love, justice, and solidarity with our neighbors. Bearing witness provides this context for ethical discernment beyond Christian community.

The church's moral witness can be disruptive and ambiguous even as it is necessary. In the years following Wogaman's protest, United Methodism experienced a denominational splintering. Between 2019 and 2024, 25 percent of United Methodist congregations in the United States disaffiliated from the UMC over the issue of homosexuality. Even when the moral path is unsettling and unclear, we can faithfully bear witness to each other. Secure in God's prevenient grace, we recognize the kinship of all of humanity. Beginning with grounded being, we bear witness to God's good creation and our part in it. We recognize the image of God in our neighbor and know that God bestows equal and inestimable worth on every human. God's prevenient grace meets us in every corner of creation. Bearing witness is a disciplined way of recognizing God's grace in the face of the world's suffering and doing something about it.

Discussion Questions

1   What stance does your church have on civil disobedience? When might be an occasion for disobeying unjust civil laws? Does the same logic hold for disobeying unjust church laws?

2   The church and its moral witness are conditioned by historical, social, and political forces. Why should faith communities bother discerning right from wrong, ethical from unethical, if we could ultimately be wrong?

3   Go out into the neighborhood and community—grocery shopping, walking, visiting the public library, and so on. Observe the people around you and those you interact with. Look for the image of God in each of them. What does this experience tell you about what God looks like?

2.2

Attentive Presence

There is nothing that falls outside of God's creation except God, and God declared it all "good." Thus, H. Richard Niebuhr asserted, "whatever is, is good."[1] Everything. Every part of creation is good. One of the tasks of Christian moral witness is to attest to this belief by being fully present, appreciating the goodness of the cosmos, the created world, in all its complexity—even when bad things happen. While all of creation is good, not everything that happens is right. Bearing witness requires that we be present and attentive. We must love God, self, and neighbor enough to pay attention.

Focused on the present, the practice of attentive presence attunes us to the needs of our neighbors. This form of love attunes us to God's redemptive action, provoking empathy for those around us. Empathy uncovers suffering wherever it exists. Attentive presence reveals to us what God is doing in the lives of our neighbors and convicts us of their reality. The moral activity of empathy prompts concern especially for the most vulnerable. Love stands against apathy and indifference to suffering. Furthermore, love awakens in us a sense of justice. Attentive presence is a way of loving the neighbor, provoking empathy for those around us and a concern for meeting their basic human needs. This is the second moment of bearing witness.

God's Wisdom

Ordinary people living out extraordinary lives of faith can be the most powerful witness to God's will for a more just world. To sense what God is doing in our midst, we just need to slow down and pay attention. The weather, politics, and even religion itself fall within the scope of the church's moral witness. To bear witness to God in the world is to endeavor to see rightly what God intends for creation and to join in. To become attuned to what God is up to in this world, we must not judge but rather listen.

Jane Dutton, a pastor in Pennsylvania, provides an example. Preaching during Epiphany, she described the wise men of Matthew 2:7-12 as "Magi of the Margins." These astrologers were not insiders to Herod's empire; they were not the chief priests

---

[1] H. Richard Niebuhr, *The Responsible Self: An Essay in Christian Moral Philosophy* (HarperSanFrancisco, 1963), 125.

and scribes of the people. Herod called for these outsiders in secret. They came from the margins of society—an unlikely place, we might suppose, for seeking witness to God's truth—and they returned home by side roads.

Dutton then proceeded to tell a story from her ministry, bearing witness to how Christ is present in the lives of people on the margins of society today.

I volunteer as a chaplain each week at Anchorage Breakfast Ministry here in Lancaster.[2] I get to welcome each and every guest every week looking into their eyes, saying "Good morning," and "I'm so glad you're here." Or "I missed you last week." I get to listen to these individuals who are struggling in some way. They may be unemployed, underemployed, homeless, recently out of prison, have a diagnosed or undiagnosed mental illness, and in general just have a tough time of it. These are the people on the margins of society. And. These are some of the most loving and generous and wise people I know. Some of these folks live without basic needs. One week after giving someone a coat the week before, he arrived at breakfast in just a sweatshirt.

"Joe, what happened to the coat I gave you?" I asked.

"I gave it to someone who needed it more," he replied.

But now you don't have a coat.

"Yeah," he said, "but I have a place to stay."

I've offered other guests warm jackets. They often tell me to give it to someone who needs it more. This is not driven by delusional thinking. This is heart-driven. This is wisdom of the heart. It is not at all uncommon for me to receive an answer to my question of, "Hey, how's today so far for you?" with, "I'm blessed. It may not look like it, Preacher Jane, but I am."[3]

Who are these poor people who gave their warm coat to someone else who needed it more? Dutton identified Joe and the other guests at Anchorage Breakfast Ministry as part of God's story. Echoing O. Henry, she concluded, "They are the magi."[4] These are the wise ones, outsiders to the modern-day empire who return home by side roads or to no home at all.

This is the nature of God's wisdom. "But God chose what is foolish in the world to shame the wise; God chose what is weak in the world to shame the strong; ... so that no one might boast in the presence of God" (1 Cor. 1:27, 29). Neither Joe nor Jane is a fool, and both show tremendous strength of character. Paul's remark about "what is foolish" and "what is weak" was not meant for them; it was meant for us. Paul was not inviting his readers, in ancient Corinth and in the world today, to look around and label others as foolish or weak. Rather, Paul was pointing his finger at us. We, the readers and bystanders, who scratch our heads in disbelief that Joe would give away his only coat or that O. Henry's Della would sell her hair or that Matthew's wise men would travel so far to offer gifts to a baby—we are the ones shamed by our foolish and weak presumptions about what God is up to in this

---

[2] In 2019, the Anchorage Breakfast Program provided no-cost meals to more than 150 people per day and operated out of First United Methodist Church in Lancaster, Pennsylvania.

[3] Jane Dutton, "Magi on the Margins," Santee Chapel, Lancaster Theological Seminary, January 3, 2018.

[4] O. Henry, "Gifts of the Magi," in *Collected Stories*, ed. Paul J. Horowitz, 763 (Dorset, 1995).

world. We are the ones who presume to know what is foolish or weak—and in the process of judging, we expose our own lack of wisdom even as we boast otherwise.

It is through prayerful listening that we learn to discern how to live into the church's moral witness. From Paul, we learn that wisdom and strength are not ours to boast. We can boast only of God. All of this is God's wisdom, for which we can only be grateful. Joe, Jane, and Della are not wise in themselves but in God. In their presence for and with each other, they bear witness to God. While prayer groups provide a means of accountability to those within our faith community (many of whom may think and act like we do), bearing witness expands our accountability to neighbors and strangers who may not share our faith at all. Missionally, we must build relationships not just with fellow Christians but with all of our neighbors.[5] Thus, by bearing witness, we try to keep our moral witness focused on what God is doing in the world. We must be attentive.

Discussion Questions

1   Do you believe that "everything that is, is good"? How would your daily attention to God's creation, to your neighbor, and to yourself change if you took this statement to heart and truly believed it? What if you could glimpse something of the divine in everything around you?

2   Do you think it was wise for Joe to give away his coat? Wise or unwise, how did Joe's action reveal God's grace at work?

3   Consider a time when someone gave you their full attention during your time of need. How did their attentive presence express neighborly love? How did you experience God's grace through this encounter?

Bearing Witness in the Present

Bearing witness requires being present for my neighbor's sake. Prayerfully attending to their stories, I "look not to [my] own interests but to the interests of others" (Phil. 2:4). How better to experience the joy of the gospel than to give ourselves over to attentiveness? Sharon Ramsay, a marriage and family therapist, described bearing witness as focusing our attention on another person to be fully present with them. She encouraged, "let our presence in the lives of others create moments for the glory of God to show up."[6] Attentive presence is an act of love leading to justice, transforming us in the process. Bearing witness is about my willingness to participate in what God is doing through my neighbor. This process begins with attentive presence.

Bearing witness, at its root, is honoring someone else's story. This is an important relational concept, particularly recognized in the field of nursing. Simply put, "bearing

---

5David W. Scott, *Crossing Boundaries: Sharing God's Good News through Mission* (Wesley's Foundery, 2019), 76.

6Sharon Ramsay, "Bearing Witness: Listening to Others Allows God to Show Up," *Presbyterian Record* 140, no. 10 (2016): 22.

witness is being present and attentive to the truth of another's experiences."[7] It is more than just being a good listener, though. It involves the moral activity of empathy. Bearing witness means decentering ourselves so that we truly empathize with the other person's perspective. We are called to bear one another's burdens. One of those burdens is our story. We each have a story to share. To bear witness is to unburden our neighbors from the agony of an untold story. We are called to be present and attentive,[8] to hear one another's stories. And then, to care for that story as if it were our own.

Sometimes these experiences are filled with joy; sometimes they are traumatic remembrances. It is especially difficult to be present for someone who is reliving a trauma. Yet, this situation is when we are needed most. According to Gabor Maté, "Trauma is not what happens to us, but what we hold inside in the absence of an empathetic witness."[9] Attentive presence is vital to emotional and spiritual health. It is for this reason that trigger warnings are important. Studying trauma may have an emotional impact based on our personal experiences of abuse, violence, oppression, etc. When our trauma history is triggered, it is advisable to seek out someone who can listen to us empathetically and nonjudgmentally. Bearing witness is a trauma-sensitive form of moral behavior. We can be the person providing attentive presence, or we can be the person in need of a compassionate listener—sometimes both, at the same time. Knowing the importance of being heard should compel us to hear one another—or to find someone who can.

We should never feel compelled to bear witness to someone else's trauma to our own detriment. Each one of us is burdened by past traumatic experiences and subject to emotional triggering in different ways. If you do not feel safe (physically, psychologically, or spiritually) bearing witness to someone else's traumatic story, you have permission to excuse yourself from being present. In fact, you should not subject yourself to vicarious trauma unnecessarily. For this reason, Pamela Cooper-White emphasized "the importance of naming, reflecting upon, and seeking ongoing support for hearing of one's own wounds."[10] The bible commands that you love yourself as you love your neighbor. Caring for your own emotional and spiritual needs is necessary to enable you to be present for others. Not all occasions for attentive presence are your responsibility or calling. Listen to your soul when it cries out, "Too much!" Nurture yourself and find respite in the care of a compassionate listener or professional counselor.

There is more to this moment of bearing witness than just showing up. We must not only be present but also attentive and not only attentive but also invested. Anne Bogart, a theatre professor, described bearing witness through her artistic lens:

> To bear witness requires the witness to also develop a point of view in relation to what one has seen. The steps from seeing to witnessing to bearing witness travel

---

[7] Rahel Naef, "Bearing Witness: A Moral Way of Engaging in the Nurse-Person Relationship," *Nursing Philosophy* 7, no. 3 (2006): 146–56, https://doi.org/10.1111/j.1466-769X.2006.00271.x.

[8] What I call "attentive presence" resonates with the idea of "being with." Samuel Wells, *A Nazareth Manifesto: Being with God* (John Wiley & Sons, 2015), 119, 125–7.

[9] Gabor Maté, "Foreword," in *In an Unspoken Voice: How the Body Releases Trauma and Restores Goodness*, ed. Peter A. Levine, xii (North Atlantic, 2010).

[10] Pamela Cooper-White, *The Cry of Tamar: Violence against Women and the Church's Response*, 2nd ed. (Fortress, 2012), 195.

from inaction to conscious action. First, we see others. Seeing does not require the responsibility of consciousness. In order to shift from seeing to witnessing, we must attempt connection, understanding and interpretation. Finally, to bear witness requires the courage to show up fully and take responsibility for one's own anxiety and to "be with" fully and compassionately. To bear witness asks for what ministers, therapists and peacemakers call a "non-anxious presence."[11]

Bogart's deep philosophical thinking about the purpose and role of theatre and other forms of artistic expression applies to the church's moral witness, too. We must not only be present but also attentive. When we practice attentive presence, we enter relationship. We experience a profound level of connection, which I call empathy. The power of being fully present with another person transcends art, therapy, and even religion. We glimpse the redemptive and renewing grace of God.

Discussion Questions

1   Consider how your body alerts you when a story is too much for you to bear. Who do you reach out to when you are at your limit or cannot hold another person's story?

2   Religious leaders must be willing and able to refer individuals to other helping professionals within a wider community of care. If you are a religious leader, create or update your list of referrals in the community. If you are a layperson, ask your religious leader about their referral list of community organizations.

3   Religious leaders often have difficulty asking for and receiving care. If you are a pastor, when is the last time *you* sought pastoral care? Write down the name of *your* pastor and reach out to them for a visit. If you are a layperson, ask your religious leader who they go to for pastoral support.

Convicting Grace and the Love Command

God not only created but also redeemed humanity. While the Holy Spirit acts prior to our awareness through prevenient grace, the Spirit also enables us to respond. We must cooperate with God, who first bestowed worth by loving us. Convicting grace, an aspect of justifying grace, prepares us to respond to God through repentance and a desire to love in return. Convicted of the need for God in our lives, we are closer to a renewed relationship with God and neighbor. This conviction precedes justification and new birth in Wesleyan theology.[12] An analogous event occurs in the moral witness of the church as we bear witness through attentive presence. Convicted

---

[11]Anne Bogart, "Bearing Witness," *SITI*, February 18, 2016, https://web.archive.org/web/20160228005129/http://siti.org/content/bearing-witness.

[12]John Wesley, "The Scripture Way of Salvation," in *John Wesley's Sermons: An Anthology*, ed. Albert C. Outler and Richard P. Heitzenrater, 372–80 (Abingdon, 1991).

of the need to love each neighbor, we attempt to enter renewed relationship with those around us. The neighbor becomes a vessel of God's grace as we pay attention to their stories and their suffering. Human empathy is the doorway to participation in divine love.

In John Wesley's understanding of salvation, convicting grace opens us fully to justifying grace, which prompts humility. Humility is Wesley's word for initial repentance.[13] Recognizing the distance between us and God, realizing the brokenness of our relationship, we repent and seek God's healing. This initial moment of recognition and repentance leads to a reorientation of our lives in relation to God. Initial repentance accepts God into our lives; living out this relationship with God requires ongoing repentance. Putting God first in my life, then, changes my relationship with everyone else. I can now see my neighbor in light of God's love for me and for them. We show humility before our neighbor by being fully present for them. Thus, the second moment of bearing witness, attentive presence, is analogous to initial repentance in Wesley's soteriology.

Empathy for our neighbors is the corollary to our humility before God. Empathy is being able to see ourselves in another person. Empathy is the ability to imagine what it would be like to walk in their footsteps. Empathy is so important to the life of faith that Jesus concluded the Sermon on the Mount with this exhortation: "In everything do to others as you would have them do to you, for this is the Law and the Prophets" (Mt. 7:12). To do so requires empathy. This is the Golden Rule, and Christianity has no exclusive claim to it. The moral requirement for empathy is an ancient truth. Just as our love for God is built on humility, our love for neighbor is built on empathy.

We cannot separate love of God and love of neighbor. One of the most prominent laws in the Jewish tradition is the *Shema*: "Hear, O Israel: The Lord is our God, the Lord alone. You shall love the Lord your God with all your heart, and with all your soul and with all your might" (Deut. 6:4-5). Monotheism, faithfulness, devotion. What more can be asked of us? The Talmud, the ancient oral tradition of law and interpretation in Judaism, notes that there are 613 commandments in the Torah, the first five books of the Hebrew Bible. So, when a Pharisee asked Jesus about the law, "Teacher, which commandment in the law is the greatest?" (Mt. 22:36), it was a question designed to stump him. Yet, Jesus offered an answer, combining the *Shema* with Leviticus 19:18.

> "You shall love the Lord your God with all your heart and with all your soul and with all your mind." This is the greatest and first commandment. And a second is like it: "You shall love your neighbor as yourself." On these two commandments hang all the Law and the Prophets.
>
> (Mt. 22:37-40)

The two laws are interconnected. Jesus's reply made it clear that there is no way to love God without also loving those created in God's image.

---

[13]See, for example, the use of the word *humility* in John Wesley, "The Image of God," in *John Wesley's Sermons: An Anthology*, ed. Outler and Heitzenrater, 14–21 (Abingdon, 1991), III.1.

Wesley taught that every commandment is an implied promise.[14] When God commands, God also enables through the Holy Spirit. God's promise through this law is that we are empowered by grace to treat others as we would want them to treat us. Through justifying grace, the Holy Spirit awakens our spiritual senses upon regeneration, allowing us to recognize Christ in our neighbor. We may then respond to God and our neighbors in humility and repentance. Repentance shows recognition—not only of sin but also of God, who stands against sin. Admittedly, it is not always easy to recognize the image of God in each other (or in ourselves). Addressing his disciples, Jesus describes the confusion of even the righteous:

> Lord, when was it that we saw you hungry and gave you food or thirsty and gave you something to drink? And when was it that we saw you a stranger and welcomed you or naked and gave you clothing? And when was it that we saw you sick or in prison and visited you?
>
> (Mt. 25:37-39)

We must look hard to see the image of God in each other. It is there, even if people have not lived into their full potential, the likeness of God.[15]

When we combine the recognition of bestowed worth prompted by prevenient grace and the empathy for neighbor empowered by justifying grace, we are drawn to bear witness to the most vulnerable persons in our community and to ensure that they have basic goods for survival. By loving our neighbors, we love Christ himself. "Truly I tell you, just as you did it to one of the least of these who are members of my family, you did it to me" (Mt. 25:40, NRSV). We are all equal in the kindom, regardless of race, ethnicity, or country of origin. We all bear the image of God. Christ is in our neighbor. Christ is in every eye, every ear, every mouth, every heart. Christ is our neighbor. Our neighbor is Christ. We have a special commitment to those whom we are most likely to overlook when seeking Christ among us.

Thus, we are commanded to give special attention to the most vulnerable persons in our community. "You shall not wrong or oppress a resident alien, for you were aliens in the land of Egypt. You shall not abuse any widow or orphan" (Exod. 22:21-22). Among the very first laws God gives the Israelites are protections for the alien, widow, and orphan. God is "Father of orphans and protector of widows" (Ps. 68:5a). The alien—also translated as immigrant or stranger—is particularly vulnerable in a political system that might render his existence "illegal." Note that God's protection for the immigrant is based on an appeal to empathy: "for you were aliens in the land of Egypt." We should be able to place ourselves in the shoes of the immigrant and treat them well. And that is not all. God not only favors the widow, orphan, and alien; God especially sides with the poor. "If you lend money to my people, to the poor among you, you shall not deal with them as a creditor; you shall not exact interest from them" (Exod. 22:25). Here, scripture attests that the poor belong to God: "my people," says God, "the poor among you."

---

[14]John Wesley, "On Perfection," II.11, http://wesley.nnu.edu/john-wesley/the-sermons-of-john-wesley-1872-edition/sermon-76-on-perfection/.

[15]The image of God is a potential; the likeness of God is that potential realized. Randy L. Maddox, *Responsible Grace: John Wesley's Practical Theology* (Kingswood, 1994), 69.

This vulnerable quartet of widows, orphans, immigrants, and the poor is prominent in the Bible.[16] "Thus says the Lord of hosts: Render true judgments, show kindness and mercy to one another; do not oppress the widow, the orphan, the alien, or the poor; and do not devise evil in your hearts against one another" (Zech. 7:9-10). Throughout the Hebrew Bible, God consistently takes the side of those who are most vulnerable. God "executes justice for the orphan and the widow"; God "loves the strangers, providing them food and clothing" (Deut. 10:18). Provisions for life's bare necessities are part of God's work.

Thus, for us to love God and love neighbor, we need to consider our neighbor's need for basic goods. As Nicholas Wolterstorff succinctly observed, "Injustice is not equally distributed."[17] The most vulnerable of society are the ones most likely to be denied rights and basic goods. We will know this if we offer them our attentive presence. It is not enough to guarantee political rights when bodies are denied sustenance. The concept of rights also includes social and economic rights. Support of human rights and basic goods cannot be separated. Thus, the provision of basic human needs should not be dependent on the ability of poor people to fend for themselves. We all have the responsibility to provide for basic human needs such as food, clothing, shelter, education, and health care.

Wesley's ministry with the poor was a central feature of his religious practice. According to Ted Jennings, Wesley weighed all activities of the Methodist movement by the criterion, "How does it benefit the poor?"[18] In Wesley's view, there was no greater obstacle to community or salvation than hoarded riches. Wesley taught Methodists, "Having first gained all you can, and secondly saved all you can, then give all you can."[19] Generous giving prevented the sin of "laying up treasures on earth."[20] Failure to give all you can was considered a sure path to spiritual destruction. Wesley instructed Methodists to give directly to the poor.

Wesley understood, on a deep level, that attentive presence with the poor raises our awareness of patterns of injustice. When we pay attention to the needs of many neighbors, we become aware of the ways in which different forms of oppression have kept us segregated, divided, or polarized. We begin to realize the ways that we are simply not in community with those persons whose stories we need to hear the most. Poverty—the lack of basic goods for survival—is a systemic reality that tests the mettle of the church's moral witness. Responding to basic needs continues to be vital to the church's moral witness. We must love the poor as we love ourselves. We must bear witness to them through attentive presence.

---

[16]For discussion of "the quartet of the vulnerable," see Nicholas Wolterstorff, *Justice: Rights and Wrongs* (Princeton University Press, 2008), 75.

[17]Wolterstorff, 79.

[18]Theodore W. Jennings, Jr., *Good News to the Poor: John Wesley's Evangelical Economics* (Kingswood, 1990), 63. Jennings argued that solidarity with the poor was the defining attribute and reason for existence of the Methodist movement (25 and throughout). Wesley also castigated wealthy churches for their failure to serve the poor.

[19]John Wesley, "The Use of Money," in *John Wesley's Sermons: An Anthology*, ed. Outler and Heitzenrater, 348–57 (Abingdon, 1991), III.1.

[20]John Wesley, "The Danger of Riches," in *John Wesley's Sermons: An Anthology*, ed. Outler and Heitzenrater, 452–63 (Abingdon, 1991), II.6, referencing Mt. 6:19.

God's redemptive activity requires us to practice empathy. God's commandment is to "love your neighbor *as yourself*." We must identify with our neighbor in order to love our neighbor. This is why the Principles of Holy Conferencing include an admonition to "strive to understand from another's point of view."[21] Even when we encounter persons within our faith community, we might fail to show empathy. We so often have difficulty empathizing with what others are thinking or experiencing. A habit of neighbor-love makes us receptive to the Holy Spirit even when we are not immediately aware of God's presence. Love can bridge the widest ignorance. But we must respond to God's invitation through humility (repentance). Justifying grace can help us see more clearly and to act more lovingly, especially to our neighbors who lack the basic goods for bodily existence. We must desire to see the image of God in our neighbors and strive to protect the most vulnerable as part of the church's moral witness.

Discussion Questions

1   Bearing witness in the present requires attention and intention. How does attentive presence differ from simply seeing or listening to someone? What else is involved?

2   Do you see a direct connection between attentive presence and the love commandment? Explain.

3   Why is it important to take time to be present with your neighbor before rushing to provide answers, goods, or services?

4   Why do you suppose God voices special protections for widows, orphans, immigrants, and the poor? What is our role in participating in this redemptive activity?

Diaconal Exemplars

My mother grew up attending church every Sunday. When she was fourteen, her Girl Scout troop visited a hospital to learn about healthcare and possible career options. She observed an occupational therapist helping children with disabilities learn to do everyday tasks. At that moment, she discerned her lifelong vocation and answered a call to serve the neediest in her community.

Her career as an occupational therapist was an expression of her faith. She witnessed to God's love through daily actions of patience and advocacy. Her passion for children led her to get involved in political lobbying at the Georgia state capitol, seeking support for handicapped persons through legislation and licensure for her profession. She served in many occupational therapy leadership capacities, at state

---

[21]UNY Communications, "The Principles of Holy Conferencing," July 8, 2016, http://www.unyumc.org/news/article/the-principles-of-holy-conferencing.

and national levels, and was so well-respected in her profession that a statewide scholarship was named in her honor. This is how her peers described her:

> In each of her roles, Linda Stephens humbly assumed leadership where she willingly worked in the foreground as well as the background to do "what needed to be done" in the name of advancing the profession of OT [occupational therapy].[22]

Her dedication to helping children with disabilities defined her life's work. Her call from God was incontrovertible; her church community's support unwavering; and her moral witness unambiguous. Like many people living out their faith through various professions, my mother was never formally commissioned by the church for her work. Bearing witness to handicapped children, she exemplified diakonia through her life's work.

Diakonia comes in many forms: lay, ordained, and consecrated. According to the DIAKONIA World Federation, diakonia is "Christian service to which all the baptized are called and which is part of the mission of Christ's church in the world."[23] Diakonia is an expression of the ministry of all Christians through service to those around us. A good example of lay diakonia is Stephen Ministry. You may be familiar with this program, which has reached 13,000 congregations and other organizations since its founding in 1975.[24] The program was named after the man in Acts 6 chosen to serve (*diakonein*) the needs of the early Christian community. Stephen, a deacon, was also the first Christian martyr. Through resources and leadership provided by Stephen Ministries St. Louis, over 600,000 laypersons have been trained as caregivers. I am one of them. According to its founder and executive director Kenneth Haugk, the goal of this program is to "equip the saints for the work of ministry, for building up the body of Christ" (Eph. 4:12). A Stephen Minister is a layperson trained to accompany another person through a season of loss, grief, or other life event. While this one-on-one ministry may provide hope and healing, the main role of a Stephen Minister is to provide attentive presence—to bear witness to the present suffering of another person.

The deacon is the ordained form of diakonia in some Lutheran, Methodist, Episcopalian, Catholic, Orthodox, and united church traditions. "From among the baptized, deacons are called by God to a lifetime of servant leadership, authorized by the Church, and ordained by a bishop."[25] In contrast to *presbyters* (ordained elders), who are called to attend to life within the church, deacons do not typically serve as pastors. United Methodist deacons are ordained "to a lifetime ministry of Word, Service, Compassion, and Justice, to both the community and the congregation in

---

[22]Georgia Occupational Therapy Association, "Awards and Recognitions: Linda Stephens Scholarship," https://www.gaota.com/recognitions-awards.

[23]DIAKONIA World Federation Executive Committee, "Diaconal Reflections: How We Experience Our Diaconal Calling in Our Diversity," 1998, https://web.archive.org/web/20160411170755/http://www.diakonia-world.org/files/theologiepapier98english.pdf.

[24]Stephen Ministries St. Louis, "History of Stephen Ministries," https://www.stephenministries.org/aboutus/default.cfm/721.

[25]*The Book of Discipline of The United Methodist Church 2020/2024* (UMPH, 2024), ¶ 328.

a ministry that connects the two."[26] In other words, deacons are called to preach, teach, lead, and serve, connecting the church and the world. Deacons serve in many different capacities, as nurses, social workers, lawyers, counselors, and teachers. For example, I am a deacon, called to the specialized ministry of teaching.

In the United Methodist tradition, there is yet another form of the diaconate that even more clearly illustrates the process of bearing witness. Deaconesses and home missioners commit themselves to a lifetime of service devoted to their specific field of labor. "Deaconesses and home missioners are professionally trained laypersons who have been led by the Holy Spirit to devote their lives to Christlike service under the authority of the Church."[27] Commissioned by and serving under the appointment of a bishop, they maintain a continuing relationship to their denomination and to their own covenant community.[28] They "function through diverse forms of service directed toward the world to make Jesus Christ known in the fullness of his ministry and mission" by the following mandates:

a) Alleviate suffering;

b) Eradicate causes of injustice and all that robs life of dignity and worth;

c) Facilitate the development of full human potential; and

d) Share in building global community through the church universal.[29]

These defining marks of diakonia touch on key aspects of bearing witness. Bearing witness provokes empathy through attentive presence for those who are suffering. Loving our neighbors, we find ways to alleviate their suffering, being especially attentive to their need for the basic goods of survival. Bearing witness, as discussed in the next chapter, also prompts us to reassess the past in light of our neighbors' suffering. Through memory and repentance, we join in eradicating the causes of injustice. In a later chapter, we will see that bearing witness facilitates the development of full human potential through solidarity as we imagine God's will for the church and global community.

Cindy Andrade Johnson is a deaconess who exemplifies bearing witness through diakonia every day through her work with refugees.[30] Johnson is a former junior high teacher who grew up in Brownsville, Texas, across the border from Matamoros, Mexico. She continues to live and work in her hometown serving immigrants trying to enter the United States. I asked what drew her to this ministry. "As a teacher," she told me, "I didn't really know that I was doing this work, working with the marginalized. I became known as a safe person to talk to." She began to hear the stories of the students she taught in Brownsville. "So many are undocumented

---

[26]*The Book of Discipline of The United Methodist Church 2020/2024,* ¶ 329.

[27]*The Book of Discipline of The United Methodist Church 2020/2024,* ¶ 1913.2.

[28]United Women in Faith, "Office of Deaconess & Home Missioner," 2025, https://uwfaith.org/what-we-do/deaconess-and-home-missioner/.

[29]*The Book of Discipline of The United Methodist Church 2020/2024,* ¶ 1913.1.

[30]The following narrative has two sources: Cindy Johnson, interview with the author, November 14, 2019; United Women in Faith, "Faith Talks with Cindy Johnson," *Podcast,* August 30, 2019, https://www.spreaker.com/episode/faith-talks-with-cindy-johnson–18959362.

because they have family on both sides of the river," she said. Her attentive presence gave her empathy for their plight and gave them confidence to trust her.

As she began building relationships with the most vulnerable persons in her community, love motivated her to try to meet their basic needs. Every week, she crosses the border to visit refugees seeking asylum in the United States.

> I go to Mexico and give food and medication to people. We have up to 500 people in tents in Mexico who live under the bridge [at the border]. I took two malnourished children to the doctor for antibiotics the other day. We have a lot of detention centers; a lot of holding places for children.

Johnson works with several organizations to alleviate immigrants' suffering, including Good Neighbor Settlement House and La Posada Providencia. She went on to say, "We're thanking God that we have this relationship. Though things are pretty bad [at the border], there's always hope. We're mandated [by Christ] to visit people in detention centers," referring to Matthew 25.

I asked her, "What motivates you and others to serve these children and their families?" She explained, "We do all this work because we are called to." Then, she shared this inherited wisdom: "You will never look into the eyes of someone whom God does not love. Always be kind." For Johnson, her kindness led to empathy, understanding, and advocacy. "We get really involved with mercy work, and that's very important, but we need to change the systems. There are a lot of policies that are not just. We have got to change the rhetoric, how we treat each other." Now, she bears witness not only through love but also through justice and solidarity (anticipating the themes of the next two chapters).

One way that Johnson advocates for refugees is to help them write their own stories. She told me of a woman who fled Zimbabwe seeking political asylum.[31] Shalom (not her real name) was the victim of sexual assault in her home country because of her activism in a political opposition movement. Vulnerable to further attack, she fled the country, eventually ending up in a detention center in California. While in detention, she learned that she was pregnant by her attacker. Officers suggested she have an abortion. Johnson met Shalom at La Posada in San Benito, Texas—the only refugee shelter that would take her. They became quick friends. Johnson reported, "She called me when she was ready to give birth, I went with her to the hospital. She invited me into the room while she was giving birth. I saw the birth of Emmanuel, who is now one year old. She asked me to be the godmother of the child." Shalom and Emmanuel still live at the refugee center. Now, Shalom and Cindy are collaborating on the Journey Project, a book of stories from refugees. Cindy and a psychologist are helping, and Shalom is in charge.

> We want to put primary source stories out so that people can read them … [the refugees] have a freedom to talk about what they went through. We keep records

---

[31]Shalom's story comes from two sources: Cindy Johnson, interview with the author, November 14, 2019; Yasmin Amer and Andrea Asuaje, "A Respite Center Helped Her Heal. Now She's Helping Other Refugees Overcome Their Trauma," *WBUR*, October 22, 2019, https://www.wbur.org/kindworld/2019/10/22/place-of-respite.

but do not publish names. We are putting them in English—translated word for word. "What was their favorite thing in their home country? What do they want to do? etc." They formulate the questions.

These first-hand accounts will be published on their website. Later, selected stories will be published in a book form. Empowering refugees to share their stories in writing, Cindy and Shalom allow us to bear witness to the realities they experience even if we cannot be there in person to hear their stories.[32]

Johnson also takes groups from the United States across the border every week to show them the reality first-hand. She described inhumane conditions in detention centers, violations of basic human rights leading to a humanitarian crisis. Migrants do not have access to adequate showering facilities, so they bathe in the Rio Grande, a dangerous and polluted river. "Working with marginalized people in the four poorest counties in the United States, on the border with Mexico, I've learned we need to advocate, to speak up whenever we can and speak up with love." She also documents the living conditions by taking sworn testimonies about what is going on. "We need transparency in these facilities. We need doctors, psychologists. We need to take care of these children." The lack of these basic human needs is robbing these children of dignity and worth. How can we help? When asked what we can do—besides sending money, thoughts, and prayers—Johnson replied with one word: "Advocacy!"

She encouraged other Christians to participate in coordinated efforts for change. "We have a lot of partners. Whenever we have an alert … we have to pick up the phone. We need to speak up. If we stay silent in the face of injustice, we're part of the problem." Many churches and their members are called to bear witness to our neighbors at the border—the refugees in our midst.

Bearing witness leads us to solidarity. Johnson is very clear that these children are already a part of our society. She considers her efforts on their behalf "an investment in the long-term health of our communities." Her relationship with refugee children is part of "building global community," to quote one of the deaconess mandates. Referring to refugee children and their families, Johnson put it like this: "We need to take care of our people [all people]. This is a worldwide issue. we need to also ask for our politicians to realize that we are part of this global world. If we isolate ourselves, how can we find a solution?" Immigrants, strangers, foreigners—these persons are the ones for whom God offers special protections. These are our neighbors. Leading the church in diakonia, Johnson responds in solidarity, for the full flourishing of all of humanity.

Discussion Questions

1   How have you participated in diakonia? Have you ever thought about discipleship this way?

---

[32]For the Lifelines Series of stories, see Yasmin Amer and Andrea Asuaje, "There's a Lot of Tragedy at the Southern Border. There's Also Profound Compassion," *WBUR*, October 25, 2019, https://www.wbur.org/kindworld/2019/10/25/lifelines-series.

2 Do you know a refugee who has settled in your community? What is their
   story? If you know their story already, consider inviting them to share with
   others in your congregation. To get to know refugees in your community,
   volunteer at a local school, women's shelter, or other service agency and
   practice attentive presence.

3 Why does bearing witness in the present lead Johnson to a keener awareness
   of injustice and a need to advocate for refugees? Is there an inevitable
   connection between love, justice, and solidarity?

From Love to Justice

Attentive presence is a profound act of love. This form of love (*agape*) is so powerful
that it breaks forth from the present, reshaping all that is past and future, too. Being
fully present for another person, especially when they are suffering, often leads
us to realize injustice. Bearing witness naturally leads us from one moment to the
next. Attentive presence, the second moment of bearing witness, leads to a need for
historical clarity, the third moment, and a desire for meaningful participation, the
fourth moment. Presence leads to awareness, which leads to advocacy. It is impossible
to isolate this moment of bearing witness.

The work of Doctors Without Borders/Médecins Sans Frontières (MSF) provides
a good example of this holistic sense of bearing witness. MSF was created in 1971 by
French physicians working for the Red Cross in Nigeria who refused to remain silent
about the atrocities they witnessed.[33] The Red Cross did not allow their doctors to
speak out about what they had seen, considering any public statement a possible
hinderance to their humanitarian work. In contrast, MSF was founded on the belief
that humanitarian efforts require a witness. Medical triage must be accompanied by
a voice for justice. MSF is committed to bearing witness:

> We believe that the principles of impartiality and neutrality are not synonymous
> with silence. When the world turns its back on crises, we are duty-bound to raise
> our voices and speak out on behalf of our patients. Our decision to do so is
> always guided by our mission to do no harm, preserve respect and dignity, and
> protect life and health.[34]

This commitment to bear witness combines band-aids with billboards, triage with
testament. The effort to meet immediate physical needs reveals transcendent human
dignity. MSF was created precisely so that doctors responding to humanitarian crises
could testify to the suffering they witnessed so that it might be stopped. Love does
not stop at triage.

Bearing witness extends the work of love further than acts of mercy. Love sees
the image of God in the neighbor. Love measures our neighbor's plight according

---

[33]Doctors Without Borders/Médecins Sans Frontières (MSF), "Who We Are," https://www.
doctorswithoutborders.org/who-we-are.
[34]MSF.

to the full flourishing God intends for each of us and takes note of the difference. Love sees the reality of suffering in light of the Resurrection and bears witness to the shadows.[35] To bear witness is to say "no" to the suffering of our neighbor. To bear witness is to speak out on behalf of our neighbor for their full human flourishing. For Doctors Without Borders, this means they act: "to alleviate suffering, protect life and health, and to restore respect for human beings and their fundamental human rights." Recognition, dignity, human rights, and basic goods all flow from being present with our neighbors, especially the most vulnerable.

Christians are called to bear witness through God's love for each of us, daring to imagine God's vision of righteousness. Bearing witness is a full-throttled, holistic endeavor to love and serve others in the name of Christ, who said, "I came that they may have life and have it abundantly" (Jn 10:10)—full human flourishing, not just survival. As a Christian, it is not enough for me to reject evil and repent of my own sin. Through baptism I have also taken on the responsibility to bear witness to my neighbor, accepting "the freedom and power God gives [me] to resist evil, injustice, and oppression in whatever forms they present themselves."[36] I cannot be silent. No matter how merciful my response, I cannot stop at mercy. I must speak out. To express neighbor-love is to be attuned to the reality of suffering in their lives and, then, not only to be aware of their suffering but to do something about it. "How does God's love abide in anyone who has the world's goods and sees a brother or sister in need and yet refuses help?" (1 Jn 3:17). Love is immediate, attending to the needs of the present. Love is also persistent, demanding justice in the face of systemic oppression.

Bearing witness to God's will for a more just world requires attentiveness to those who bear the image of God. In what may seem the most unlikely of places, we encounter the risen Christ. Referring to her service at Anchorage Breakfast Ministry, Jane Dutton shared this reflection: "I was sick a few weeks ago and missed my regular Monday. The next week more than several people asked how I was, said they missed me, and said they had prayed for me. God's love is pouring out in both directions. God is at work on the margins and in the margins."[37] Dutton's attentive presence to Joe and others on the margins of her community brought her into closer relationship, not only with them but also with God.

Cindy Johnson shared a similar response: "I see God every day because of what these people [refugees] are doing. That gives me such energy."[38] During her podcast interview, a caller asked, "When you encounter migrants who have been mistreated, what is the message of faith that you share with them?" She replied that we need to turn the question around: "They share faith with me! We both share our faith. We're doing what God's calling us to do. We're taking care of our families. They have such faith. I just reinforce their faith."[39] Indeed, Johnson and Dutton both express the truth that God is already here—a mystery, beyond understanding, but a real, tangible mystery, nonetheless. To this truth, we bear witness.

---

[35] Shelly Rambo, *Spirit and Trauma: A Theology of Remaining* (Westminster John Knox, 2010), 41.
[36] *The United Methodist Hymnal: Book of United Methodist Worship* (UMPH, 1989), 34.
[37] Dutton, "Magi on the Margins."
[38] Cindy Johnson, interview with the author, November 14, 2019.
[39] United Women in Faith, "Faith Talks with Cindy Johnson."

Discussion Questions

1 How are issues of homelessness and immigration related to trauma? Not every instance of being unhoused or immigrating to a foreign land results in an experience of trauma. Why do you think the author chose these topics as illustrations?

2 Trauma-informed response is not dependent on a diagnosis of trauma. Practicing attentive presence, for example, can be an expression of love for all neighbors, not just those with trauma histories, as exemplified by Dutton, Johnson, MSF, and others. How might you be more attentively present when interacting with immigrants in your community?

A Glimpse of the Holy

Bearing witness in the present embodies the love command in all of its fullness: loving God and loving my neighbor as myself. Bearing witness is about my being present for someone else in their times of difficulty. Shedding "selfish ambition or empty conceit," I seek to be filled with humility (Phil. 2:3). Humility begins simply by paying attention to your neighbor as you would have them pay attention to you. It is about allowing that person's story to come through while being attuned to the Spirit in our midst. It is about glimpsing the image of God in my neighbor and seeking to follow the example of Christ by being present with them. To bear witness means not only hearing my neighbor's story but also seeing my neighbor in their fullness. Empathy reveals a glimpse of the holy.

Humility is the fitting response for me, a person with a relative degree of social power and privilege, whose primary sin may be pride. Feminist and womanist theological ethicists offer a different perspective based on experiences of oppression. For example, Jacquelyn Grant argued, "for women of color, the sin is not the lack of humility, but the sin is too much humility."[40] We can still bear witness to others while asserting ourselves. In Jane's story, above, Joe asserts himself as an agent with equal standing. His self-giving is not coerced; he gives his coat out of generosity, gratitude, and love for his neighbor.

Love recklessly! This is the Christian imperative—extravagant, generous, reckless love. Neighbor-love serves everyone. Every person we encounter is a Christ-encounter, a Godly moment of divine presence. Yet, sharing love indiscriminately with every neighbor can seem impersonal. It is not. Love leads me not to unmoved apathy but rather to passionate advocacy. Love is biased in its regard for those who are suffering. When I love my neighbor, I make their well-being my priority. When my neighbor is suffering, love leads me to speak out on their behalf against all forms of injustice. Empathy in the face of suffering prompts me to call out past injustices and to imagine more just ways of relating. Love moves me beyond mercy toward justice-making, the next moment of bearing witness.

---

[40]Jacquelyn Grant, "The Sin of Servanthood and the Deliverance of Discipleship," in *A Troubling in My Soul: Womanist Perspectives on Evil and Suffering*, ed. Emilie M. Townes, 199–218 (Orbis, 1993), 215.

2.3
Historical Clarity

Bearing witness to suffering is disconcerting. It can be uncomfortable to be present with people in times of pain, loneliness, and loss. It is heart-wrenching to encounter persons lacking basic goods of survival—food, healthcare, shelter, and physical safety. Accompanying my neighbor through their trauma can result in compassion fatigue or vicarious trauma.[1] It is risky work, attentive presence. Furthermore, love has a way of creating within us a righteous discontent, causing us to seek causes and explanations, prompting us to see patterns and connections. Through attentive presence with our neighbors in times of suffering, we are led to moments of realization. All is not well—and we are partially to blame. The empathy arising from attentive presence leads us to the next moment of bearing witness: historical clarity.

A moment of historical clarity gives us the opportunity to realize personal and social responsibility for the world around us. When we see Christ in our neighbors and hear the stories of their lives, we are convicted of realities beyond ourselves and made aware of our failings. Recognizing our common humanity and equal worth before God, convicted of the reality of their suffering and need for basic goods, questions arise. Where did their suffering come from? In what ways am I complicit? How has our community failed to care for its most vulnerable members? Reassessing our past in light of these present ills enables us to name injustices and recognize systemic oppressions. The plight of one person might appear simply unfortunate; the plight of an entire group of people might indicate problems in need of collective repentance. How shall we respond?

This chapter exercises historical clarity by exploring how Christians have responded to moral challenges in the world around us. What witness have we offered—both individually and as a church—on issues such as eugenics, Doctrine of Discovery, climate change, racism, and poverty? What is the fruit of our faith, and how can we cultivate a more faithful witness? How can we bear witness to God's will for a more just world by reckoning with our past? How can we call out injustice and advocate for those who have suffered because of our own iniquities and failings as a church? Memory can lead to repentance. Bearing witness through

---

[1]For more information, see Pamela Cooper-White, *The Cry of Tamar: Violence against Women and the Church's Response*, 2nd ed. (Fortress, 2012), 195; Karen A. McClintock, *Trauma-Informed Pastoral Care: How to Respond When Things Fall Apart* (Fortress, 2022), 107–22.

historical clarity shapes our moral witness to account for victims of injustice as we work toward healing relationships. It is only by reckoning with our past that we can prepare ourselves for meaningful participation in God's preferred future.

The Grace of Doing Nothing

Memory is the mode of transcendence that enables us to respond to God's forgiveness through repentance for both personal and social sin. Understanding sin as brokenness, we can see that individuals as well as institutions and all of society suffer from sin. Individuals as well as groups need healing in their relationships. Through a process of repentance, we identify injustices and begin preparing for the future work of reparation and restitution. We join with God to repair broken relationships. This is the third moment of bearing witness.

Historical clarity is, in some ways, the most difficult moment of bearing witness. Memory exposes patterns of oppression, confronting us with our past. For example, while it is true that "All lives matter," it is also true that certain lives have historically faced discrimination, injustice, incarceration, lynching, and enslavement due to the color of their skin. This pattern continues today, as documented by legal scholar Michelle Alexander in *The New Jim Crow: Mass Incarceration in the Age of Colorblindness*.[2] Thus, when we say, "Black lives matter," we are speaking from an historically informed awareness that all is not okay even today with the way our society treats persons of color. As a white Methodist, I must learn to view the present as part of the pattern of racial injustice perpetuated by my white ancestors, my community, and my church. Awakened to patterns of injustice in the lives of our neighbors, we reassess the past and repent, fully assured of God's forgiveness. Bearing witness to my African American neighbors prompts me to reckon with this past.

Historical clarity is the repentant pause between love and justice, a pivotal point of introspection before full-throated advocacy. H. Richard Niebuhr poetically described this moment of repentance as "The Grace of Doing Nothing": "The inactivity of radical Christianity ... is the inaction of those who do not judge their neighbors because they cannot fool themselves into a sense of superior righteousness. It is not the inactivity of a resigned patience, but of a patience that is full of hope and is based on faith."[3] Niebuhr went on to acknowledge the interconnectedness of the world in sin and the need for works of mercy as we await the healing grace of God. Bearing witness prepares us for this "inactivity." Attending to the stories of victims of injustice, we are forced to reckon with our sins, individual and collective. It is only by mapping these depths that we can fully engage in the meaningful participation in God's good work that completes the process of bearing witness. However, we cannot rush to reconciliation without first doing the hard work of repentance. This

---

[2]Michelle Alexander, *The New Jim Crow: Mass Incarceration in the Age of Colorblindness* (New Press, 2012).

[3]H. Richard Niebuhr, "The Grace of Doing Nothing," in *An Eerdmans Reader in Contemporary Political Theology*, ed. William T. Cavanaugh, Jeffrey W. Bailey, and Craig Hovey, 254–8 (Eerdmans, 2012), 258.

exercise of memory enables renewed perspective and understanding, and it takes time. Repentance requires preparation.

We must reckon with our own past. What have we done or failed to do? How have we contributed to evil, injustice, and oppression in the lives of those around us? Sometimes we must move through stages of grieving before we can come to a point of accepting the reality of brokenness and before we can honestly wrestle with our complicity in it. This moment calls for repentance as we live into the forgiveness God has already promised us. Being forgiven does not mean forgetting the past, for repentance is an exercise of memory. Nor can we presume to repent if we are not also attentively present for those neighbors with whom we seek healing. Repentance also requires personal and communal restitution, creating healthier mindsets, more equitable structures of power, and new forms of accountability within the church and other institutions. Going forward, accepting God's forgiveness means reassessing the past in light of God's will for healing and reconciliation.

Acts of Preparation

1   Read Psalm 130 with a partner or group. Listen to the depths from which others cry out. Sit with the injustice of their experiences. Bear witness to their suffering.

2   Consider one overwhelming moral issue facing your community and the world today: climate emergency, drug abuse and addiction, systemic racism, poverty, etc. Engage in a silent meditation for the purpose of listening to your body and the emotions it reveals: anger, despondency, fear, hope. Journal your feelings.

3   Participate in public worship with your congregation or other faith community. Pay attention to the opportunities for repentance and forgiveness. How does liturgy help us with the task of reckoning with our past?

Navigating Grief

Jenny Phillips is called to environmental justice and dedicates much of her ministry to helping others enter a moment of historical clarity.[4] Her ministry includes helping people find what they need in terms of community resources. For example, she helps people in remote areas without electricity to write grants for solar panels. There are many poor, rural communities across the globe that have few resources to deal with direct losses due to climate change: dislocation, malnutrition, and economic upheaval. Providing electricity through solar panel installation is one way to help these communities become more resilient to climate events—the effects of climate degradation they had very little to do with. Most of her time, though, is spent

---

[4]The following is based on Jenny Phillips, interview with the author, August 15, 2019.

working with people privileged enough not to suffer directly from the impacts of climate change.

How do people insulated from the most devastating effects of their own consumption and energy use reckon with their complicity in climate degradation? Phillips is very intentional in this aspect of her pastoral ministry. When privileged people experience vicarious suffering, fearing what kind of world their children will have, she accompanies them through a process of grieving.

> Often with groups that I work with, I talk about grief and the stages of grief in terms of how people respond to issues of climate change. Starts with denial. I don't argue anymore. I used to. Now I take a more pastoral approach as I'm encountering a person who is grieving. "How will it rock their world if what they are hearing is actually true?" Some don't want the changes that need to happen—in the face of very clear scientific data. Denial. Then, anger. Pointing the finger at others. Anger at God, who is supposed to be in control of all of this. Bargaining: "If I drive a hybrid car, if I use cloth grocery bags, ..." However, systemic change is now required. Depression. A sense of powerlessness or hopelessness. Acceptance. Not accepting that everything will unfold in worst case scenario, but [asking] what change is required to create a world ...
>
> We bounce through all these stages of grief every day. I experience all of these stages; we'll never be done with that. The existential suffering is very real, and the church has a role to play in helping people deal with it. We need these people—affluent folks with wealth—to demand the change that needs to happen in the world.

Phillips's work is clearly informed by Elisabeth Kübler-Ross's five stages of grieving: denial, anger, bargaining, depression, and acceptance.[5]

Grieving is a natural response to suffering and loss, even when the suffering and loss are not directly our own. Grief can enable a person to deal with feelings they may not fully understand. The process of grieving can help us bear witness to realities that at first seem distant and abstract. Facilitating this process, Phillips maintains an attentive presence as God's grace works through her and all the people she encounters. When they enter the stage of acceptance, she stands ready to assist them with the work of reckoning with their past.[6] Phillips serves as a midwife to repentance, helping people birth their nascent moral witness in relation to climate change.

Repentance is the way we seek to be right with God and one another, as individuals and as a church. Repentance, *metanoia*, calls for turning from the ways of the past and preventing future wrongs. The first step of repentance is admitting wrong and feeling remorse about it. We reassess the past in light of the suffering we have witnessed. It involves admitting our own failure to act. It involves admitting our own misdeeds. It involves confessing sins of commission and omission: "we have rebelled

---

[5] Elisabeth Kübler-Ross, *On Death and Dying* (Simon & Schuster/Touchstone, 1969).

[6] Phillips is not alone in this work. "Ecological Grief" is one of five programmatic themes of the BTS Center in Portland, Maine, which cultivates and nurtures "Spiritual Leadership for a Climate-Changed World." https://thebtscenter.org/.

against [God's] love, ... we have not heard the cry of the needy."[7] Repentance begins with confession of sin and saying, "I'm sorry." That step is vital, but there is more. The second step is to cease our wrongdoing. We must turn from old patterns of hurt and harm toward new patterns of health and love. Repentance requires an intent not to repeat the offense.

Recognition of our sin brings a double awareness of our moral agency: we failed, and we can do better. Just as attentive presence leads to a conviction that our neighbor's suffering is real, historical clarity convicts us that we had a hand in that suffering. Through attentive presence, I listen fully to another person, respond with empathy, and consider my need to repent of actions that caused harm and injustice. With remorse for past actions, I can ask for and accept the forgiveness of God and mindfully turn away from repeating that same wrongful action. Then, once I have reassessed the past and my role in it, I can consider how the church and I might make amends. The third step is to attempt to fix what we have broken, if doing so does not cause further harm. Through grace, we can repair past harm and dismantle systems of injustice. Empowered by God's forgiving grace, we can enter into right (just) relationships with God and neighbor. We can build social structures conducive to well-being. We can work toward reconciliation. The church's moral witness mirrors the continual repentance of our life in Christ.

Some clarifications and cautions are needed. The process of forgiveness and repentance is not a transactional exchange. I can repent without receiving forgiveness from the person I have wronged; I can forgive prior to any sign of repentance by someone who has wronged me. Also, in many situations, it is not possible to achieve reconciliation or renewed relationship. For example, in cases involving an abuse of power, the most just outcome may require no continued relationship between the victim and perpetrator. Furthermore, forgiveness requires ongoing accountability. A person who has abused a position of power should not be reinstated without demonstrable restitution and other elements of justice-making, including stringent oversight and added protections for the vulnerable going forward.[8] Additionally, I can reckon with my own complicity in social sin and systemic wrongdoings without a juridical determination of the guilty party. For collective failings, our repentance can contribute to a more just society despite a lack of closure or reconciliation.

A Wesleyan theology of salvation helps us understand repentance as part of the church's moral witness. Initially, in the life of faith, repentance is a grace-enabled response to a newfound conviction that I have fallen short of what God intends for my life. Initial repentance—the kind that leads to justification and new birth—is a leap of faith. It is "a conviction ... [un]mitigated by a sense of forgiveness."[9] In other words, the first time we repent can be frightening because we do so without an assurance that God will forgive us. Once we experience God's forgiving, justifying grace in our

---

[7]"A Service of Word and Table II," in *The United Methodist Hymnal: Book of United Methodist Worship*, 12 (UMPH, 1989).

[8]See, for example, Lauren D. Sawyer, Emily Cohen, and Annie Mesaros, eds., *Responding to Spiritual Leader Misconduct: A Handbook* (FaithTrust Institute, 2022), 90–2, 98–9, https://faithtrustinstitute.org/.

[9]Randy L. Maddox, *Responsible Grace: John Wesley's Practical Theology* (Kingswood, 1994), 165.

lives, the practice of repentance is less frightening. It becomes a spiritual discipline. We can be assured of God's forgiveness because we have already experienced it. I think it is common, however, to relive the initial uncertainty of repentance again and again. Like a trauma, the memory of initially confronting our brokenness before God replays itself throughout our lives. While deep in our hearts we may have assurance of God's forgiveness, wisps of doubt cloud our vision. Repentance requires faith every time, and every time it makes our faith stronger. A healthy faith community can support us in this journey of spiritual maturation. Thus, continued repentance, as evidenced by the Holy Communion liturgy, is essential to growth in our individual and collective life of faith. It is part of the church's moral witness.

Historical clarity builds on attentive presence by being honest about where we are and how we got here. This step can be difficult for people trying to understand an injustice and who do not suffer its immediate effects. Phillips shared with me a story to illustrate this difficulty. She was the "voice of faith" on a discussion panel about food poverty, energy access, and other pressing issues facing low-income communities of color in Atlanta, Georgia. Vulnerable people often have the least power to address these concerns. The attendees at this event were not the vulnerable ones. The audience in this local church consisted mainly of affluent white people with no direct experience of these problems in their community. Perhaps they had not borne adequate witness to their poor neighbors. For the most part, they had not felt the adverse effects of poverty or climate change but were nevertheless worried about the climate emergency they hear so much about.

During the question-and-answer portion of the event, an older white man asked her, "Pastor, I just need to know, are we going to be okay?" Her response challenged him to transcend his own experience:

> We are definitely not okay right now ... globally, people are not okay. While the people in this room may remain shielded from the worst effects of climate change, the most vulnerable persons in the world will not be shielded ... there is this disconnect on who the "we" is: affluent church members in the U.S. or global humanity. We have more choice right now than we're ever going to have to respond to climate change. The longer we wait to take significant action, the fewer possibilities there are for intervention.

The "disconnect" Phillips named can be repaired by bearing witness to the victims of climate change. Injustice is not distributed equally. We must seek historical clarity to understand our world, past and present, and our part in it. Reflecting back on this episode, she reaffirmed her witness, telling me, "We are part of a larger community. When brethren are suffering, the body of Christ is suffering. We are not okay right now." It is the great challenge of her ministry, to help people recognize their own power and agency to change the world. We must repent of our past, unjust ways and bear witness to our neighbors before we can join in what God is already doing to repair and reconcile this world.

How can we receive God's forgiveness if we remain unrepentant? Seeing that everything is not okay in the world is a necessary preparation for repentance. This preparation may involve multiple stages of grief. Recognizing that we all have dirty hands when it comes to systemic injustices, such as climate change, could cause us to despair if it were not for the promise of forgiveness. And even if we are not paralyzed with inaction through despair, we can easily become overwhelmed trying to save the world. Yet it is not through our own power but through power of the Holy Spirit that we join in the work of justice. The Good News is that God has already forgiven us and is already making all things new.

We are forgiven. God bathes us in waters of baptism, and our billions of individual rivulets converge to wash away the deficiencies of the past. "But let justice roll down like water and righteousness like an ever-flowing stream" (Amos 5:24). We are meant to join in God's justice-making. Through baptism, we are called to advocate for God's justice. It is the role of prophets like Phillips to awaken people to their complicity in the problems of the world and to encourage them to remember their baptism: "Do you accept the freedom and power God gives you to resist evil, injustice, and oppression in whatever forms they present themselves?"[10]

Discussion Questions

1   How do your baptismal vows shape the way you live out your life? Do you believe that God gives you the power to resist injustice and oppression in your community? How does the liturgy of Holy Communion empower and sustain you in this work?

2   How does belonging to a community of faith strengthen your moral witness? Do you believe that together, we as the church can make a positive difference in this world, even against such intractable problems as climate change, poverty, and racism?

3   Consider your personal journey through the stages of grief on issues facing your community. What are you in denial about? What are you angry about? What are you bargaining about? What are you depressed about? How has a measure of acceptance of the reality of a problem prepared and enabled you to begin working toward justice?

Repentance as an Act of Justice

Bearing witness to the sufferings of this world is a way of proclaiming that, in the name of God, we will not stand idly by. "For it is not the hearers of the law who are righteous in God's sight but the doers of the law who will be justified" (Rom. 2:13). We are called to resist injustice. The Hebrew prophets had some poetic ways of describing God's justice. Justice is dry bones living again. Justice is the unimaginable peace of the lion lying down with the lamb. Justice is what God does—for us, through us, despite us—to restore and make new all of creation. This section explores how reckoning with our past can enable right relationships, how the ministry of memory can enable discipleship, and how repentance can be an act of justice.

---

[10]*The United Methodist Hymnal*, 33.

Because God's justice is so hard to grasp, the prophets often begin by telling us what God's justice is not. Some folks mistakenly separate justice from worship, as if loving neighbor and loving God were two separate things. When we worship, we should ask, "With what shall I come before the Lord and bow myself before God on high?" (Mic. 6:6). Not sacrifices or burnt offerings, said Micah, but only our repentant selves: "what does the Lord require of you but to do justice and to love kindness and to walk humbly with your God?" (Mic. 6:8). Micah's witness is not alone. Amos also warns against substituting pageantry for equity, as if God's righteous appetite could be sated with a choice farm animal and loud, musical praises. "I hate, I despise your festivals, and I take no delight in your solemn assemblies … the offerings of well-being of your fatted animals I will not look upon. Take away from me the noise of your songs; I will not listen to the melody of your harps" (Amos 5:21-23). Was God's displeasure, as communicated through the prophet Amos, due to our ancestors' failure to bear witness through justice-making?

Worship can neither be separated from justice nor substitute for the sacrifices necessary outside of the sanctuary. To emerge from the waters of baptism and swim in the stream of righteousness, we must not only worship God but also bear witness to our neighbors. "For just as the body without the spirit is dead, so faith without works is also dead" (Jas 2:26). Baptism propels us to put our faith into action. There is continuity between the sacraments, liturgy, and everyday life. The double love commandment is, in fact, a single command. We cannot claim to love God and fail to love our neighbors and ourselves. Thus, we cannot claim to love our neighbors and fail to bear witness to their suffering. Furthermore, we cannot bear witness to the suffering of others without attending to our own traumatic healing. Victim-survivors of trauma should not be coerced into jeopardizing their own well-being under the guise of love for the neighbor.

Acts of repentance connect our moral witness and worship of God. The liturgy of Holy Communion shapes us for the task. Responding to God's invitation "to live in peace with one another," we confess our sin, accept God's forgiveness, and become ambassadors of Christ, "offer[ing] one another signs of reconciliation and love."[11] Then, recalling God's salvation history, from creation to deliverance to redemption, we give thanks for God's new covenant through Christ Jesus. The contrast between God's faithful actions and our own failures—as individuals, as a people, as a church—provides the historical clarity so important when bearing witness. Offering ourselves "as a holy and living sacrifice, in union with Christ's offering for us," we proclaim our faith and ask for God's blessing: "By your Spirit make us one with Christ, one with each other, and one in ministry to all the world." Make us one! This is not about me alone. This is about our life together. Bearing witness to these truths, we become the church again and again. Through the nourishment of Holy Communion, we are equipped to bear witness to God's will for a more just world. This is what it means to prepare for right relationships, justice.

Repentance is not an abstract exercise. For example, as a white Christian in the United States, I struggle with how to respond to injustices perpetuated generations ago against Native Americans. My ancestors played a role in the destruction of native

---

[11]*The United Methodist Hymnal*, 15–16.

peoples. I continue to benefit from social structures and inheritances that privilege me and other white people in the United States. What can white people do to turn from a sinful mindset, one that distorted the gospel to the extent that it resulted in the subjugation of native peoples in the name of Christianity and civilization? How can I repent? How can *we* repent?

Repenting as a Church

The United Methodist Church (UMC) provides some examples of bearing witness as a church—many other denominations can provide their own examples. In 2008, this denomination repented for past Methodist support of eugenics.[12] Like many primarily white Protestants around the turn of the twentieth century, Methodists advocated "race betterment" by supporting forced sterilization laws and laws restricting interracial marriage. The 2008 statement warned, "The overt racism of the eugenic campaigns of the last century is no longer acceptable in today's civic square or pulpits, but the impetus toward eugenics remains." There are still broken relationships; there is still justice-work to be done. The resolution expressed concern about new biotechnologies involving human reproduction and embryo selection. Racism and other mindsets of superiority still shape decision-making at individual and policy levels. Relationships are still in need of healing through God's grace. After recounting the history of injustices, this church offered a statement of formal apology and lament for "Methodist support of eugenics policies." This was not the first time United Methodists repented of their moral failures as a church.

The UMC engaged in an "Act of Repentance for Racism" in 2000, adopting a formal resolution of that title and performing a liturgical act of repentance.[13] Focused on the treatment of African Americans by the UMC and its predecessors, this formal resolution sought historical clarity and confessed past wrongs through remembrance and remorse. This action was part of a longer process: "confession and repentance for racism is but a first step toward the changing of hearts leading to healing and wholeness." Bearing witness requires letting go of old prejudices and entering into right relationship between the perpetrators and the victims of injustice—though the moral responsibilities of victim and perpetrator differ significantly.[14] Bearing witness demands a reallocation of power and privilege. It causes us to let go of old mindsets, changing not only the way we act but also the way we think. Thus, the UMC adopted a study guide on the church's role in racism, recommended church-wide study, and requested that every annual conference "engage in a liturgical act of repentance" the following year. The UMC still has a long journey of racial reconciliation ahead of it.

---

[12]"Repentance for Support of Eugenics," Resolution 3185 in *The Book of Resolutions of The United Methodist Church 2008*, 340–6 (UMPH, 2008).

[13]"Act of Repentance for Racism," Resolution 149 in *The Book of Resolutions of The United Methodist Church 2000*, 384–5 (UMPH, 2000).

[14]When righting relationships, the demands on perpetrators are distinct from the demands on victims, even though our experiences can mutually inform our understanding of God. James Newton Poling, *Rethinking Faith: A Constructive Practical Theology* (Fortress, 2011).

Healing and reconciliation cannot happen unless white people seek historical clarity and offer restitution. This formal act of repentance was but one moment in a larger process of bearing witness to each other and to God.

The UMC is also repenting for its history of mistreatment of Native Americans and other Indigenous persons. The scholarship of Homer Noley provided important preparation for this task. Supported by the General Commission on Archives and History in the mid-1980s, Noley wrote a history, *First White Frost: Native Americans and United Methodism*.[15] His research brought into sharp relief the way in which Europeans initially questioned the humanity of "man-like creatures inhabiting the Americas," the significance of John Wesley's recognizing Native people "as members of the family of God" and "as recipients of God's grace," and the importance of "a Ministry of Presence" when ministering to and with Native Americans.[16] The first two moments of bearing witness—recognition and presence—are clearly evident.

In 1988, the UMC began to reconsider its relationships with Native Americans in preparation for the 500th anniversary of Columbus's "discovery" of the Americas. The Doctrine of Discovery originates from fifteenth-century Roman Catholic papal writings declaring lands and peoples discovered outside of Christendom to be subject to their Christian conquerors. In other words, the pope declared that Christian European nations had a divine right to dominate Indigenous peoples and their lands. Soon, European Protestants, too, embraced the mentality of this papal edict. While Pope Paul III clarified in 1537 that Indigenous persons should not be deprived of their liberty and property, the colonizers and missionaries continued to subjugate, enslave, and steal from the peoples they encountered in Africa and the Americas—all in the name of Christ. The Roman Catholic Church and others remained complicit in their silence, insufficient advocacy, and active participation in oppression. This philosophy of cultural superiority became law in Western Europe. European immigrants brought this attitude of privilege and entitlement with them to North America. The Doctrine of Discovery entered US federal law in 1823. Two hundred years later, on March 30, 2023, the Vatican issued a statement formally repudiating the original papal writings, acknowledging their terrible effects and asking for pardon.[17]

White Methodists participated fully in these politics of white superiority. Reckoning with its past in 1992, the UMC adopted a resolution confessing the church's sin and offering a formal apology to Native Americans.[18] Then, this church entered into a process of repentance to redress its failures, resolving, "While it is difficult to judge past events in light of contemporary moral sensibilities, Christians have the responsibility to understand them and face up to their contemporary consequences."[19]

---

[15]Homer Noley, *First White Frost: Native Americans and United Methodism* (Abingdon, 1991).

[16]Noley, 18, 48, 229–30, respectively.

[17]Raymond J. de Souza, "The 'Doctrine of Discovery' and the Catholic Church," *National Catholic Register*, April 4, 2023, https://www.ncregister.com/commentaries/the-doctrine-of-discovery-and-the-catholic-church.

[18]"Confession to Native Americans," in *The Book of Resolutions of The United Methodist Church 1992*, 210–11 (UMPH, 1992).

[19]"Toward a New Beginning Beyond 1992," in *The Book of Resolutions 1992*, 386–92.

In other words, the UMC bore witness through its collective memory of its own oppression, exploitation, and domination of Indigenous peoples, persons of color, and "others suffering under structures of domination." This statement of moral witness began with recognition of equality (the first moment of bearing witness): "As people of faith, we confess that God is the creator of all that exists and that all humans are created equal in dignity, rights, and responsibilities."[20] This is not a trivial confession, as Noley's history reminds us. Recognition eventually enabled empathy, which then brought about awareness and a desire to change. "Therefore, we must challenge all value systems and structures which in theory and/or practice devalue human beings and rob them of their dignity and their relationship to the rest of God's creation which sustains us all."[21] Challenging the attitudes contributing to broken relationships is part of repentance. The UMC understood its moral witness in the context of resurrection and new beginnings as it recommended exploring the return of native lands to Indigenous peoples—a plan for restitution.

The UMC's moral witness for Indigenous peoples continued. In 1996, the General Conference supported restitution to the Cheyenne and Arapaho Tribes of Oklahoma for the Sand Creek Massacre of 1864—an attack led and enabled by Methodists. Repeated resolutions in 2000, 2004, and 2008 affirmed the need for healing relationships with Indigenous persons. This denomination's "Act of Repentance and Healing for Indigenous Persons" on April 27, 2012, provided continued opportunity for historical clarity. Another 2012 resolution, "Trail of Repentance and Healing," recognized that a process of healing relationships with Indigenous persons must include study, self-examination, and confession. The resolution specified several parts of this process, corresponding to specific moments of bearing witness:

- Attentive presence: "building relationships with Indigenous persons … through listening and being present with Indigenous persons";
- Historical clarity: "discovering the ongoing impact of historic traumas" and "confessing our own participation in the continuing effects of that trauma";
- Meaningful participation: "working beside Indigenous persons to seek solutions to current problems" and "advocating and resourcing programs that are self-determined by native and Indigenous persons to be part of the healing process."[22]

Thus, these actions of love, justice, and solidarity were built on the recognition of equal dignity proclaimed by the UMC twenty years earlier. Bearing witness is an ongoing process within the life of faith.

---

[20]"Toward a New Beginning Beyond 1992," 388.

[21]"Toward a New Beginning Beyond 1992," 388.

[22]"Trail of Repentance and Healing," Resolution 3324 in *The Book of Resolutions of The United Methodist Church 2012*, 420–2 (UMPH, 2012).

The Sand Creek Massacre

Methodist involvement in the Sand Creek Massacre provides a case study for historical clarity. Acknowledging the wrongs done to Cheyenne, Arapaho, and other native peoples by white Methodist settlers in the nineteenth century is one part of repentance. The 2012 General Conference adopted a petition calling for "full disclosure" of those persons involved in the 1864 Sand Creek Massacre, one of the worst atrocities committed against native peoples in North America and one led and abetted by Methodists. This disclosure was presented to General Conference 2016 in a report by Gary L. Roberts, a historian and United Methodist layperson. Subsequently published as *Massacre at Sand Creek: How Methodists Were Involved in an American Tragedy*, Robert's report documented how white Methodists treated Native Americans and the mindset that enabled them to rationalize and justify the events of November 29, 1864, at Sand Creek in the Colorado Territory.[23] On that day, US Army soldiers set upon a peaceful encampment of Cheyenne and Arapaho peoples, slaughtering hundreds of women, children, and elderly after luring away most of the adult men. The mindset that enabled this slaughter of innocents remains a social sin of which white US Methodists still need to repent.

According to Roberts, understanding the complexities of Indian-white relationships involves realizing the distinct ways of seeing diverse cultures and differing mindsets involved. Native Americans and Euro-Americans have different ways of seeing the world: one cyclic and the other linear (Roberts, 10–11). Within these distinct ways of seeing are diverse cultures, languages, and traditions. There are multiple Indigenous peoples in North America, just as there are multiple European peoples. These differences or similarities in themselves do not determine how individuals and entire peoples might relate to each other, though. Mindsets shape the way different people and peoples interact. The prevailing Anglo-American mindset in the nineteenth century was one of cultural, religious, and technological superiority (14). Roberts traced the development of this mindset through the history of Western Christendom, embedded in a triumphalist theological narrative and expressed in the Roman Empire, the medieval Crusades, and the European Doctrine of Discovery (19–24). To this general European mindset, the English added "a deeply embedded sense of Anglo-Saxon superiority" (23). Roberts described the effects of this mindset as ranging from "benign paternalism" to "militant contempt and even violence" (231–2).

This Anglo-American mindset prevented significant relationship-building with Native Americans. Attempted Methodist missions among Native Americans largely faltered as white evangelists and missionaries rarely invested sufficient time to learn about native peoples' ways of seeing, their cultures, and their languages. Roberts explained:

> The old "anti-Indian sublime" was as fundamental to Methodist thinking as grace or sanctification. The best that could be said of Methodist efforts among Indian

---

[23]Gary L. Roberts, *Massacre at Sand Creek: How Methodists Were Involved in an American Tragedy* (Abingdon, 2016).

people was that enough was done to make the annual reports of the Missionary Society respectable. But there was no aggressive or enthusiastic support for the effort beyond a few missionary spirits. There was no heart for Indian missions because the soul of Methodism was bound up in American exceptionalism.

(Roberts, 178)

A sense of superiority proved a barrier to relationships and a justification for oppression. White Methodists embraced an Anglo-American mindset as completely consistent with—indeed as an expression of—their faith. They embraced a civic theology blurring Christian and US identities.

While the United States began to develop a sense of national identity, Methodism was spreading rapidly among Anglo-American settlers. White Methodists and other Euro-Americans considered the "Indian" as a "savage other" in need of civilization and salvation (39). Methodists prioritized the former, trying to civilize Indigenous peoples.

Methodists, like other Americans, acted toward them on the basis of this image of the savage and never attempted to know Indigenous people or to learn what they thought, knew, believed, valued, or felt. The country's growth blended with biblical notions of "chosen people" and "the promised land," to make the "savage other" even more alien to the principles of the Church. What emerged was a "civic theology" that linked Anglo civilization and Christian evangelization. Unlike the Methodists of the Revolutionary era, Methodists were now [by the 1850s] moving into the political arena. Loyalty to the Union was a religious duty, and Christianization was essential to civilization.[24]

This description shows a failure to bear witness as a church. White Methodists did not bear witness through grounded being, failing to recognize the essential equality of Native Americans. They did not bear witness through attentive presence, failing to get to know Native Americans, failing to love them as neighbors. These failures made it impossible for them to bear witness through historical clarity: not sensing any injustice and not seeing any victims, there was nothing in their mind or heart to repent of. They had cut themselves off from meaningful participation in God's work of reconciliation and *shalom*.

The Anglo-American mindset of superiority seemed to justify domination of native peoples, and every incremental achievement of greater domination fed back into an even greater sense of divine favor. A nationalistic mission driven by a sense of Manifest Destiny created a self-fulfilling circumstance in which white Methodists understood their faith through the lens of their nation and the progress of their nation as evidence of the truth of their faith. "Methodism had become an establishment church," according to Roberts, embracing "American exceptionalism and destiny as tenets of Church policy and ministry" (234). Once white Methodists made this turn to a "civic theology," it became nearly impossible for them to critique US policies

---

[24]Roberts, 57, citing Jeffrey Williams, *Religion and Violence in Early American Methodism: Taking the Kingdom by Force* (Indiana University Press, 2010), 95–130.

and the injustices perpetrated by its dominant white culture without also implicating Christianity itself. This explanation, however, does not excuse the church for taking so long to acknowledge its sins against Native American peoples.

To reckon with this part of Methodism's past, Roberts was given the task of determining the responsibility of two prominent white male Methodist leaders, as well as the Methodist Episcopal Church, for the attack at Sand Creek (222). His conclusions were unambiguous. Methodist layman John Evans, founder of Northwestern University and namesake of Evanston, Illinois, was governor of the Territory of Colorado at the time. Roberts concluded: "John Evans, more than any other person, was responsible for the conditions that made the Sand Creek Massacre possible" (223). John Milton Chivington, an ordained Methodist elder and colonel in the US Army, led the attack "to further his own ambitions," according to Roberts (226). Chivington was already known as "the fighting parson" (72). Although the Sand Creek Massacre was widely condemned at the time, the Methodist Episcopal Church remained silent (230–1, 237). Roberts wrote, "What stands out most strikingly in the Methodist response to Sand Creek and the events that followed, however, is indifference. Sand Creek was simply not important enough to the Church to matter" (235).

The pervasive Anglo-American mindset shaped by a civic theology among Methodists seems to have been the most significant enabling factor in the tragedy of Sand Creek. Very few white Methodists transcended this mindset, which blinded them to the injustices to which they contributed. The historical clarity offered by Roberts's report helps me bear witness to these injustices and helps the church repent.

Discussion Questions

1   Consider the liturgy in your congregational worship services. How is repentance ritually enacted? What has this meant for you in the past? What additional meaning might this have for you in light of this study?

2   Have you ever thought about repentance as an act of justice? If justice is about righting relationships, how does repentance help us do this?

3   How has the pervasive "Anglo-American mind-set of superiority" affected you and the relationships you have with people of other races and ethnicities?

Seeking Right Relationship

Mindsets can be changed. Repentance helps me turn from past ways of thinking. My harmful mindset and the UMC's structures of paternalism must be changed to heal relationships with Indigenous peoples. Indeed, healed and healing relationships are the key to helping white US United Methodists like me to overcome the mindset of superiority we have inherited. Before we can move to meaningful participation in God's good future, the fourth moment of bearing witness, we must seek historical clarity and repent. Roberts put it this way: "The different ways of seeing must be understood and valued before words like 'peace' and 'reconciliation' can have meaning, purpose, or hope of reality" (12). After recognizing that all is not okay in this world, we must seek right relationships.

Seeking Historical Clarity

Historical clarity leading to repentance is a necessary moment in the process of bearing witness. The Council of Bishops offers leadership. Following the 2012 Act of Repentance and Healing for Indigenous Persons, the Council mapped a process for healing. Through "A Statement from the Council of Bishops as We Embark on a Journey Toward Healing Relationships with Indigenous Peoples," the bishops described how they would bear witness to God and neighbor:

> Today, as the Council of Bishops on behalf of The United Methodist Church, we stop to listen to our own hearts and our own voices. History is not only a body of information stored in archives for reference and study waiting to be mined by scholars and researchers. It is a living, breathing phenomenon that resides in us and among us framing our understanding of ourselves and each other. The history we recall in this moment continues to weigh upon all of us. Together we grieve the history which still weighs upon Indigenous people around the world and Native Americans in the United States.[25]

In this moment of bearing witness, the Council named injustice and sought to learn from the past. The Council began this moment with an intentional pause: "we stop to listen." This posture indicated not only attentive presence but also an attitude of repentance. Then, they acknowledged the difficulty of the moral activity of memory: "The history we recall in this moment continues to weigh upon all of us." It is a moral burden we must carry, recognizing the brokenness of past relationships and confessing our role in breaking them.

Reckoning with the past is not easy. The bishops were honest in admitting that their preparation for repentance involved a process of grieving. Then, the Preamble to their letter continued with a confession of the church's complicity in a violent history of killing, forced removal, destruction, massacre, imprisonment, and genocidal policies. Following this confession, the bishops sought wisdom, not only from the Bible but also from the Indigenous peoples they had harmed: the Lakota White Buffalo Calf Woman, Black Elk, the Traditional Elders Circle, Black Hawk, and Queen Lili'uokalani. They offered attentive presence by listening to the words of the deceased. They sought clarity from this history in order to lead the church in being convicted of its sin.

---

[25]Council of Bishops of the UMC, "A Statement from the Council of Bishops as We Embark on a Journey toward Healing Relationships with Indigenous Peoples," April 30, 2012, https://web.archive.org/web/20200921061104/https://www.epaumc.org/archives/2012-general-conference/2012/04/act-of-repentance-and-healing-for-indigenous-persons/.

After these acts of preparation, the Council offered a statement of repentance. These words revealed a heartfelt desire to enter into a new mindset and to heal broken relationships.

> As the Council of Bishops, we are here to repent and express remorse for the church's past conduct in its relationships with Native and Indigenous peoples in all the places where we have extended the mission of the church for over two hundred years. We are here to commit ourselves to addressing the wrong and asking for the forgiveness of those who have been wronged by failing them so profoundly. We confess to God, acknowledging our guilt, resolving to cease the harm, pledging ourselves to live differently, reversing the damage that has been done through our participation in violence, maltreatment and neglect of Native and Indigenous peoples so that we may bring about healing and restoration to all.

This posture of repentance began with remorse and included a commitment to redress past harms. They sought forgiveness on behalf of themselves and their church. Theirs was a full, robust understanding of repentance, including confession, ceasing harm, intent to change, restitution, and a desire for healing and restoration.

The statement of repentance continued. The Council recognized the systemic nature of the injustices, including oppression by the institutional church. The Council also recognized the presence of God among Indigenous peoples, seeking to "learn from them spiritual values" that would benefit the church and world. Our bishops sought relationships of equality and mutuality among Indigenous and non-Indigenous persons. They envisioned a two-way street of grace in which we learn from and benefit each other. This new attitude, this changed mindset, served as a rebuke to the previous mindset of superiority that had facilitated hurt and destruction, such as the Sand Creek Massacre. The bishops also sought to avoid empty words: "Our work in healing broken relationships must be specific, actionable and accountable." They prioritized future mutuality over past paternalism.

Addressing "our Native and Indigenous brothers and sisters" on behalf of themselves and the church they represent, the bishops confessed past and current failures:

> We acknowledge the pain of your nation peoples and our sinful behavior in these events. We know that past history has been filled with violence against you. We have confiscated your land. We have recklessly destroyed your cultures. Today we acknowledge that all this is not in the past.

The Council admitted ongoing fault on behalf of the UMC and its members, including continued neglect of our Indigenous neighbors' human rights and basic needs, "the critical issues of hunger, health, employment, and sovereignty." Seeking to bear witness to their neighbors, they resolved not to forget: "We must not yield to historical amnesia." Seeking right relationships, they prayed for forgiveness:

> We pray to God to give us a new heart and a new spirit through Jesus Christ, who breaks down the dividing walls of hostility, so that we may truly repent of our grave sins, petition for forgiveness, and work towards healing.

Then, the Council, as part of its plan of repentance, offered specific items of commitment, education, and advocacy as well as continued repentance.

An Act of Restitution

The UMC's continued repentance has resulted in concrete acts of restitution, as envisioned by the Council of Bishops in their 2012 Statement. One significant example of restitution occurred on Saturday, September 21, 2019, when the UMC returned land in Upper Sandusky, Ohio, to the Wyandot/te People.[26] The property, entrusted to the Methodist Episcopal Church in 1843, includes a burial ground and the mission church where Methodist Missionary John Stewart began his work with the Wyandot/te. "In Wyandot/te we say tizameh (pronounced tih-zhuh-may), 'thank you,'" said Billy Friend, chief of the Wyandotte Nation of Oklahoma.[27]

This land restitution is part of the ongoing work of repentance. Speakers at the ceremony noted the importance of this step even as they acknowledged the need for further repentance and healing. Chebon Kernell, executive secretary of the UMC's Native American Comprehensive Plan, remarked,

A new chapter of recognition and intentionality began with a statement by The United Methodist Council of Bishops in 2012 about embarking on a journey toward healing relationships with Indigenous people. And so, we are in a steady, growing, yet incomplete attempt to come to a place of healing.

Repentance is a journey undertaken in partnership, the foundation of new, more just relationships. The two resident bishops in Ohio, Tracy Malone and Gregory Palmer, were both present. Jointly, they offered a commitment echoing the Council's 2012 Statement: "We will seek resources and opportunities for justice, and we will seek to strengthen and support leadership development in Native American communities. We will work toward healing." Indeed, the theme of healing came up again and again, not as a completed task but as a goal toward which their witness was aimed.

Dan Hawk, chair of the East Ohio Conference Native American Awareness Committee, expressed most eloquently the significance of restitution as part of a larger process of repentance:

John Wesley drawing on John the Baptist talked about bringing forth fruits of repentance and part of our whole Methodist ethos is that it's not just enough to say, 'I'm sorry.' We look toward repairing the damage and healing the hurt and this is one small but, I think, significant step in repentance, reconciliation, restoration, one step in a long journey but it tangibly lives out our commitment

---

[26]General Board of Global Ministries, "Sacred Native American Lands Will Be Returned to Wyandotte Nation," August 26, 2019, https://www.umcmission.org/share-our-work/news-stories/2019/august/sacred-native-american-lands-will-be-returned-to-wyandotte-nation.

[27]Quotations are from Rick Wolcott, "Remembrance, Repentance and Restoration: Denomination Returns Entrusted Land to the Wyandot/te Nation," *East Ohio Conference News*, September 24, 2019, https://eocumcnews.com/2019/09/24/remembrance-repentance-and-restoration-denomination-returns-entrusted-land-to-the-wyandot-te-nation/.

to walk in acts of repentance and even though it's a small plot of land the very fact that we're giving back land speaks volumes, I believe, about us and to our Indigenous brothers and sisters.

For Hawk, Palmer, Malone, Kernell, Friend, and others present, it was clear that restoring land to the Wyandot/te People served as a tangible expression of a repentant church. This small act could not by itself right centuries of wrong. However, it was a necessary step in reckoning with a harmful past. The real fruit of repentance is in the relationships that sprout from it.

The Necessity of Love in the Work of Repentance

Tweedy Sombrero Navarrete spoke to me about bearing witness and the UMC's efforts at repentance with Indigenous persons.[28] Navarrete is Dine' (Navajo) and a pastor in Arizona. She has served both Native American and Anglo congregations. She had a lot to say about ministry, relationships, and repentance—particularly the love borne by attentive presence.

When I asked her about encountering Christ in a neighbor, she told me about her mentor. Harry Long was a lay pastor for Native American Fellowship Ministries in downtown Phoenix. "He was a humble servant, very encouraging. He epitomized what I wanted to be. Always so gracious," she said. As she told me about Long, I could tell she was particularly influenced by his attentive presence. She told me she felt like an adopted daughter, and even after his death, she is still close to his family, his children. The kin-dom, indeed! From her description of him, she clearly perceived that he bore witness to everyone around him, not just her. She explained, "He was always walking among the homeless, wanting to hear their stories." His witness radiated through the community. Fellowship Ministries served a large number of homeless people and gained a reputation for hospitality. "A lot of people knew where our church was. We had a clothing bank and a food bank and sweat lodges in the back." When Long was ready to retire, he encouraged the bishop to appoint Navarrete as pastor and supported her through the transition.

Long's posture of attentive presence set the tone for Navarrete's ministry. "A lot of the native people found safety on the grounds of the church," she told me. She meant this literally. During the summer, she explained, their small shelter overflowed with people, who would find places to sleep in the churchyard. The parsonage was next door to the church, and ministry began at her doorstep.

> I found myself just walking among the homeless there, at midnight, to see if they needed anything, if they needed prayer. I wasn't afraid. I was a single woman. It might have been dangerous, but I didn't feel that. Sometimes my daughter would join me. I was never afraid. I was among people who needed to be cared for, loved. I was constantly going out to just be with them. We never feared. I really felt they were protecting us. It became this very respectful time to be with each other, just knowing they had a place to come to. We were there for them all the time.

28Tweedy Sombrero Navarrete, interview with the author, December 5, 2019.

This kin-dom participation was built on her willingness to bear witness to those around her, to recognize their inherent dignity, and to empathize. I could tell she loved these neighbors. Looking back on this work, she described the downtown fellowship as one of the happiest times of her ministry.[29]

Bearing witness in the Anglo congregations she served often required her to tear down walls of prejudice. She was the target of open hostility by congregants who told her they did not want a Native pastor. Their attitudes and ways of talking were filled with hurtful stereotypes and caricatures of "drunk Indians," who would presumably urinate in the living room if they were allowed inside a house. She told me she spends a lot of effort on education within Anglo congregations throughout the community.

> I taught a class at two churches that were racist. I taught about Native Americans, and I took forty people on an immersion trip to a reservation. When we were done, they were more knowledgeable than before. When I first went to those churches, they said "we don't want no drunk Indians."

Perhaps her embodied, loving presence made a difference for the forty people in this class and for other Anglos in these congregations. Establishing loving relationships takes time. Bearing witness always begins with recognition of the image of God in the other person and learning to empathize with them as fellow humans in the kin-dom.

Without a foundation of dignity and love, attempts at repentance falter. When I asked her about the "Act of Repentance and Healing for Indigenous Persons" at General Conference 2012, she told me she was against it. Her congregations were not ready for repentance. She explained,

> I was serving an Anglo church at the time. The people were asking, "Why are we apologizing? Why do we have to do that?" So, we hadn't done our job. If those are the kinds of questions you're asking, we need to do some teaching.

This depiction sounded to me like a congregation stuck in various stages of grieving. Broken relationships cannot be healed when there is no acknowledgment of brokenness. Navarrete seemed to be pointing to a large disconnect between UMC policies of repentance and repentance as an everyday practice grounded in historical clarity. We must interrogate our own power and privilege. We must examine the structures of the church and its complicity, not only at Sand Creek in 1864 but also in our local communities today. Not least, healing and repentance must be built on attentive presence, empathy for the neighbor. Can there be repentance without love?

Navarrete also felt that the Act of Repentance was too focused on the past. "We didn't address where we are now and where we are going in the future. We got stuck at Sand Creek." She would like the UMC to put more effort into strengthening

---

[29] Tweedy Sombrero Navarrete, "In Ministry as a Native American," *Response*, November 2017, https://web.archive.org/web/20210517152213/https://www.unitedmethodistwomen.org/news/in-ministry-as-a-native-american.

Native congregations and helping Native Americans become pastors. In her eyes, the formal Act of Repentance did not address current problems or relationships. As a result, she has seen little progress: "We're still fighting the same old fight. People still come in and tell us that we can't be Christian and Native at the same time." As an Anglo, I felt she was asking for much more attentive presence from people like me— more recognition of dignity, more empathy, more love, and less show and pageantry at General Conference. Without structural changes in this church, the UMC, old patterns of behavior and privilege re-emerge. Addressing social sin requires not only being present or dignifying the "other" but also an attentive presence to one's own discomfort and blind spots when it comes to confronting historical oppression with deeper clarity.

Meanwhile, Navarrete continues to bear witness in significant and personal ways among the Anglos she serves. She told me about an encounter at Shepherd of the Valley United Methodist Church, a congregation she served at the time. "I went up to this young man, gave him a bottle of water, and listened to his story. He was new to being homeless. He was kicked out because he's gay. He told me 'I'm finding some comfort here [at the church]. I just need to charge my phone.' Then I prayed with him." Love does not stop at triage, but neither can justice survive without love. The process of bearing witness cannot be abbreviated or shortcut. We cannot condense the healing of millions of broken relationships into one ceremonial act of repentance, no matter how well-intentioned. Yet, we cannot fully participate in what God is doing in this world without seeking healing for our brokenness.

She offered her thoughts on where to go from here. "How do we move from insensitivity to knowledge? I work on trying to help people be more knowledgeable about what they say and how they say it. I try to teach them. It needs to be done. Education. Being sensitive to all persons, LGBTQ, racial, ethnic, all people." Education, yes. And I would also add words to what is implied in all her ministry: bearing witness through grounded being, attentive presence, and historical clarity as we move toward God's preferred future.

Reckoning with the past is a difficult moment of bearing witness. We are tempted to deny current realities. We might prefer to forget and be forgiven. We may want to rush to "reconcile" before taking appropriate responsibility for learning about the past, our role in it, and seeking to offer restitution to those to whom it is due.[30] But, attentive presence with our neighbors confronts us with a mirror of convicting grace, reflecting our own brokenness, individually and as a church. We can see that all is not okay in the world. Historical clarity, then, demands repentance in preparation for meaningful participation in God's good future.

Discussion Questions

1   Think of a time when someone asked for your forgiveness. How did this act of repentance contribute to repairing a broken relationship?

---

[30]In her "theology of remaining," Shelly Rambo warned against rushing to redemption, arguing that dominant redemption narratives are not helpful when dealing with traumatic suffering. *Spirit and Trauma: A Theology of Remaining* (Westminster John Knox, 2010), 156–8.

2 Have you or someone you know participated in a collective act of repentance
   for a specific purpose, such as those of the UMC, discussed above? Discuss
   with a prayer partner or group what that experience was like. What lasting
   effects did it have?

3 Were you surprised that Navarrete opposed the UMC's Act of Repentance?
   What questions would you like to ask her to help you understand her
   perspective? If you were not surprised, what would you like to say to her or
   other Native Americans about this situation?

2.4
Meaningful Participation

Dealing with the compounding and enduring legacy of historical sin can be an overwhelming—perhaps impossible—task. When we immerse ourselves in the moment of historical clarity, when we truly glimpse the enormity of our failings as a church and as a society, when we begin to realize the pervasiveness of injustice all around us—how do we avoid moral paralysis?

The process of bearing witness prepares us. Recognition of equal dignity in the kin-dom of God occurs in the first moment, grounded being. Prompted by prevenient grace, we develop support for human rights in response to the image of God in our neighbor. Empathy for the most vulnerable persons in community occurs in the second moment, attentive presence. Prompted by justifying grace and convicted of our responsibility, we respond in love to meet basic human needs. Memory of our past complicity in current systems of oppression occurs in the third moment, historical clarity. Prompted further by justifying and forgiving grace, we seek to repair broken relationships with the victims of injustice, engaging in acts of repentance. God's bestowed worth, redemption, and forgiveness prepare us for meaningful participation in God's work of reconciliation and *shalom*.

The fourth and final moment of bearing witness reckons with God's preferred future. Holiness, discipleship, and sanctification are nurtured in community as we seek the mind of Christ and imagine God's will. Meaningful participation in God's will for creation requires us to imagine God's justice through the eyes of our neighbors, especially those least well-off, for whom injustice is a constant reality. God heals broken relationships and enables new ones as we embrace *shalom* and a new vision of abundant living. Imagining God's justice, we enter into solidarity with our neighbors and all of creation.

Prayerful Action

Grace Musuka is a missionary who lives by "informed prayer and prayerful action"—the motto of World Day of Prayer. She provides leadership training for women in central Africa and is based in Zimbabwe, her birthplace.[1] World Day of Prayer is a global ecumenical movement led by Christian women who welcome all to join in prayer and action for peace and justice.[2] The women of Zimbabwe chose the theme for World Day of Prayer 2020, "Rise! Take Your Mat and Walk," based on John 5:2-9a.[3] This passage "suggest[s] that we should not be afraid to act on the word of God. God is offering us the steps for personal and social transformation."[4] Musuka and others interpreted Jesus' encounter to be a call to act in love for peace and reconciliation. God's grace requires our response. Prayer is preliminary to action.

Musuka connects informed prayer and prayerful action in ways that make a difference in the lives of those around her. She began her ministry as a regional missionary in 2012 by conducting a needs assessment: going to each of her six assigned countries (Cameroon, the Democratic Republic of Congo, Malawi, Namibia, Tanzania, and Zimbabwe) and listening to women tell their stories.[5] Assured of God's prevenient grace, she listens without rushing to judgment. Helping women write their own stories is a first step in teaching them to be self-sufficient. During an interview exploring women's empowerment in Africa and the ecumenical 2020 World Day of Prayer, she shared her own story. She said that she often goes to Bible verses in prayer. One of her favorites is, "I can do all things through [Christ] who strengthens me" (Phil. 4:13).[6] This verse has inspired her to witness in her community and in communities around her, joining in action for peace and justice.

When asked what we in the United States can pray for, she named some very specific needs in Zimbabwe, including more schools and basic necessities. "We need peace. We need to be economically empowered. We have basic needs for families and children, education, health issues."[7] She was also quick to remind us, "Jesus has no feet but ours; no hands but ours." Before putting our feet and hands to use for Jesus' sake, we need guidance. Where shall we walk? What shall we do?

Prayerful Activities

1   Listen to the interview of Grace Musuka with a group or study partner. What does her witness inspire you to pray about or hope for?

2   How does prayer lead to action? Consider examples from your own faith life, your congregation, and wider community.

---

[1] United Women in Faith, "Grace Musuka," https://uwfaith.org/wp-content/uploads/2023/08/RegionalMissionaryBios.pdf.

[2] World Day of Prayer International Committee, https://worlddayofprayer.net; World Day of Prayer USA, http://www.wdp-usa.org.

[3] World Day of Prayer Committee of Zimbabwe, "Rise! Take Your Mat and Walk," https://worlddayofprayer.net/zimbabwe-2020.html#/.

[4] World Day of Prayer Committee of Zimbabwe.

[5] United Women in Faith, "Faith Talks with Grace Musaka," *podcast*, November 7, 2019, https://www.spreaker.com/episode/faith-talks-with-grace-musaka–20006424.

[6] United Women in Faith.

[7] United Women in Faith.

3   How do you know what to pray for? With a prayer partner or group, intentionally listen to the needs of persons in the community in which your congregation is situated. Then, pray fervently!

The Threshold of Hope

One version of God's future is found in Isaiah, "For I am about to create new heavens and a new earth" (65:17a). How can we participate in this vision of righteousness? Pamela Brubaker, a Mennonite pastor, reflected on the prophet's depiction of hope in light of her experience on a ten-day cross-cultural immersion with the Guatemalan community in LaGrange, Georgia, in 2019. Preaching on Isaiah 65:17-25, she descried bearing witness to the experiences of Guatemalan immigrants.[8]

> I visited Stewart Detention Center which imprisons almost 2000 men, not for crimes such as murder or embezzlement but for not having been born in this country. I saw the terrible conditions there. I met dozens of families who traveled many hours to see their loved ones for their allotted one hour of visitation per week only to wait for many hours because there are only five visitation windows for those 2000 men. In fact, I saw family members who traveled many hours, waited many hours and then were turned away.

Her host family, Anton and Charlotte Flores, were US citizens who spent over thirty years working with immigrants denied opportunities to jobs, education, housing, earning power, and dignity because they lack citizenship status.

She spent time with youth in the community. The father of two of the youth had spent months in Stewart Detention Center before being deported; their mother supported them and worked to build up their community. Another youth, a senior in high school, impressed her as particularly smart and fun, an avid reader who was intentional about how she spent her time. Brubaker shared, "I will never forget when I casually asked her about her plans for college, knowing, as a former high school teacher, that colleges compete for students like her. She stoically told me that she was fifteen when DACA [Deferred Action for Childhood Arrivals] was rescinded, and she couldn't go to college." Had Brubaker not taken the risk and effort to be personally present with this youth, she may never have learned, on a personal level, this part of the experience of being an undocumented immigrant. We cannot realize the kin-dom without face-to-face relationships.

After being attentively present with individuals in this community very different from her own, Brubaker perceived society differently. The people she met and the realities they shared caused her to reckon with the past.

> I learned of the deep connections between slavery and Jim Crow laws of the past and current national attitudes and policies around immigration, and the racism

---

[8]Pamela Brubaker, Sermon, Santee Chapel, Lancaster Theological Seminary, November 19, 2019.

and white supremacy that drives both. The town of LaGrange grew up around a cotton plantation, and the estate and college at its center were built by African American enslaved people. There is a street named Redline Alley, which once separated the poor black sharecroppers from the well-to-do white community, and it now marks the boundary between the immigrant population and the wealthier people. The Callaway family, who owned that plantation, are honored everywhere in that town, but there is little credit given to the many enslaved people whose blood and sweat built the town.

This past came alive in an unexpected way as she and some of the Guatemalan youth traveled to nearby Montgomery, Alabama, to visit the Legacy Museum.

One of its purposes is to help educate the public and to tell the truth about our country's history around slavery and lynching. There was one exhibit where we watched a holographic representation of a mother and her children being brutally separated as they were sold, and I will never forget as Bryant turned to me and said, "That is happening to my family and to so many others at the southern border."

This potent mixture of past and present convicted Brubaker of her own complicity in the plight of immigrants to the United States. Having borne witness to these neighbors, she could no longer ignore the injustices that she might have overlooked previously.

I witnessed a court case where a Guatemalan man was driving a truck with a trailer, and he was stopped by the police, although he was breaking no laws. Since he did not have a license, he was fined over $1000 and given a misdemeanor. I don't know the outcome of his case, but he was either sent to Stewart [Detention Center], or he was back driving without a license (because he cannot get one without legal status), or he could choose not to drive and lose his job, his livelihood, and his ability to support his family.

All these experiences of bearing witness with a Guatemalan community in Georgia profoundly reshaped how she understood the hope found in Isaiah 65:17-25.

These words were written by the prophet Isaiah, son of Amoz, during a time of political turmoil in the eighth century BCE. The Assyrian empire had invaded Israel and Judah. The Hebrews, returning from exile, were under foreign occupation in their homeland. Amidst this suffering, Isaiah proclaimed God's preferred future: "I [God] will rejoice in Jerusalem and delight in my people; no more shall the sound of weeping be heard in it or the cry of distress" (Isa. 65:19). Through this prophet, we hear God's intention for humanity, community, and creation: long lives, safe shelter, productive vineyards, fruitful labor, and blessed children for generations. God will anticipate and respond to every need. In this vision, "The wolf and the lamb shall feed together" (Isa. 65:25a). There will be no more hurt and destruction.

Brubaker reflected on her spiritual growth in relation to these words:

At one time, some years back this passage is one that I would have loved to preach on. It is filled with words of hope: God creating a new heaven and earth,

God delighting in God's people, the sound of weeping and distress is no more, God answering before we call. It's beautiful. Honestly, I would have taken these words, and simply picked them up out of context from their place in the Hebrew Bible and said what made sense to me from where I stand. My sermon probably would have been one of hope, but if I am honest, a shallow and easier hope. I look back on my [earlier] self and see someone who would have had little awareness of my social location and all that is entailed in it, and I would have thought little of the person or persons who penned these words and what they and their people were experiencing and their history.

She admitted that, despite a difficult childhood, her context of being a white, heterosexual American Christian had shielded her from extreme adversities of poverty, oppression, displacement, and powerlessness. "But the Guatemalan community that I lived with would understand much better than me. They, like the Hebrews, understand living under oppression."

Bearing witness through recognition and love had recast for her what God's justice looks like. Her attentive presence with Bryant and other Guatemalan youth gave her enough insight to realize that God was working through them in ways that would change her life and relationship with God and neighbor.

I look with awe at the hope and faith that is present in the Hebrew people in this passage, these words resonate with trust for God to bring goodness and life after centuries of trauma, and it parallels the faith in God and the hope and joy that I experienced with the Guatemalan people that I lived with, which was beautiful and inspiring. Both of these communities knew hope borne out of trauma and oppression ... I remember what I would have done in the past with this passage, placed myself in the perspective of the Hebrew people. But now, if I am honest, I feel more connected with the culture of the Persians, who were in power, not the Hebrews. And in my preparation for this sermon, I kept getting stuck here. I'm supposed to offer us some wisdom. But I know I need to listen around these issues a lot more than I talk.

In this confession, Brubaker described her need to reckon with the past and present before offering hope for the future, although she did not express words or a framework for this process. Nevertheless, grace had prompted within her an intuitive understanding of bearing witness.

Eventually, God got me to this place, that is where I need to end this sermon with listening, especially when it comes to places where I carry privilege. I must live in the tension and discomfort of being a white American Christian, of being part of a culture that has been the oppressive one, and allow God to use my discomfort to teach me and transform me. I realize that we are not all the same here, we come from very different places, each of us, many of us do not carry the privilege that I do. If it makes sense in your context, I invite you also into a posture of listening and learning. And if not, if you stand in a very different place, I stand in the discomfort of saying I don't know what to say, I am here not as a teacher but as a learner. I want to listen.

Through these words, she approached the final moment of bearing witness, ready to reckon with God's future. Her "soul waits for the Lord" (Ps. 130:6), even as she admitted discomfort. She brought us to the threshold of hope, not certain what to do with Isaiah's depiction of God's vision of righteousness. Brubaker left us poised for meaningful participation in the full flourishing of all of creation.

Discussion Questions

1   Brubaker ended her sermon with the intent to listen. What emotional and spiritual impact did you feel when she resisted rushing to proclaim a word of hope?

2   Brubaker's experience bearing witness to Guatemalan neighbors changed her perspective on the world and God's presence within it. After a moment of historical clarity, she recognized the tension and discomfort of her own social location and sought to be transformed by God. Which aspects of her situation do you identify with? Which aspects of your situation are different from hers?

3   Imagine the transformation God might enact in Brubaker's life and your own. What does this hope look like?

Full Flourishing

Reconciliation and full flourishing are the ultimate aims of Christian moral witness. Paul proclaimed, "see, everything has become new!" (2 Cor. 5:17, NRSV), affirming the idea that God is still speaking, even today. Paul also declared, "Look, now is the acceptable time; look, now is the day of salvation!" (2 Cor. 6:2). It is clear he did not intend to limit his declaration to the day on which he wrote this passage. Rather, Paul was pointing to the eternal present of God's saving action.

To join in God's salvation in the present moment is the call of discipleship, the motivation for the church's moral witness. Discipleship can be expressed in many ways, such as proclamation, testimony, teaching, and worship. One mode of discipleship is diakonia, as described in Chapter 1.4. Through baptism, Christians join in "the diaconate of all believers" as we bear witness within and with our communities.[9] Paul illustrated this ministry in 2 Corinthians 5:17-20, offering a holistic evangelical mandate to become ambassadors for Christ, entrusted with the ministry (*diakonīan*) of reconciliation. This powerful diaconal responsibility involves justice-making and extravagant welcome, pertinent to race relations, immigration, LGBTQIA+ advocacy, and many other arenas in which humans have built obstacles to human flourishing. To overcome our divisions, to heal relationships, and to experience reconciliation, we are called to lives of holiness through diakonia.

---

[9] WCC and ACT Alliance, *Called to Transformation: Ecumenical Diakonia* (WCC, 2022), 16, https://www.oikoumene.org/resources/publications/ecumenical-diakonia.

Holiness is the life of faith through which we are enabled, by the power of the Spirit, to grow in Christ-likeness. David Field, an ecumenical leader in Methodism, defined holiness as "the gracious work of God in human persons, which transforms us so that our lives are characterized by love for God and our fellow human beings."[10] God works in us, with our cooperation, as we mature in faith. God's grace not only precedes our understanding and awakens us in humility, it not only renews the image of God within us, but it also enables us to grow. The restored image of God is but the potential to grow into the likeness of God.[11] Whereas justification is what God does for us, putting us in right relationship to God, sanctification is what God does in us, allowing us to grow in faith and love.[12] Through the sanctifying work of the Holy Spirit, we are enabled not only to live in grace but also to grow in grace. Holiness can be understood as the transforming work of the Holy Spirit in our lives. In other words, holiness is the process through which the image of God is restored in each of us as we grow in Christ-likeness. Holiness is how God matures or "perfects" us in love.

Christian perfection is the term Methodists use for entire sanctification. Christian perfection is not an end point in the life of faith; it is best understood as a state of maturity. John Wesley explained: "Christian perfection therefore does not imply (as some men [and women] seem to have imagined) an exemption either from ignorance or mistake, or infirmities or temptations. Indeed, it is only another term for holiness."[13] It is through growth in holiness that we seek to have the mind of Christ. As Paul taught the Philippians, "Let the same mind be in you that was in Christ Jesus ... work on your own salvation with fear and trembling, for it is God who is at work in you, enabling you both to will and to work for his good pleasure" (Phil. 2:5, 12c–13). We grow as Christians when we seek the mind of Christ, attempting to live a life of holiness. Wesley taught that the sanctified life is full of peace, joy, faith, hope, and love. This means fulfilling all of God's commandments—not as a way of earning salvation but as a fruit of sanctification. Living God's law is a response to God's love for us. Every command of God is an implicit promise that God enables us to fulfill. "I give you a new commandment, that you love one another. Just as I have loved you, you also should love one another" (Jn 13:34). God empowers us to love, to have faith, and to hope.

Discipleship is the name for our participation in God's work, which can find expression in diakonia. Growth in Christlikeness allows us to love each other, to encourage the development of each person's full human potential. Flourishing is for everyone, not just for the select few or the demonstrably pious. Bearing God's full image and redeemed through Christ's universal atonement, every person is invited to

---

[10]David N. Field, *Bid Our Jarring Conflicts Cease: A Wesleyan Theology and Praxis of Church Unity* (Foundery, 2017), xv.

[11]Randy L. Maddox, *Responsible Grace: John Wesley's Practical Theology* (Kingswood, 1994), 66–9; John Wesley, "The New Birth," in *John Wesley's Sermons: An Anthology*, ed. Outler and Heitzenrater, 336–45 (Abingdon, 1991), II.4.

[12]John Wesley, "Justification by Faith," in *John Wesley's Sermons: An Anthology*, ed. Outler and Heitzenrater, 112–21 (Abingdon, 1991), II.1.

[13]John Wesley, "Christian Perfection," in *John Wesley's Sermons: An Anthology*, ed. Outler and Heitzenrater, 70–84 (Abingdon, 1991), I.9.

flourish. As the good shepherd, Jesus proclaimed, "I came that they may have life and have it abundantly" (Jn 10:10b). The church's witness to human flourishing includes an affirmation that God's grace is available to all and a commitment to live together in Christian community, welcoming, forgiving, and loving one another. This is the work of new creation. We witness to God's renewing and reconciling work through our commitment to assist every person to realize their full human potential so that all of God's creation may flourish.

Solidarity in Community

We cannot reach our full potential alone; Christian faith is a group project. To mature as Christians means to live into Christlikeness in a community of faith. This involves personal growth as well as social awareness. Faith always includes a social dimension. To nurture the potential of Christlikeness in ourselves and our neighbors is the communal task of being church together. A distinctly Wesleyan approach claims, "Scriptural holiness entails more than personal piety; love of God is always linked with love of neighbor, a passion for justice and renewal in the life of the world."[14] Thus, community is vital to learning to love our neighbors and the world around us.

Recently returned from a trip to Palestine in 2019, Liz Fulmer shared with me her experience of bearing witness in community.[15] She was amazed at what she had learned by staying with a Palestinian family. Marevat and Anwar are Palestinian Christians who regularly host international visitors in their home in Bethlehem. Fulmer told me that at first, they seemed reticent to talk about the occupation, preferring to show the pleasures of everyday life. Eventually, though, they spoke about the daily reality of living as occupied people, a people whose very existence is widely ignored and even denied in US media.

Fulmer described her visit to Palestine, and this home visit in particular, as a political transgression of sorts. Without generalizing about all of Israel or all Israeli people, she spoke about her experience as a way of bearing witness to the existence of Palestine and its people:

> You get the impression that the powers that be do not really want you to make relationships with the Palestinian people. We were told not to say that we were visiting Palestine but only to say that we were visiting the Holy Land. We could talk about the more famous sites but were advised to avoid saying that we were visiting Nablus or Ramallah, which are off the beaten path. This is an intimidation tactic to limit where people can travel and what people can talk about. There's an effort to control the narrative so that tourists, especially Americans, don't get any information that could invalidate the Palestinian stereotype that is so frequently presented in the news media.

---

14. *The Book of Discipline of The United Methodist Church 2020/2024* (UMPH, 2024), ¶ 102, p. 53.
15. Elizabeth Fulmer, interview with the author, June 27, 2019.

> To forge relationships with Palestinians—to go beyond the superficial caricature—is seen as a danger, because when you meet and learn from the Palestinians you can share their stories more widely, thereby causing conflict with the mainstream messaging ... So, to enter into a relationship anyway is bold and holy.

From this experience, Fulmer realized that bearing witness to the Palestinians was politically risky and morally necessary. As she departed the home of Marevat and Anwar, she promised them, "I see you, I see that you are here, and when we leave this place, we will tell people that you are here." She promised to continue bearing witness. Through this witness, she committed herself to imagine God's justice embracing the people of Palestine. She committed herself to solidarity.

Holiness involves serving others by building up a community. The church should not only provide basic goods for survival but also nurture the conditions for living our best. Through Christian community, we recognize that one cannot live a full life alone. We need the nurture, support, and accountability of community. By bearing witness to her Palestinian hosts, Fulmer became part of their community of support. She and others radiate their moral witness through cooperative ministries. For example, Zaki Labib Zaki, a pastor in Illinois, provides trauma counseling and medical missions to displaced persons:

> A community meal and time of fellowship followed [the medical clinic], and we visited, and often prayed, with lots of refugees. More than one person told us they found "real hope" while listening to the message of the Gospel ... Other refugees told us that the gatherings and community meals nurtured, not just their hungry bodies, but also their souls and made them feel "human again" for the first time since they were forced to flee from their homes and become refugees.[16]

Medical care, a shared meal, Gospel readings—these are the ingredients to solidarity in community. This is an example of glimpsing meaningful participation in God's will for a more just world. Living into our full potential requires solidarity in community.

Community extends to all of creation. The UMC uses the phrase "abundant living" to express solidarity with all of creation, emphasizing environmental sustainability. The 1996 resolution, "God's Vision of Abundant Living," offered "a theology of 'enough'" to counter rampant consumerism and exploitation of the environment.[17] Claiming that "the whole of creation contains all that is necessary to sustain itself," this resolution presented a vision in which "abundant living" means "providing not only for the needs of this generation, but also for generations to come." The resolution demanded individual and corporate response to the global, environmental

---

[16]General Board of Church and Society, "Church and Society Ethnic Local Church Grant Supports Middle East Migrants," https://www.umcjustice.org/news-and-stories/church-and-society-ethnic-local-church-grant-supports-middle-east-migrants-869.

[17]"God's Vision of Abundant Living," in *The Book of Resolutions of The United Methodist Church 1996*, 454 (UMPH, 1996).

crisis: "We have a choice: We can be sustainers, or exploiters, of creation." This idea of abundant life as a sustainable and just lifestyle also factored into this church's 2016 resolution on climate change: "the Church must address [climate justice] so that abundant life is ensured for our children and future generations."[18] Here, abundant life refers to the ability to provide for basic human needs and the potential for full human flourishing—essential elements for justice in the UMC's social witness. Holiness is nothing less than our full participation in God's mission, through which we and the rest of creation are transformed toward *shalom*.

Shalom is peace, wholeness, fulfillment. It is "the complete and harmonious interrelatedness of all creation," according to the UMC's moral witness on "Environmental Stewardship."[19] This 1984 resolution defined stewardship as "how we bring all of the resources at our disposal into efficient use in our participation in the saving activity of God." Thus, *shalom* provides a guiding vision for the UMC's moral witness. Imagining this good future that God has in store for us, we join in as stewards of creation: "Stewardship, then, is to become involved wherever wholeness is lacking and to work in harmony with God's saving activity to reconcile, to reunite, to heal, to make whole." Reflecting on how we can use the resources of the land for healing, health, and integrity, Jenny Phillips suggested beginning with wonder.

> I think that as humans we have not lost our capacity for wonder at the majesty of God's creation. Part of what we're doing in the Earthkeepers programs is making sure that we're not taking that for granted; we're naming it and calling it out, giving people permission to make those connections.[20]

When people work together in community, inclusive of each other as well as non-human creation, we can glimpse God's preferred future. With its focus on healing of creation, the UMC's witness echoes the Jewish concept *tikkun olam*, meaning "repair of the world." Mary Elizabeth Moore, Dean Emerita of the Boston University School of Theology, explored this concept as "a vision of social, political, and religious transformation."[21] "*Tikkun olam* is grounded in hope for the restoration of the world, or the restoration of justice and righteousness," she explained. It is a vision of God's preferred future for creation in which we participate.

Meaningful participation in solidarity with the environment is an essential part of the church's moral witness. (We will explore bearing witness to all of creation in Chapter 3.2.) Phillips observed, though, that "One of the ways we get uncomfortable is fear that we might have to get rid of our buildings etc." The point is that care for the environment is not opposed to human community. God's good future includes us and the things we have created. She explained, "A passage I lean on is Revelation 22:1-5, depicting a city of God—an infrastructure, a built environment that is integrated with trees, etc. It is powerful." A vision of *shalom* includes all of it. Just

---

₁₈"Climate Change and the Church's Response," Resolution 1035 in *The Book of Resolutions of The United Methodist Church 2016*, 82 (UMPH, 2016).

₁₉"Environmental Stewardship," in *The Book of Resolutions of The United Methodist Church 1984*, 334 (UMPH, 1984).

₂₀Jenny Phillips, interview with the author, August 15, 2019.

₂₁Mary Elizabeth Moore, *Ministering with the Earth* (Chalice, 1998), 4.

as the wolf and lamb dwell together in Isaiah's vision, the city street rests next to the river in John's Revelation. The image of a holy city is also present in Psalms 46 and 48. This is why the church's moral witness must be animated by a solidarity that extends to all of creation. This understanding is so important that United Methodist bishops adopted a new phrase for it: "environmental holiness."[22] Environmental holiness requires conversion to a life of discipleship that understands a common calling to participate in God's redemption, reconciliation, and healing of all creation to realize *shalom*. The church is called to proclaim this inbreaking reality through its moral witness.

Imagining God's future as *shalom* helps us to understand the interconnectedness of all parts of the church's moral witness. God's "vision of shalom" means "wholeness and harmony" for all of creation, with which God is in covenant and which Christ came to redeem, and to which humanity is completely interrelated.[23] This includes not only what we typically think of as "the natural world" but also humanity and its institutions. A UMC resolution, "Environmental Justice for a Sustainable Future" put it this way: "We believe that at the center of the vision of *shalom* is the integration of environmental, economic, and social justice."[24] Such an expansive moral witness requires imagination.

Risk-taking imagination requires the commitment of a community. Each moment of bearing witness is an act of community. The examples of historical clarity presented in Chapter 2.3 illustrate the commitment needed. Just as the work restoring land to the Wyandot/te People required the effort of many people and cooperation between institutions, imagining a future in solidarity with each other requires community building and healing. Perceiving a lack of commitment to this work within her congregation, Tweedy Sombrero Navarrete suggested that the UMC was not ready for the work of repentance, much less the work of imagining a future together. Just as there could be no repentance without love, there can be no meaningful participation in God's good future without solidarity in community.[25]

Discussion Questions

1   The fourth moment of bearing witness invokes our imagination. What does *shalom* look like—for you, your church, your community, and the world? What would it be like to exercise environmental holiness in your everyday life? In the community? In national and international politics?

---

[22]Council of Bishops of the UMC, *God's Renewed Creation: Call to Hope and Action. Foundation Document*, 2009, https://web.archive.org/web/20220120212523/http://hopeandaction.org/main/wp-content/uploads/2010/03/Foundation-Doc-Eng-Handout-2-col.pdf

[23]"Caring for Creation: A Call to Stewardship and Justice," Resolution 1033 in *The Book of Resolutions of The United Methodist Church 2016*, 68 (UMPH, 2016).

[24]"Environmental Justice for a Sustainable Future," in *The Book of Resolutions of The United Methodist Church 1992*, 63 (UMPH, 1992).

[25]My understanding of solidarity is commensurate with that of Samuel Wells, *A Nazareth Manifesto: Being with God* (John Wiley & Sons, 2015), 78.

2　In what ways does your community fall short of what God intends for us? What would full flourishing look like in your neighborhood and municipality?

3　How can you engage in the ministry of reconciliation with the most vulnerable persons in your community? How can you practice the ministry of reconciliation with the most polluted and neglected parts of the environment in your community? What would solidarity mean in your context?

Imagining God's Justice

Imagining God's justice as we reckon with the future brings us from attentive presence through historical clarity to a position of advocacy. What is God's will for a more just world, and how can we turn this vision into prayerful action? Carol Napier, a layperson in Georgia, offers one example. She petitioned to amend the UMC's constitution in 2016.

> As the Holy Scripture reveals, both men and women are made in the image of God and, therefore, men and women are of equal value in the eyes of God. The United Methodist Church acknowledges the long history of discrimination against women and girls. The United Methodist Church shall confront and seek to eliminate discrimination against women and girls, whether in organizations or in individuals, in every facet of its life and in society at large. The United Methodist Church shall work collaboratively with others to address concerns that threaten the cause of women's and girl's equality and well-being.[26]

This constitutional amendment was ratified in November 2019, supported by over 90 per cent of the votes at the General Conference and annual conferences of the UMC. Similar legislation had been proposed and rejected by the UMC for decades.

This addition to the UMCs, Constitution is a symbol of the much longer work of bearing witness. Notice the moments of bearing witness evident within its text: recognition of full equality and dignity; reassessment of the past and confession of injustice; intention to repair broken relationships and to address systemic oppression; and a commitment to solidarity and full flourishing (well-being). Napier explained her motivation: "I introduced this constitutional amendment for all the girls around the world who are raised in churches that tell them in subtle and not so subtle ways that they are second-class citizen—and for the women, who have worked so hard to eliminate sexism in the church."[27] Napier's advocacy arose, no doubt, from years of personal experience and attentive presence with other women and girls who had suffered from sexism. The resulting constitutional amendment, now a prominent

---

[26]Heather Hahn, "Church Ratifies Women's Equality Amendment," *UM News*, November 6, 2019, https://www.umnews.org/en/news/church-ratifies-womens-equality-amendment.
[27]Hahn.

part of the church's moral witness, challenges us to imagine anew God's will for a more just world.

It is difficult to imagine what God's justice looks like, especially in our world today. In 2013, I was invited to the Anna Howard Shaw Center at Boston University School of Theology to do just that. The theme of this 29th annual Women in the World conference was "Economic Justice for Ministry in the 21st Century." Participants shared a common conviction: "The church today cannot be silent on issues of economic justice."[28] The material conditions of human existence matter to God and to the church. Poverty, inequality, oppression, and all forms of injustice cry out for neighbor-love. We knew that we needed to pay attention to power and privilege and to lift up marginalized voices. We also recognized the common but inadequate tendency to separate love from justice, to attempt to satisfy the demands of neighbor-love through mercy only. "Society is very comfortable with the God of Compassion, but much less comfortable with the God of Justice," confessed the conference organizers. We asked ourselves, as United Methodists, what could we do "to be clear on the meaning of God's justice and to embody that justice in the world today"? As we gathered for a full day of prayer, study, and fellowship, we challenged each other to consider not only justice in society but also justice within the church.

Justice for Women

My presentation, "Imagining God's Justice," examined the status and role of women in church and society. I was invited to speak to this conference because of my work at the General Commission on the Status and Role of Women. This agency of the UMC's General Conference advocates for the full participation and inclusion of women in the church, challenges the church to confront institutional sexism, and helps church leaders address issues of sexual harassment and abuse in ministry settings. Preventing and addressing sexual abuse between adults in the church was the focus of my ministry. In this work, I heard the stories of women in ministry in many different contexts and encountered economic injustices facing women in ministry. I explored the connections between economic justice for ministry and the sin of sexual violence against women, the meaning of God's justice, and how the church may imaginatively embody that justice in the world. I bore witness to many stories of injustice.

Three stories from my work illustrated a range of attitudes and realities in the UMC. In the same week, I received two email inquiries. The first was from a woman who inquired, "Our church has women in leadership—we have a woman pastor and a woman bishop. What more can the Commission do for us or with us?" The second inquiry was from a female member of a committee on ministry in another region. She requested biblical and theological study materials to give to a male candidate who did not understand why the UMC ordains women. At the same time, a complaint

---

[28]The quotations in this paragraph come from the conference description. Boston University School of Theology Anna Howard Shaw Center, "2013 Women in the World Conference," http://www.bu.edu/shaw/events/women-in-the-world-conference/2013-women-in-the-world-conference/.

of clergy sexual misconduct was pending resolution in a third annual conference. A woman I will call Christina (not her real name) was let go from her staff-position at a local church because of the Staff-Parish Relations Committee's discomfort with her allegation that the former pastor had exploited her for his own sexual gratification. She was fired for whistleblowing.

Bearing witness immerses us in the messiness of life and the struggles of our neighbors. My attentive presence to these three women attuned me to a range of different experiences. What do we make of the sometimes-conflicting evidence of personal stories such as these? How do we move from personal anecdotes to a comprehensive picture of what is really going on in the world? An anecdote is the truth of an individual in a particular time and place. These stories reflect the lived, daily experiences of women—*lo cotidiando*, as mujerista theologian Ada María Isasi-Díaz wrote about so passionately and persuasively.[29] When anecdotes are collected together, they become statistics, indicating what is true for many individuals at many times and places. When these statistics reveal patterns, we gain a broader outlook as patterns of injustice indicate systemic oppression. These stories reveal not only statistical trends but also a fuller picture of the daily struggles of women and girls facing abuse and exploitation from within their own communities of faith.

Bearing witness helps us all to imagine and live into God's justice. Bearing witness to these stories empowers women to join together to claim their own moral agency. When the lived experiences are shared and supported in a community of faith, they become a liberating, historical project of reclaiming moral agency. For Isasi-Díaz, justice was a personal, embodied journey of faith, the goal of which is liberation. She taught that life is found *en la lucha*, in the struggle: "the struggle to be self-determining within the context of community and in view of the common good, and to have the material conditions needed to develop into the fullness of our capacity."[30] (Her viewpoint resonates strongly with that of Grace Musuka and the theme of the 2020 World Day of Prayer.) Bearing witness to women's stories also helps men to see a reality different from their own and to join with women in this struggle. When we bear witness to one another's stories, we participate in God's liberating action. Joining in God's mission, the *missio Dei*, is not something we can delegate. Bearing witness to the truth of these experiences is an act of discipleship.

The Sin of Violence

Violence is the most significant factor impacting the well-being and equality of women, perpetuating and reinforcing worldwide economic and social injustices. Marjorie Suchocki, a process theologian, identified the original sin of humanity as rebellion against the well-being of creation in her book *The Fall to Violence*.[31] Not pride, not lust, but rather the unnecessary reliance on violence is the fundamental

---

[29] Ada María Isasi-Díaz, *La Lucha Continues: Mujerista Theology* (Orbis, 2004), 92–106.
[30] Ada María Isasi-Díaz, *En La Lucha / In the Struggle: Elaborating a Mujerista Theology* (Fortress, 2004), x.
[31] Marjorie Hewitt Suchocki, *The Fall to Violence: Original Sin in Relational Theology* (Continuum, 1994).

expression of sin. Sexual harassment and abuse are one form of this violence. The reliance on violence to subjugate women inflicts "wounds of the spirit," as ethicist Traci West described the combined effects of shame, sexual sin, and violence.[32] Based on his work with individuals on both sides of sexual violence, theologian James Poling suggested that the authentic church for both victims and abusers needs to be a "community of nonviolent resistance" that is "attuned to the human problem of abuse of power and ... systems of domination that institutionalize power in abusive ways."[33] We must recognize violence as sinful before we can imagine God's alternative.

Structures of violence are used to control and dominate some groups of people at the expense of others. It is our historical and current reality that structures of violence across the globe create economic injustices disproportionately impacting women. According to the Ms. Foundation for Women, "physical violations of women and children are fundamentally grounded in issues of power and control—and therefore, related to women's relatively weak economic status."[34] Violence, discrimination, and access to basic goods are intertwined. Author Eve Ensler (who since goes by "V") was less diplomatic in her assessment: "The mechanism of violence is what destroys women, controls women, diminishes women and keeps women in their so-called place."[35] Gender-based violence derails economic justice at the outset. When women suffer sexual abuse and harassment in the church, as well as in the home, neighborhood, and workplace, power is being used against them to create inequities. Unequal access to rights and goods then leads to greater disparities of power. Abuse of power sustains a negative feedback loop.

Let us return to the story of Christina. When she reported being the victim of clergy sexual abuse, it did not matter whether her salary had been commensurate with male staff. What mattered most at that moment was her personal safety. What mattered next were the basic human needs of food, shelter, and health care. As a single mother of two small children who relied on her for their sole support, being fired in retaliation for her truth-telling left her with no salary and no health benefits. Her abuser—and the church community colluding with him—had robbed her of the basic capability to flourish at that point in her life. A life free of violent coercion is a fundamental human need. Without this capability, full human flourishing is compromised.[36]

We can disrupt cycles of violence and abuse. Our hope lies in our God-given capacity to transcend violence through memory, empathy, and imagination, to use Suchocki's terms. These distinct moments of bearing witness equip us for hope. It is humanity's uniqueness within creation that, even when enmeshed in an inheritance

---

[32]Traci C. West, *Wounds of the Spirit: Black Women, Violence, and Resistance Ethics* (New York University Press, 1999), 209.

[33]James Newton Poling, *Rethinking Faith: A Constructive Practical Theology* (Fortress, 2011), 86.

[34]Ms. Foundation for Women, "More to Do: The Road to Equality for Women in the United States," 2013 Special Report, 30.

[35]Quoted by Nicholas D. Kristof and Sheryl WuDunn, *Half the Sky* (Alfred Knopf, 2009), 61.

[36]Both Suchocki and Isasi-Díaz make this connection. Isasi-Díaz, *En La Lucha*, 43; Suchocki, *The Fall to Violence*, 67.

and social structure of violence, we can—through God's grace—imagine and act upon alternatives. Violence need no longer dictate our relationships with one another. We can imagine God's justice providing a better way.

Exemplars of Moral Witness

When we bear witness as the church, we do so with bodies scarred from lifetimes of violence. To bear witness is to speak the truth of what we know about violence in this world, to call out the ways in which violence is used to perpetuate economic injustices against women, and to imagine that the church can be a place of justice. We must bear witness to each other. Through prevenient, justifying, and sanctifying grace, God empowers us to become the kin-dom we are meant to be. Grounded as creatures loved equally by God, we bear witness through attentive presence with our neighbors, historical clarity about our own failures, and meaningful participation in God's preferred future. When we bear witness as a church, we do so as the broken, resurrected body of Christ. The church's moral witness is lived out in as many ways as there are members of the body of Christ. Can you imagine the possibilities?

Eunice Musa Iliya, an ordained elder, works to improve the lives of women in Nigeria.[37] She was one of only three women elders in Nigeria when she was ordained in 2000. I first met her when she served on the board of directors of the Women's Commission. She described to me a context in which many women were illiterate, and few were allowed to work outside the home. "Women are treated as property, less than human."[38] This need has defined her ministry. In 2013, as principal of the Women's Leadership Training Institute, she empowered women "to believe in who they are and have the confidence that they are equal in the image and likeness of God … there's nothing that they cannot do because they are also human." Reflecting on this experience in ministry, she shared, "It was quite amazing and very fulfilling to have a church that can give women hope, that can give them a positive self-image."[39] She also addressed the sexual violence of rape and incest by holding the first-ever sexual ethics training event for clergy in Nigeria in 2013. Later, she was appointed general superintendent of the Southern Conference of the UMC Nigeria Episcopal Area. When asked about her hope for the women of Nigeria, she replied, "I'd like to see women empowered to speak for themselves. I'd like to see young women see themselves as created in the image and likeness of God."[40] When I imagine God's justice, I picture Eunice Iliya empowering women in Nigeria.

Marilyn Zehring is a laywoman who is passionate about social justice and mission.[41] She finds inspiration in Jane Addams, the late nineteenth- and early

---

[37]United Methodist Development Center, "UMC Pastor Working to Improve Lives of Women in Nigeria," https://web.archive.org/web/20170212221039/http://umcdc.paramoredev.com/stories/umc-pastor-working-to-improve-lives-of-women-in-nigeria.

[38]Eunice Musa Iliya, interview with the author, February 2013.

[39]Iliya, interview with the author.

[40]United Methodist Development Center, "UMC Pastor Working."

[41]Marilyn Zehring, interview with the author, November 12, 2019.

twentieth-century social reformer who co-founded Hull House in Chicago in 1889. As a teenager, she read a biography about Addams and visited the neighborhood near Hull House with her Methodist Youth Fellowship from her hometown in Nebraska. This experience transformed her. Zehring told me she began to see a whole different world. The trip made her want to help people and address social problems. As an adult, she later served as a director of the Women's Division. "We went to the Tennessee state capitol for an immigration rally. A woman approached me who lived in the area; she had gotten discouraged and stopped going to rallies. The woman said, 'Seeing all of you women here has made a difference in my life and I will be coming back!'" Zehring realized that her embodied witness does make a difference. She reflected, "I felt that God was using me to let this woman know that what she was doing was important." She continues to be active in United Women in Faith and the Christian social witness group in her congregation. Along with this group, she is instrumental in promoting adult education through newsletter articles, fair trade sales, and hosting guest speakers in her local church. She works on issues of immigration, sex trafficking, gun violence, racial justice, and interreligious dialogue. These educational efforts are not without risk. Her congregation received threats in response to inviting a local Imam to speak about Islam. When I imagine God's justice, I picture Marilyn Zehring raising awareness of social issues in Columbus, Nebraska.

HiRho Park is a practical theologian, Christian educator, and ordained elder.[42] She is passionate about empowering women's leadership in the church. She shared, "My call is to provide higher education by using technology for those who do not have access otherwise, so that they may live an abundant life." She is also a leader in the Women Coaching Women program. Drawing on her research and expertise with clergywomen and intercultural competence,[43] she provided a two-week training for about forty-five women leaders in Zimbabwe and about fifty women in the Philippines in 2019. When I asked what kind of struggles women leaders face in the Philippines, she responded, "sexism, discrimination, roadblocks to women speaking up; racial, ethnic, and classism issues." Referring to the combination of sexism, racism, and classism, she said, "Triple burdens are still alive. We try to help them to speak up about their own issues." She explained, "Coaching begins by listening. By having somebody listen to their stories, women experience healing and confirmation of God's grace." Clearly, her attentive presence makes a difference. She told me, "This is a truly lifechanging experience for many clergywomen. Women usually comment, 'It changed my life.'" When I imagine God's justice, I picture HiRho Park coaching women leaders.

---

[42]HiRho Park, interview with the author, August 5, 2019.

[43]HiRho Park, *Develop Intercultural Competence: How to Lead Cross-Racial and Cross-Cultural Churches* (General Board of Higher Education and Ministry, 2018); HiRho Park and Susan Willhauck, eds., *Breaking through the Stained Glass Ceiling: Women Pastoring Large Churches* (General Board of Higher Education and Ministry, 2013).

Transformation

Do not expect to remain the same when God is making of you "a new creation" (2 Cor. 5:17). When we seek to participate in God's will for a more just world, we will be changed. God invites us to participate in salvation now, as we are. We become ambassadors for Christ, entrusted with the message of reconciliation. Once we capture a glimpse of God's reconciling vision, our vision changes: "From now on, therefore, we regard no one from a human point of view; ... see, everything has become new!" (2 Cor. 5:16-17, NRSV). As you bear witness to this new reality, prepare to be transformed, again and again!

Garlinda Burton, a deaconess and former president and director of the Nashville Freedom School Partnership and former general secretary of the General Commission on the Status and Role of Women in the UMC, shared such a transformation in her own walk of faith.[44] "When I first joined Hobson Church in Nashville, I was out of my element," she said. She described growing up being heavily involved in a relatively safe church community in a middle-class Black neighborhood. Joining Hobson in her forties, church became a much different experience. "A lot of parents at Hobson were in extreme poverty." She estimated 60–70 percent of the church membership were indigent, and many struggled with addiction.

She witnessed poverty firsthand in the children's ministry. "We had to feed the children—and everyone else—before Sunday School and after worship every week and at other church activities." As a Sunday School teacher, she took particular interest in one family.

> The first awareness [for me] was these four children, siblings, were hungry. They didn't have any structure at home. One of the boys had a mental illness; the only girl had been sexually abused; their cousin had been sexually abused, also. So, God called me to become more than a typical Sunday School teacher.

Burton began caring for this family in direct ways. She drove the four children to and from church every Sunday. She helped with feeding them and the rest of Hobson's Sunday School children before and after church. Burton accompanied the four siblings as they grew up and still keeps up with them in their thirties.

This experience has been life-changing for all of them. Encountering such extreme poverty within her church community challenged Burton's understanding of ministry. She offered this witness:

> What has convicted me over the years, in ministries with children and youth, especially children at risk because of poverty, violence, and addiction ... is realizing the church had to be more than Bible lessons and children's church. God has called the Christian community to care for the whole person. God had actually provided those things for me. As a Christian, I was called. I was convicted.

---

[44]Garlinda Burton, interview with the author, July 10, 2019.

Burton went on to talk about the impact that these experiences had on her understanding of the church.

> Hobson was a game-changer for me. For example, indigent folks in our congregation often led the way on giving and tithing. One time, a sister friend at Hobson who didn't have any money—she had gotten high the night before—put a scratch-off lottery ticket worth $50 in the offering plate. That was all she had. But she gave it freely.
>
> It was my church family at Hobson that taught us that we are all to give what we have to the church and to each other. We can't sit back on God's grace and act self-satisfied and smug about how blessed and good we are. As people of God, we should work for everyone to have the experience of a liberating, soul-changing community.

This community of faith, Hobson UMC, challenged Burton far beyond her comfort zone. She now bears witness both to the debilitating effects of poverty and the transforming work of God to liberate the oppressed. I imagine this is God's will for a more just world.

The renewal of all creation includes each and every one of us in solidarity. As we imagine God's justice, we find meaningful participation by challenging and transcending structures of violence. When we imagine radical solidarity with every person and all of creation and attempt to see God in these relationships, we bear witness to the possibilities God gives us for a new creation. Growing in Christ-likeness, we become the church's moral witness. The holy disruption of God's grace in our lives will transform us.

Discussion Questions

1   What injustice have you experienced or are vulnerable to experiencing that you would passionately like to see rectified or changed?

2   To help create a more just world, consider your capacity for attentive presence and meaningful participation. Think of ways to meet people who could benefit from an attentive presence. What can you do to connect with people who have experienced injustice?

3   Iliya, Zehring, and Park each bear witness to God's good future. Who are the people in your congregation and community who inspire you through their witness?

4   Have you or anyone you know experienced the kind of transformation Burton describes? How might bearing witness to others enable you to participate meaningfully in what God is doing in your community?

PART THREE

Contemporary Challenges

3.1

Racism and Sexual Violence

This is the first of three chapters addressing contemporary challenges in Christian social ethics. The topics are complex: racism and sexual violence; climate change and empire; abuse of power and institutional betrayal. Many other topics could have been considered. For example, the fault lines of past generations' racial codes—slavery, Jim Crow, red lining—still define the social landscape of many communities in the United States and find new expression in immigration policies and mass incarceration. The issue of immigration came up in previous chapters, as did the Doctrine of Discovery and attacks on Indigenous peoples. None of these issues occurs in isolation; they are interconnected, systemic issues.

My choice of these three challenges is strategic: each contributes to a deeper understanding of trauma-informed Christian ethics. The challenge of abuse and betrayal is an issue critical to faith communities, threatening their integrity and missional viability. This challenge helps us understand group dynamics and the possibilities of healing in community, emphasizing communal aspects of the four moments of bearing witness. Likewise, the challenge of climate change and empire increases our capacity to bear witness, broadening the scope beyond humanity to include all of creation as potentially traumatized subjects. Examining climate change in the context of empire also reveals hidden power dynamics that must be confronted when addressing injustices. Similarly, the challenge of racism and sexual violence presents hard cases for testing and refining an ethic of bearing witness.

Racialized, gender-based sexual violence strengthens the methodology and practice of bearing witness by centering the experiences and perspectives of Black and brown women. Drawing on trauma studies and Black feminist theology and ethics, particularly the defiant and resistance ethics of Traci West, this chapter explores bearing witness as a liberative, moral act spanning compassion to politics. West's intersectional and antiracist lens shapes the process of bearing witness by prioritizing the experiences of Black women survivors of sexual violence as a primary source of ethical reflection. To expose and redress patterns of systemic patriarchy and racism, trauma-informed Christian ethics requires intersectional power analysis and solidarity with persons whose viewpoints are different from our own—regardless of your demographic location. By bearing witness to our neighbor's suffering, we join in solidarity with trauma survivors.

Guided by West, this chapter explores how persons of relative privilege can bear witness to victim-survivors of sexual trauma. Reframed as a process of liberation committed to antiracism, bearing witness seeks to enable liberative practices of social action in the current era of multiple and intersecting social and personal traumas. As author, my position of privilege in relation to structures of systemic violence and racism shapes my viewpoint, resonating with Elisabeth Vasko's theology of "compassionate witnessing" and Rebecca Todd Peters' "solidarity ethics" approach to economic globalization.[1] This ethic also finds common cause with a restorative justice approach to Christian responsibility, addressing how privilege can be used in solidarity with survivors to work toward moral repair.[2] The learning is generalizable. Bearing witness in the context of gender-based, racialized sexual trauma strengthens our capacity to address the suffering caused by other traumas.

Power and Agency

During a remarkable career of advocacy and scholarship, Traci West has provided tools for Black women to claim and exercise moral agency. Offering resistance, disruption, and defiance, West draws on deep wells of spiritual, communal, and intrapersonal resources to challenge systems of oppression. West empowers women of color to overcome trauma compounded by layers of racism, patriarchy, heterosexism, and classism. She enhances moral agency and moral community by bearing witness to their experiences of trauma.

What resources does West's Black feminist ethics provide to relatively privileged persons seeking to contribute to the survival, healing, and flourishing of Black women survivors of sexual trauma? For example, what does West's resistance ethics say to a white, heterosexual, cis-gender, affluent male, such as this author? West's writings expose how heterosexism, racism, and colonial legacies shape the experience and perpetuation of sexual violence. She provides antiracist guidance for relationships of solidarity across social power differentials with victim-survivors of sexual trauma. Morally supportive relationships require recognizing and empowering the survivor's moral agency while also providing support, safety, and protection. For persons with relative social privilege, this can be a difficult endeavor.

The history of feminist theological ethics reveals a constant struggle to engage in self-critical analysis and to avoid reifying the social distinctions and power structures under critique. For example, Valerie Saiving's critique of Reinhold Niebuhr's theological anthropology, which universalized the male perspective, has itself been critiqued for "essentializing the experience of white upper-middle-class women."[3] Black women offered a contrasting perspective based on their divergent experiences of moral agency. In her groundbreaking *Black Womanist Ethics*, Katie

---

[1] Elisabeth T. Vasko, *Beyond Apathy: A Theology for Bystanders* (Fortress, 2015), 7, 25; Rebecca Todd Peters, *Solidarity Ethics: Transformation in a Globalized World* (Fortress, 2014), 30.

[2] Wonchul Shin and Elizabeth M. Bounds, "Treating Moral Harm as Social Harm: Toward a Restorative Ethics of Christian Responsibility," *Journal of the Society of Christian Ethics* 37, no. 2 (2017): 153–69.

[3] Elizabeth L. Hinson-Hasty, "Introductory Comments for Panel on Niebuhr and Feminism," *Niebuhr Society, Annual Meeting of the American Academy of Religion*, Chicago, November 17, 2012; Valerie Saiving Goldstein, "The Human Situation: A Feminine View," *The Journal of Religion* 40, no. 2 (1960): 100–12.

Cannon asserted important "differences between ethics of life under oppression and established moral approaches which take for granted freedom and a wide range of choices."[4] The trajectory of white feminist studies in religion exemplified the "established moral approaches" that Cannon sought to challenge.

Both Saiving and Cannon offered critiques of ethical approaches that failed to account for their own moral agency. But what of the agency of the victim? Those who write about trauma often emphasize the victim's lack of agency. Jennifer Beste explored the devastating theological consequences of trauma, depicting traumatic debilitation that could be perceived as entirely disempowering to the victim.[5] Serene Jones suggested that only "the intervention of an external agent" could "break the hold of [traumatic] violence upon its victim."[6] Likewise, Judith Herman emphasized "the traumatized person's sense of unpredictability and helplessness."[7] Are victim-survivors powerless, though? As an activist-scholar, West recognizes and empowers Black women's moral agency through intersectional analysis grounded in the experiences of women of color.[8] As shown below, West's defiant and resistance ethic recognizes the victim-survivor as a moral agent whose inner resources contribute to her own survival.

Discussion Questions

1   Why is self-critical analysis necessary to Christian social ethics? How does your social location shape your moral actions and decision-making?

2   West offers a form of Christian ethics characterized by resistance, disruption, and defiance. Why does the author question the relevance of this form of ethics for himself?

Bearing Witness as a Moral Act

Bearing witness to survivors of trauma is a form of social action for liberation. Writing intentionally from a feminist perspective and eschewing the supposed "moral neutrality" of her profession, Herman asserted, "The therapist is called upon to bear witness to a crime. She must affirm a position of solidarity with the victim."[9] To bear witness to trauma is to know that this injustice should not have happened. Bearing witness "involves an understanding of the fundamental

---

[4]Katie G. Cannon, *Black Womanist Ethics* (Scholars, 1988), 5–6.

[5]Jennifer Erin Beste, *God and the Victim: Traumatic Intrusions on Grace and Freedom* (Oxford University Press, 2007), 106–8, 127.

[6]Serene Jones, *Trauma + Grace: Theology in a Ruptured World*, 2nd ed. (Westminster John Knox, 2019), 77.

[7]Judith L. Herman, *Trauma and Recovery: The Aftermath of Violence—From Domestic Abuse to Political Terror* (Basic Books, [1992]2015), 47.

[8]Carolyn Bratnober, "Traci C. West: Disruptive Activism, Ministry, and Scholarship," in *Challenging Bias against Women Academics in Religion*, Women in Religion vol. 2, ed. Colleen D. Hurting, 105–24 (Atla Open Press, 2021), 114, https://doi.org/10.31046/atlaopenpress.46.

[9]Herman, *Trauma and Recovery*, 4 and 135.

injustice of the traumatic experience and the need for a resolution that restores some sense of justice."[10] Bearing witness is not confined to therapeutic relations; it is the moral activity of anyone desiring to love their neighbor, the victim-survivor of trauma. Bearing witness is a process by which the listener, the observer, the neighbor becomes part of the narrative by taking sides with the oppressed. West serves as an essential guide to this moral activity of bearing witness.

In *Disruptive Christian Ethics*, West related multiple stories of women survivors of trauma to illustrate her method of social ethics. For example, María González suffered sexual harassment by her supervisor while participating in a workfare program in New York City, and she was not the only welfare recipient to encounter discrimination and harassment in this program, according to a lawsuit filed by the US Justice Department on behalf of these victims.[11] West's purpose in presenting the harrowing details of María's case is to encourage her reader to bear witness to the atrocities countenanced in US society, the brunt of which economically marginalized women of color bear disproportionately. Her standing as a moral agent and survivor calls me to recognize my own particularity in a social location much different from hers. How can I become an ally to María? The care with which West presented her story, refusing to allow María to become a stand-in for all victim-survivors, challenges us to engage with María's particularity as a moral agent. Presenting María's experience in tandem with the experiences of other women, West refuses to allow her readers to construct a single story about victim-survivors.[12] To bear witness to María is to become part of her story and to find our way toward a role characterized by love, justice, and solidarity with her.

In the same book, West examined newspaper accounts of an investigation of sexual violations of women by police officers in Hartford, Connecticut.[13] Here, she illustrated the ways in which women were not only victimized sexually but also stripped of dignity and worth through journalistic depictions that focused mainly on their status as prostitutes rather than the traumas they endured at the hands of law enforcement. In defiance of these oppressive, cultural norms, West asserted a "commitment to human well-being and dignity" as a litmus test for Christian ethics.[14] A liberative Christian ethic requires "Christians to engage in an ongoing struggle for sustained, systemic changes," and, West asserted, "hope for ethical relationships is only found in one's participation in the process of becoming a more compassionate society."[15] Bearing witness to trauma survivors is thus a profound, moral act, based on human dignity and compassionate relationships engaged in the struggle for systemic justice.

The act of bearing witness to trauma brings unjust structures to light, exposing violence for what it is. West observed: "Ironically, violence functions as a catalyst for

---

[10]Herman, 135.

[11]Traci C. West, *Disruptive Christian Ethics: When Racism and Women's Lives Matter* (Westminster John Knox, 2006), xiii.

[12]Chimamanda Ngozi Adichie, "The Danger of a Single Story," *TEDGlobal*, 2009, https://www.ted.com/talks/chimamanda_ngozi_adichie_the_danger_of_a_single_story.

[13]West, *Disruptive Christian Ethics*, 50–1.

[14]West, 54.

[15]West, 52.

both ... the power of domination and resistance to that power."[16] To bear witness to the trauma survivor neighbor is to become involved, to stake moral ground, and to engage in the struggle. Herman argued, "these attacks ... remind us that creating a protected space where survivors can speak their truth is an act of liberation. They remind us that bearing witness ... is an act of solidarity."[17] Such solidarity is dangerous. Herman asserted, "To speak publicly about one's knowledge of atrocities is to invite the stigma that attaches to victims."[18] There is no middle ground for an uninvolved bystander. Herman warned that when threatened, the powerful will respond by attacking those who witness to trauma.[19] Thus, a trauma-informed Christian ethic must bear witness to violence in a way that takes sides with the oppressed.

Traumatic Ruptures

Liberation theology is rooted in the experience of oppression and the moral agency of the marginalized. For example, in her *mujerista* theology, Ada María Isasi-Díaz adopted concepts developed in Paulo Freire's *Pedagogy of the Oppressed*, identifying conscientization as an essential part of liberation.[20] The corollary themes *suffering* and *survival* are likewise central to liberative ethics. Working toward liberation from a Black feminist perspective, West pioneered a scholarly conversation between theology and trauma studies, identifying male violence against Black women as causing not only suffering but also, and more precisely, trauma.[21] Trauma is the result of an experience that overwhelms a person's normal coping mechanisms; it is the wound resulting from experience(s) of terror.[22] A distinctive feature of trauma is the way it ruptures relationships across time, space, and community.[23]

---

[16]Traci C. West, *Solidarity and Defiant Spirituality: Africana Lessons on Religion, Racism, and Ending Gender Violence* (New York University Press, 2019), 218.

[17]Herman, *Trauma and Recovery*, 247.

[18]Herman, 2.

[19]Herman, 246.

[20]Ada María Isasi-Díaz, *En La Lucha/In the Struggle: Elaborating a Mujerista Theology* (Fortress, 2004), 161–2.

[21]West was one of the first religious scholars to engage Judith Herman's seminal work on trauma and recovery. Traci C. West, *Wounds of the Spirit: Black Women, Violence, and Resistance Ethics* (New York University Press, 1999), 55.

[22]Trauma can be experienced through single events or long-term stressors, such as systemic racism, extreme poverty, or emotional neglect. The cumulative traumatic effect of long-term stressors is called *complex trauma*. Trauma has "lasting adverse effects on the individual's functioning and mental, physical, social, emotional, or spiritual well-being." Substance Abuse and Mental Health Services Administration (SAMHSA), "SAMHSA's Concept of Trauma and Guidance for a Trauma-Informed Approach" (HHS Publication No. (SMA) 14–4884. SAMHSA, 2014), 7, https://store.samhsa.gov/product/SAMHSA-s-Concept-of-Trauma-and-Guidance-for-a-Trauma-Informed-Approach/SMA14-4884.

[23]Can rupture contribute to the good? Sara Wilhelm Garbers asserted, "Liberative political ethics and theologies indeed recognize our need to be ruptured by the real of human suffering." Karen Ross, Megan K. McCabe, and Sara Wilhelm Garbers, "Christian Sexual Ethics and the #MeToo Movement: Three Moments of Reflection on Sexual Violence and Women's Bodies," *Journal of the Society of Christian Ethics* 39, no. 2 (2019): 353. However, I would clarify that the victim-survivor of sexual violence does not need the rupture of suffering; rather, the bystanders and the ones bearing witness to trauma need to allow the reality of suffering to rupture our collusion with the systems of oppression that enable such violence.

Trauma creates temporal distortion by rupturing one's narrative self. Mind and body, if one can even speak of them separately, continue to respond to environmental triggers as if the danger were ever-present. Besser van der Kolk explained, "trauma is not just an event that took place sometime in the past; it is also the imprint left by that experience on mind, brain, and body."[24] Van der Kolk provided a memorable image for this aspect of trauma, explaining that while the conscious mind may be unaware of the ongoing effects of trauma, "the body continues to keep the score."[25] For the survivor, not only the effects of trauma but also the trauma itself persists, shaping every moment. This creates a disruption in how one experiences time. Traumatic memories reside in a perpetual present, refusing integration into the past and curtailing future possibilities. Shelly Rambo claimed that "the central problem of trauma is a temporal one" and that "the recovery of a narrative is an integral part of trauma healing."[26] This epistemological rupturing severely impairs one's sense of self.

Trauma ruptures relationships with self, others, and God. Trauma is fully embodied, yet beyond comprehension. Resmaa Menakem grounded his work on racialized trauma by attending to embodiment, claiming, "without a clear and present focus on the body, trauma cannot be fully addressed."[27] Rambo described this aspect of trauma in terms of body and word: "the body experiences trauma in ways that escape cognitive functioning and awareness."[28] Even when recognized, this embodied knowledge of the trauma eludes words: "All trauma is preverbal."[29] Without recourse to language, Rambo claimed, "traumatic suffering breaks down one's social world, severing bonds of trust that are essential for establishing a sense of self."[30] As a result, Van der Kolk asserted, "survivors of trauma often begin to fear that they are damaged to the core and beyond redemption."[31] Those aspects of the trauma that can be remembered or spoken are often experienced as shame: the traumatized person may be ashamed about feeling overwhelmed and powerless during the traumatic event.[32] Thus, Herman asserted, "psychological trauma is an affliction of the powerless."[33] However, West resisted this shame, countering "the helpless victim" trope by advocating for the victim-survivor's agency.

West defiantly opposes depictions of powerlessness, describing ruptured relationships as layers of invisibility, fracturing community ties. West symbolized her recognition of the moral agency of those harmed by violence and sexual abuse

---

[24]Besser A. van der Kolk, *The Body Keeps the Score: Brain, Mind, and Body in the Healing of Trauma* (Penguin, 2014), 21.

[25]van der Kolk, 46.

[26]Shelly Rambo, *Spirit and Trauma: A Theology of Remaining* (Westminster John Knox, 2010), 19 and 21.

[27]Resmaa Menakem, *My Grandmother's Hands: Racialize Trauma and the Pathways to Mending Our Hearts and Bodies* (Central Recovery, 2017), 58.

[28]Rambo, *Spirit and Trauma*, 21.

[29]van der Kolk, *The Body Keeps the Score*, 43.

[30]Rambo, *Spirit and Trauma*, 21.

[31]van der Kolk, *The Body Keeps the Score*, 2.

[32]van der Kolk, 13.

[33]Herman, *Trauma and Recovery*, 33.

by adopting the term *victim-survivor*.[34] In *Wounds of the Spirit*, she challenged her readers to appreciate the survivor's "help-seeking efforts" even when they do not conform to our expectations.[35] An excerpt of the trial transcript involving one of the women in Hartford violated by a police officer reveals how this victim-survivor used her power for self-preservation. When asked why she did not report the crime to the police, she responded, "I was concerned because he is an officer. Who was I going to tell? ... Because I was a prostitute and he's law enforcement. Nobody's going to believe me."[36] Her decision not to report the officer immediately was an exercise of moral agency for her own well-being. West bore witness by affirming and supporting this survivor's ability to resist oppression, particularly when she chose to protect herself from further harm.

Discussion Questions

1   The author describes bearing witness as a dangerous form of social action. Why would someone showing compassion to a victim-survivor of sexual violence be at risk? What social and political consequences might the modern-day Good Samaritan suffer for such benevolence?

2   Write down five adjectives that come to mind when describing a victim of sexual abuse. Then, write down five adjectives that come to mind when describing a *survivor* of sexual abuse. Compare your lists and share them with a classmate or colleague. How do your perceptions of blame, agency, and power shape your assumptions about victim-survivors of sexual trauma?

3   An ethic of liberation takes sides with the oppressed using an intersectional lens to examine racism, patriarchy, heterosexism, colonialism, classism, and other forms of oppression. What tensions do you perceive between recognizing systemic oppressions and asserting that victim-survivors have agency and are not powerless?

Bearing Witness to Trauma

Bearing witness to the truth of the neighbor's experience of trauma is made difficult because of traumatic ruptures. Narrative ruptures interfere with the survivor's ability to put into words the traumatic parts of their story. Relational ruptures interfere with the survivor's ability to be fully present to themselves, others, and God. Social ruptures interfere with the survivor's ability to assert the truth of their experience in the face of perpetrators and systems of power intent on rendering the reality of trauma invisible. To bear witness to a trauma survivor "entails attesting to the temporal distortions and epistemological ruptures" of "suffering that does not go away."[37] The hope of resistance

---

[34]Bratnober, "Traci C. West," 111; West, *Wounds of the Spirit*, 1.
[35]West, 57–67, 152.
[36]West, *Disruptive Christian Ethics*, 53.
[37]Rambo, *Spirit and Trauma*, 15.

to traumatic violence is grounded in the human capacity to transcend ruptures of time, space, and community. Navigating this terrain requires an ethic that can span from compassion to politics.

Bearing witness to traumatic violence prioritizes the truth as experienced by the trauma survivor, even and especially when that truth eludes expression in language. It is a form of "the poetics of testimony," to use Rebecca Chopp's description of a way to "speak of the unspeakable."[38] To bear witness theologically is to seek new ways to communicate about sin, God, and salvation when the old words do not suffice. Seeking to activate the theological imagination, Rambo suggested, "The challenge of theological discourse is to articulate a different orientation to suffering that can speak to the invisibility, gaps, and repetitions constituting trauma."[39] This reorientation requires attention to transcendence, which Chopp defined not in the sense of being wholly other to human experience but rather as "a matter of the power and spirit of transfiguration."[40] Bearing witness embraces the spirit of transfiguration, seeking to promote healing after the trauma of sexual violence.

Sexual traumas are the manifestations in particular bodies—often women of color—of social and material disparities enabling and colluding with abuses of power. This reality highlights the critical importance of feminist religious discourse and especially West's intersectional, antiracist approach to Black feminist ethics. Healing from traumatic ruptures requires what West termed a "defiant spirituality" to confront distorted power relations directly.[41] Thus, bearing witness is a set of antiracist, liberative practices, rooted in love and justice, with the aim of solidarity with victim-survivors. Transcending traumatic ruptures, we can recognize and resist the ways social oppressions perpetuate sexual violence.

As presented and discussed in Chapter 1.3, a trauma-informed social ethic of bearing witness, drawing upon trauma studies and the work of process theologian Marjorie Suchocki, provides a way of bearing witness to victim-survivors. This model consists of practices of social action arranged in four perspectival moments: existence, present, past, and future (see Table 3.1.1). However, ruptures are not neatly isolated temporally or spatially, and these moments of reckoning are intermingled in practice. For example, West's project of "truthful cultural translations" for the purpose of antiviolence solidarity includes all these modes and moments: recognition of intrinsic dignity as a shared moral understanding; empathy as a relational commitment; memory as a tool for interpreting scripture and tradition; and imagination as a guide for the entire enterprise of "ending gender-based violence."[42] Human capacities for recognition, empathy, memory, and imagination pertain to present, past, and future simultaneously. Thus, each of the four moments of bearing witness reinforces the others and does not function separately.

---

[38] Rebecca S. Chopp, "Theology and the Poetics of Testimony," *Criterion* 37, no. 1 (1998): 6. See also Jones, *Trauma + Grace*, 79; Rambo, *Spirit and Trauma*, 164–5.
[39] Rambo, 169.
[40] Chopp, "Theology and the Poetics of Testimony," 10.
[41] West, *Solidarity and Defiant Spirituality*, 218.
[42] West, 107–8.

TABLE 3.1.1 *Bearing Witness against Racism and Sexual Violence*

Perspectival Moment	Mode of Transcendence	Moral Theme	Practice of Social Action	West's Moral Emphases
I. Existence	recognition	dignity	grounded being	diversity, difference, shared humanity
II. Present	empathy	love	attentive presence	embodied wisdom, particularity
III. Past	memory	justice	historical clarity	intersectional power analysis
IV. Future	imagination	solidarity	meaningful participation	reciprocal learning, strategic alliances, human freedom

Grounded Being and Dignity

Our equal status as created beings provides a theological starting point for a trauma-informed response to sexual violence. Realizing the widespread occurrence of trauma, bearing witness begins with recognition of our shared bond of human dignity, a foundational commitment of West and other feminist ethicists.[43] Furthermore, West challenges us to avoid universalizing the neighbor when recognizing our shared humanity. We must also recognize our neighbor's difference, seeing the diversity of humanity as part of our shared humanity.

The practice of grounded being recognizes the human dignity of the trauma survivor. Because the experience of trauma disrupts one's relationship to self—what West called "mind-body-spirit wholeness and dignity," shame often replaces dignity in the mind of the victim-survivor.[44] Suchocki described the effects of sexual abuse as "a cascading system of negative self-esteem transmitted through the medium of guilty feelings."[45] West observed that feelings of shame are compounded by ever-present societal devaluations based on race, gender, and sexual orientation, leading to self-blame and alienation from one's faith community.[46] Feelings of shame, guilt, and loss of human agency can rob the survivor of a full sense of dignity and worth. In fact, perpetrators of actual or threatened sexual violence often intend to do just that!

---

[43]West, *Disruptive Christian Ethics*, 54. See also Peters, *Solidarity Ethics*, 117.
[44]West, *Solidarity and Defiant Spirituality*, 153.
[45]Marjorie Hewitt Suchocki, *The Fall to Violence: Original Sin in Relational Theology* (Continuum, 1994), 138. See also van der Kolk, *The Body Keeps the Score*, 13, 104.
[46]West, *Wounds of the Spirit*, 67–76.

Reckoning with created existence is to view every part of creation as good and to recognize our neighbor as "very good" (Gen. 1:4, 10, 12, 18, 21, 25, 31). Recognizing that our neighbor is created in the image of God means that our neighbor's human dignity is equal to our own; it is to affirm with West our "equal human freedom to live without being targeted for violence and discrimination."[47] In the case brought against police officers in Hartford, the news media contributed to the trauma of the sexual violations by failing to portray the victim-survivors with full and equal human dignity. According to West, "the women who were assaulted were primarily referred to as 'prostitutes'" and "the term 'victim' was rarely used."[48] These women experienced violation initially through sexual assault and later through demeaning depictions in the community.

West's act of recognition, seeing women as neighbors with equal human dignity, bore witness to their trauma. Reckoning with created existence entails fundamental commitments to human equality and human rights, including the right to freedom from the threat of violence and the opportunity for flourishing. These commitments cannot be realized through a supposed "universal" neighbor. An antiracist, trauma-informed ethic must begin specifically with West's affirmation of "black women's intrinsic equality, worth, and dignity."[49] We are each loved fully and equally by God.

Recognition of shared, human dignity is essential to bearing witness to survivors of sexual assault. An "unequivocal affirmation of one's individual worth" is a spiritual necessity for Black women victim-survivors, asserted West.[50] This essential "entitlement to human dignity" cannot be taken for granted, given that sexual assault often threatens a woman's "moral right to exist."[51] As one bearing witness, I can participate in moral repair by recognizing the dignity God has already bestowed on the survivor of trauma. To recognize the full, human dignity of those persons most often targeted for sexual violence—women; Black women; gay, lesbian, and transgender persons—is, in West's words, "a spiritual witness to the process of beingness," a witness that "signals freedom."[52] The very act of recognition can be liberative for me as well as my neighbor.

Through the act of recognition, I see not only common humanity but also diversity and difference.[53] Dissonance between my preconceptions and the embodied reality of my neighbor raises, as West emphasized, "potentially constructive" uncertainties requiring translation and no small amount of humility on the part of persons with relatively greater power and privilege.[54] Such recognition and affirmation acknowledge not only our shared, created existence but also the wonderfully unique qualities that make each person a beloved child of God despite the strata of structural sin disproportionately weighing down on Black and brown bodies, particularly women.

---

[47] West, *Solidarity and Defiant Spirituality*, 211.
[48] West, *Disruptive Christian Ethics*, 51.
[49] West, *Solidarity and Defiant Spirituality*, 108.
[50] West, 49.
[51] West, 197.
[52] West, 197.
[53] West, 238.
[54] West, 239.

Discussion Question

1   West challenges us to recognize the person who is our neighbor. If each person is, in certain respects, like all others, like some others, and like no other, how might we recognize María González, for example? Practice seeing her in terms of shared humanity, difference, and diversity.

Attentive Presence and Love

Trauma-informed response to sexual violence proceeds with empathy and love in the present. Recognizing the signs and symptoms of trauma, we meet the trauma survivor where they are. As Menakem asserted, "to a traumatized body there is only *now*."[55] For many survivors, the experience of trauma refuses integration into the past. Flashbacks, sensory triggers, increased stress hormones—all these responses of the trauma survivor are geared toward one end: survival. The temporal rupture of trauma, though, keeps the body ready to go on high alert at all times. The fight, flight, freeze, or fawn response is only one trigger away, responding to prior trauma as it replays itself again and again. The survivor's only full point of temporal connection is the eternal, traumatic present. Reckoning with the present, we can bear witness to our neighbor through attentive presence. Recognition of the victim-survivor's particularity is essential to feminist and antiracist discourses, which seek to value concrete (rather than generalized or universal) human experience as sources of moral insight. This form of neighbor-love requires an embodied wisdom that I call empathy.

Empathy engages body and mind together; it is embodied wisdom, affective and passionate.[56] However, when artificially separated into emotional and cognitive components, West asserted, empathy is "unreliable … as a basis for antiviolence activism."[57] Empathy requires reason, not just emotion. To avoid such a simplistic distinction, empathy must be characterized by what West termed "embodied sensory and emotional experiences … [that] can help to morally discipline one's responses to the other in the encounter."[58] This rational, fully embodied empathy is necessary for antiviolence activism.[59] As a mode of self-transcendence, empathy opens us to the possibility of being changed and transformed by the trauma survivor who is our neighbor. According to Suchocki, "self-transcendence through empathy emerges when one relates to the other as the related other who is also a subject."[60]

---

[55]Menakem, *My Grandmother's Hands*, xv, original emphasis.

[56]My understanding of empathy is resonant with Pamela Cooper-White's definition, based on the work of Heinz Kohut: empathy is an observational stance attentive to the perspectives of other, allowing them to "feel recognized and understood." Pamela Cooper-White, *Shared Wisdom: Use of the Self in Pastoral Care and Counseling* (Fortress, 2004), 178.

[57]West, *Solidarity and Defiant Spirituality*, 154. Here, West responded to Paul Bloom, who distinguished between "emotional empathy" and "cognitive empathy." West argued for reason over emotion. Paul Bloom, *Against Empathy: The Case for Rational Compassion* (HarperCollins, 2016), 16–17.

[58]West, *Solidarity and Defiant Spirituality*, 8.

[59]West, 8, 37, 154.

[60]Suchocki, *The Fall to Violence*, 40; see also 147.

For Rebecca Todd Peters, concrete relationships expressed as mutual partnerships between the relatively privileged and the marginalized provide the starting point for solidarity.[61] Elisabeth Vasko described this kind of empathy-wed-to-social-action as compassion.[62]

Empathy recognizes a trauma survivor as a moral agent with the power to resist injustice and contribute to her own well-being. Countering the feeling of helplessness experienced by a trauma survivor, empathy claims space for the survivor's agency.[63] Empathy is a "form of interpretative care requir[ing] a balance of connection and honoring of difference."[64] Empathetic, attentive presence can bridge divisions, "crossing identity borders" and other human-created barriers that would keep us separated.[65] Empathy requires that the person bearing witness be honest with themself about their relative privilege, seeking to learn from the perspective of those who do not share that privilege.[66] Empathy attuned to particularity addresses, in part, the dilemma posed by West: "How does one transcend race *and* pay attention to racial oppression?"[67] A liberative ethic seeking broad applicability must allow us to unmask intersectional oppressions. Thus, violence against Black women must be understood as gendered and racialized.

While recognition sees the universal shared human dignity in each neighbor, attentive presence meets the trauma survivor in her concrete, social, economic, raced, and gendered location. How might empathy disrupt the layers of trauma experienced by Black, female survivors of rape, for example? West cited the story of Yvonne, who was abducted and raped at twelve years of age.[68] Yvonne immediately reported the assault to her family and the police and underwent a physical examination at the hospital, revealing bleeding and a dislocated arm. Yet, no one believed her, including her grandmother—something she did not learn until years later. Reflecting on the incident as an adult, Yvonne wrote, "Where I lived in the South, any time a black woman said she was raped she was never believed."[69]

A trauma-informed ethic seeks not only to realize the ubiquity of trauma in society generally but also to identify and name the reality of trauma in the lives of individuals—in Yvonne's case, a rape perpetrated when she was twelve years old. At the least, attentive presence entails believing the survivor. One cannot be empathetic to a person whose story one disbelieves. In Yvonne's case, simply being believed may have provided the sense of safety so necessary for trauma healing and recovery. Bearing witness to Yvonne requires overcoming the layers of classism, racism, and sexism that conspire to convince bystanders that her story could not possibly be

---

[61]Peters, *Solidarity Ethics*, 115.
[62]Vasko, *Beyond Apathy*, 86.
[63]West, *Solidarity and Defiant Spirituality*, 154, 206.
[64]Jennifer Baldwin, *Trauma-Sensitive Theology: Thinking Theologically in the Era of Trauma* (Cascade, 2018), 84.
[65]West, *Solidarity and Defiant Spirituality*, 198.
[66]Peters, *Solidarity Ethics*, 83.
[67]West, *Disruptive Christian Ethics*, 56, original emphasis.
[68]West, 57–8, citing Charlotte Pierce-Baker, *Surviving the Silence: Black Women's Stories of Rape* (W. W. Norton, 1998), 138–9.
[69]West, 58, citing Pierce-Baker, 124.

true because she is poor, Black, and female. Thus, bearing witness through attentive presence demands deep listening by the relatively privileged bystander.[70] Bearing witness attempts to reestablish the human connections ruptured through trauma, to love the neighbor who has survived trauma, and to be changed through the encounter.

Admittedly, identifying empathy with love can be problematic. West voiced a healthy distrust of common Christian conceptions. "Christian love rhetoric has traditionally enjoyed an unperturbed attachment to transphobic and misogynist denials of gender equality," observed West; the rhetoric of Christian love, "that problematic love framework," is a tool of oppression.[71] West explained: "An understanding of harm-free Christian love as the most authentic representation of Christianity denies the prevalent, *authentic* reality of the Christian gender-based violence and spiritual abuse interwoven throughout Christian practices of love."[72] A more authentic Christian practice, what I am calling empathetic love through attentive presence, centers the agency of the survivor. Empathy is a necessary, though insufficient, mode of transcendence for bearing witness to our neighbors who have experienced trauma. Empathetic love must also be vigilant, using social analysis to uncover patterns of racism, with "particular attention in the context of dismantling support for gender violence."[73] Thus, attentive presence must be accompanied by historical clarity.

Discussion Questions

1 West expressed distrust for Christian rhetoric about love that fails to account for particularity. To appreciate her point, consider the ways that appeals to "love" have abetted racial injustice by avoiding conflict and difficult conversations.

2 West also expressed distrust for any conception of empathy that separates head and heart. A person expressing empathy as fully embodied wisdom must be open to being transformed by the encounter. How have you been changed by being attentively present to someone in need of help?

Historical Clarity and Justice

Historical clarity allows us to view trauma histories through the lens of justice. Trauma has an etiology. Instead of the blame-laden query, "What's wrong with you?" a trauma-informed neighbor learns to ask, "What has happened to you?" Through historical clarity, we can expose systems of violence, including internalized oppression. The practice of historical clarity allows us, along with West, to observe

---

[70]Peters, *Solidarity Ethics*, 63; Vasko, *Beyond Apathy*, 223; West, *Solidarity and Defiant Spirituality*, 84, 239.

[71]West, *Solidarity and Defiant Spirituality*, 237–8.

[72]West, 237–8.

[73]West, 237; Vasko, *Beyond Apathy*, 224.

that "contemporary moral patterns are rooted in and were initiated within particular racist historical relations."[74] Such an observation requires an intersectional analysis of power. Trauma has an identifiable history, and an ethical response to trauma must seek clarity about this past and participate in concrete acts of justice-making in solidarity with survivors.

Reckoning with the past utilizes memory as a mode of transcendence. The trauma survivor struggles with a past that will not go away. Memory of trauma can be dangerous, disrupting the survivor's sense of safety and exposing "the systems they call to account."[75] Violations include both individual traumas as well systems of violence, such as "that history of societally sanctioned devaluation" of Black women and girls discussed by West.[76] That no one believed Yvonne's report of rape illustrates this kind of societal devaluation, which she endured following the sexual assault. Bearing witness, the privileged bystander can become an ally through this danger.

Bearing witness to victim-survivors of trauma engages what Suchocki termed "transformative memory": a "remembrance of the past as *past*, opening one to a new present ... for the sake of well-being."[77] According to Suchocki, memory allows us to experience guilt for our complicity in unnecessary violence and to exercise the freedom to overcome it through forgiveness.[78] Done with "the fullest possible knowledge," she asserted, "forgiveness is the ground of transformation."[79] However, Suchocki elided the distinction between violator and violated, ignoring the fact that neither the historic circumstances nor the relative degree of power and vulnerability are shared equally.[80]

While all of humanity is complicit in and culpable for structures of violence to some degree, the moral responsibilities of the one bearing witness are distinct from those of the victim-survivor. For victim-survivors, West observed, "memory work" is "a particular type of gender justice spirituality."[81] Indiscriminate calls for forgiveness inevitably prove unjust and cause further harm.[82] Survivors of trauma do not need or deserve the feelings of guilt that they invariably experience. The emotional and spiritual consequences of this dynamic of shame and self-blame are exacerbated by systems of patriarchy, heterosexism, and racism and further enabled by the Christian emphasis on forgiveness, which West described as "a moral assault" on Black women.[83]

Thus, West expressed deep concern about Christian practices of confession, preferring the word "admission." West asserted that "admissions of Christians' culpability in homophobic violence must be distinguishable from traditional Christian theological emphases on confession of sin and pursuit of forgiveness," which are

---

[74]West, *Solidarity and Defiant Spirituality*, 68.

[75]Ross, McCabe, and Wilhelm Garbers, "Christian Sexual Ethics," 354–5.

[76]West, *Solidarity and Defiant Spirituality*, 110.

[77]Suchocki, *The Fall to Violence*, 150.

[78]Suchocki, 137.

[79]Suchocki, 151, 146, respectively.

[80]Suchocki, 147–9.

[81]West, *Solidarity and Defiant Spirituality*, 190.

[82]Beste, *God and the Victim*, 117; Pamela Cooper-White, *The Cry of Tamar: Violence against Women and the Church's Response*, 2nd ed. (Fortress, 2012), 251–5; West, *Wounds of the Spirit*, 76.

[83]West, 55–88, especially 76.

"too self-indulgently transactional" and do not necessarily entail "participation in change that ends violence."[84] For bystanders, Vasko suggested "the language of lament" as a means of recognizing the effects of structural violence on "the sinned against" and acknowledging collective guilt and responsibility.[85] For those bearing witness to trauma survivors, admission and lament must be combined with concrete acts of moral repair. In a word, transformative memory requires the work of justice.

Specifically, the practice of historical clarity requires the work of *restorative justice*. The framework of restorative justice utilized by Wonchul Shin and Elizabeth M. Bounds helpfully addresses the moral harm caused by situations of "ongoing degradation and humiliation,"[86] such as contributed to the layers of trauma experienced by Yvonne, María, and others. Restorative justice expands moral responsibility beyond personal blame, locating moral harm in structural injustices and implicating the entire community in collective responsibility for "both active intervention and relational healing."[87] Furthermore, the "broader notion of responsibility present in restorative justice" underscores my critique of Suchocki, above, "suggest[ing] that multiple social relations may lead to differentiated social responsibilities."[88] Thus, the ongoing work of feminist attention to gender-based violence and trauma must attend to intersectional power differentials. Bearing witness must see not only universal, human dignity but also the historical and social scars and constraints we bear disproportionately. We are neither complicit in the same way nor responsible in the same way.

An intersectional power analysis examines the ways that race, gender, class, and other social categories shape and distort relationships between individuals and communities. Bearing witness to survivors of sexual violence and other traumas entails identifying past harms, righting relationships, and offering restitution. For example, bringing historical clarity to Yvonne's case includes naming the structures of racism that prevented others from believing her, affirming the veracity of her story and, more generally, the integrity of her "counterpublic voice" and the societal value of her role as "a bearer of truth," publicly validating her experience, and actively working to repair and restore her full standing in the community.[89] This kind of restorative justice-making can lead the one bearing witness to reckon imaginatively with the future, engaging in meaningful participation through solidarity.

Discussion Question

1   Historical clarity requires knowledge of how social categories have been used to privilege or oppress persons in the past. For example, what do you know about the history of political rights of women, African Americans, or persons with disabilities in your community?

---

[84]West, *Solidarity and Defiant Spirituality*, 209–10.
[85]Vasko, *Beyond Apathy*, 118–19. See also discussion of repentance in Beste, *God and the Victim*, 115, 119.
[86]Shin and Bounds, "Treating Moral Harm," 155.
[87]Shin and Bounds, 156, 161.
[88]Shin and Bounds, 163.
[89]West, *Disruptive Christian Ethics*, 59–62.

Meaningful Participation and Solidarity

The practice of meaningful participation is the fourth moment of bearing witness, working toward a better future in solidarity with victim-survivors of sexual violence. As we bear witness to our neighbors by reckoning with the future, West guides us in practicing reciprocal learning, entering strategic alliances, and envisioning human freedom.

Trauma disrupts one's ability to imagine a future beyond traumatic interference. During recovery, according to Herman, "the survivor reclaims her world" by "creating a future."[90] This stage of healing involves learning to defend oneself, reconciling with oneself, reconnecting with others, and finding a mission, perhaps through social action.[91] None of this can be done for the victim-survivor: she must be empowered to exercise her own voice and flourish as a full, moral agent.[92] The healing process requires support from persons who can offer "essential messages of hope," according to Pamela Cooper-White, including an affirmation of the survivor's agency and the persistence of God's love amidst suffering.[93] Neighbors bearing witness can become allies in the survivor's recovery and healing by joining in solidarity to imagine a more life-empowering future.

Reckoning with the future requires exercising imagination in tandem with the work of justice. Suchocki described the naming of sin as the bridge from past to future: "[moral] vision is inherently operative within the very pronouncement of a social situation as sinful."[94] By offering truthful acknowledgment of past violence and owning up to our complicity and collective responsibility, we can offer new possibilities for survivors of trauma, for ourselves, and our communities. West named "the development of moral and spiritual imagination" as an important and underutilized tool of religious communities. "Religion at its best," she stated, "trains the believer to actively engage the world as it is while providing a lens for imagining what the world ought to be."[95] Recognizing past and present structures of violence gives clarity about what needs to be different and potentially uncovers positive examples to encourage imaginative possibilities. For example, West cited a "legacy of antiracist confrontations … steeped in a belief in the unseen possibility of human freedom" as providing courage for survivors.[96] The work of imagining new futures in solidarity with survivors of trauma is vital to participation in societal transformation.

Solidarity requires survivors and those bearing witness to invest in a relationship that can be mutually transforming. West identified "solidarity as [a] strategic and spiritual practice" involving "reciprocal learning."[97] West observed, "Once we train ourselves to perceive the means that individual victim-survivors utilize for their

---

[90] Herman, *Trauma and Recovery*, 196.
[91] Herman, 197–208.
[92] Herman, 133–4.
[93] Cooper-White, *The Cry of Tamar*, 246.
[94] Suchocki, *The Fall to Violence*, 157.
[95] West, *Solidarity and Defiant Spirituality*, 52 and 176.
[96] West, 214.
[97] West, 183 and 195.

survival and liberation, our ability to envision broader possibilities for women-empowering change increases."[98] Bearing witness to survivors of sexual violence, we must be open to change, in both our perspective and our actions. "To embark on this journey with survivors," wrote Jennifer Beste, "involves a willingness to disrupt our sense of well-being, comfort, and security and to be challenged in our view of ourselves, our world, and God."[99] Resisting doing further harm through solidarity is the necessary follow-through to an ethic that practices love and justice for and with our neighbors who are trauma survivors. "For privileged bystanders," asserted Vasko, "our redemption will be worked out through a liberative praxis marked by compassionate solidarity."[100] West noted that this "solidarity-building work" includes "collective action and cultivation of firm alliances."[101] It is a form of political action.

Discussion Question

1   West described a kind of human freedom characterized by reciprocity, allyship, and solidarity. Compare and contrast this vision of freedom to the "American Dream" (whatever that means to you). Which vision of freedom more closely aligns with the values of your faith community? Which vision of freedom more closely aligns with the practices of your faith community?

Bearing Witness as Political Action

When trauma ruptures relationships and community, it reveals unjust power relations. Traumatic ruptures disturb the status quo, individually and politically, exposing what West termed, "the moral gaps that violence maintains."[102] Trauma presents an embodied witness to violence, calling attention to injustice and implicating the powerful and the power structures that support them. This exposure can endanger the victim-survivor of trauma. Trauma is not merely an individual's struggle in response to terror and violence but also a phenomenon with inherent societal and political dimensions.

Since power structures tend to blame the victim and others oppressed by those structures, trauma survivors need allies. We know about María González and other victims of workplace sexual harassment in New York, in part, because someone bore witness to her story, believed her, and joined in a legal fight to address the violations. Solidarity with trauma survivors requires bearing witness to their experiences, hearing their testimonies, and joining them in resistance. Acknowledging the existence of trauma is a political undertaking, noted Herman, requiring the support of a movement.[103] The "Me Too" movement initiated by Tarana Burke illustrates

---

[98]West, *Wounds of the Spirit*, 180.
[99]Beste, *God and the Victim*, 126.
[100]Vasko, *Beyond Apathy*, 219.
[101]West, *Solidarity and Defiant Spirituality*, 198.
[102]West, 218.
[103]Herman, *Trauma and Recovery*, 9.

both the kind of politics in which allies can join in solidarity and the importance of being vigilant to racism within feminist discourse—her call to action failed to gain traction until it was repeated by a white celebrity.[104] Meaningful participation in solidarity with survivors—combined with a commitment to antiracism—can repair structures of violence through collective action, such as public policy advocacy.

Envisioning Human Wholeness and Well-Being

This chapter has provided a trauma-informed framework for interpreting West's resistance ethics, complementing her work by developing an ethic of bearing witness to victim-survivors. In turn, West's resistance, disruptive, and defiant mode of Christian social ethics hones an ethic of bearing witness by drawing attention to diversity, difference, and shared humanity; insisting on embodied wisdom and particularity; offering the tools of intersectional power analysis; and practicing reciprocal learning, entering strategic alliances, and envisioning human freedom. For example, her approach to ethics shows that expressions of mere compassion are insufficient for addressing traumatic ruptures. Relatively privileged allies require the moral guidance of her antiracist, intersectional lens to bear witness to the lived reality of victim-survivors of trauma.

West offered antiracist conditions for support and empowerment of Black women survivors of sexual violence applicable to each moment of bearing witness. Recognition must lead to a dignity amid embodied difference as well as common humanity. Empathy must lead to a love that honors the survivor's agency and particularity through an embodied wisdom open to mutual transformation. Memory must lead to restorative justice centered on the well-being of the survivor, addressing intersectional oppressions while repairing moral harm through collective responsibility. Imagination must lead to a solidarity of strategic alliances open to mutual learning and imagining human freedom. The process of bearing witness through love, justice, and solidarity provides the possibility for relatively privileged allies to work in solidarity with survivors of trauma toward liberation.

Each moment of bearing witness can bring bystanders and survivors into a closer relationship, demanding that we transcend the limitations of our own perspectives as we seek to redress the structures of privilege that condone and collude with racialized, sexual violence. This ethical framework, though, is no guarantee of authentic solidarity. It is an ongoing struggle for persons of relative privilege to become aware of the structures of power and privilege in which we are all embedded. This kind of conscientization can only occur through solidarity with persons with less power. Understood and practiced in solidarity with survivors, particularly Black women survivors, bearing witness can enable new, liberative practices *if* we, along

---

[104]Tarana Burke, "Me Too Is a Movement, Not a Moment," *TEDWomen*, 2018, https://www.ted.com/talks/tarana_burke_me_too_is_a_movement_not_a_moment?language=en; Sandra E. Garcia, "The Woman Who Created #MeToo Long before Hashtags," *The New York Times*, October 20, 2017, https://www.nytimes.com/2017/10/20/us/me-too-movement-tarana-burke.html.

with West, "maintain an ethical vision of human wholeness and well-being that is directly responsive to the converging form of violence confronted by women."[105] With this vision in mind, bearing witness is an imaginative, hope-filled, moral intervention in the midst of the struggle to survive, seeking transcendence in traumatic spaces and healing and justice in a world awash with trauma.

Discussion Questions

1 Increase your awareness of sexual violence and racism by researching the prevalence of gender- and race-based violence in your community.

2 Contact a local service provider (YWCA, Coalition Against Rape, NAACP, women's shelter, sexual assault prevention center, and so forth) for information about becoming an ally. What do you and your faith community need to know about supporting their work?

---

[105]West, *Wounds of the Spirit*, 181.

3.2

Climate Change and Empire

How shall we love the world that God so loves? Responding faithfully to the climate crisis begins with recognizing the traumatic effects of climate change on humans and non-humans alike. Psychological trauma is a protective response experienced through single events or long-term stressors, such as systemic racism, extreme poverty, emotional neglect, or the effects of climate change. A trauma-informed approach to climate change has the potential to expand human moral vision, enhancing collective agency and increasing resilience. This chapter addresses anthropogenic climate change as an unprecedented moral problem in the context of empire, requiring a reevaluation of inherited ethics and theology.

Much of creation is suffering from trauma—including ourselves. In 2017, the American Psychological Association reported that "climate change has acute and chronic impacts, directly and indirectly, on individual well-being."[1] Mental health practitioners have even identified "pre-traumatic stress response (a before-the-fact version of classic PTSD)" in persons who anticipate and fear the long-term deleterious effects of climate change.[2] The trauma extends beyond our human neighbors. Plants, animals, and entire ecosystems evidence new stresses due to a warming planet. In this chapter, I focus on bearing witness to the natural world of which we are a part, and the *world* I have in mind is not just Earth but the cosmos [*kosmon*], the entire creation.

Anthropogenic climate change is an unprecedented problem. Because of its global scope and systemic causes, moral actors have difficulty recognizing it as an ethical problem with human causes in which they participate. The climate crisis is also bound up in structures of empire, which militate against effective moral action. Adopting a trauma-informed approach to the climate crisis prompts us to consider the suffering, agency, and wisdom of all of creation through recognition, empathy, memory, and imagination. Bearing witness to the traumatic sufferings of creation challenges inherited theological and ethical understandings of God, humanity, and our relationships with each other and all of creation. Thus, bearing witness to

---

[1]Susan Clayton, Christie Manning, Kirra Krygsman, and Meighen Speiser, *Mental Health and Our Changing Climate: Impacts, Implications, and Guidance* (American Psychological Association and ecoAmerica, 2017), 22.

[2]Susan Clayton et al., 57.

non-human creation makes possible the kind of alternative relationships necessary to participate in God's salvific work to reconcile and make new all of creation.

An Unprecedented Moral Problem

Anthropogenic climate change is an unprecedented problem that challenges inherited understandings of theology and ethics. It is a structural problem, caused by systems and patterns of behavior involving billions of moral actors over long periods of time, and can be addressed only through collective moral agency when recognized as such. To see climate change as a problem is to recognize that it is beyond the natural, normal, or inevitable course of events, that it is harmful, and that we can do something about it. To quote the movement 350.org: "It's warming. It's us. We're sure. It's bad. We can fix it."[3] Recognizing the increase of greenhouse gases, such as carbon dioxide, in Earth's atmosphere as a *problem*, however, is part of the ethical challenge of addressing the climate crisis.

Outright denial that the Earth is warming due to human activity is not a credible stance, though this view is widespread in the United States—a country with 4 percent of the Earth's population that consumes 16 percent of the Earth's energy.[4] Some climate skeptics counter that current atmospheric and meteorological measurements are natural fluctuations within "normal" parameters. Others argue that global warming is not a situation that can be changed. Ronald Heifetz's well-known distinction between technical work and adaptive work comes to mind. Technical work is required to apply known solutions to known problems, but "adaptive work is needed when one is faced with a situation that is not a problem but is instead a changed condition."[5] Is climate change a condition requiring adaptation or a problem requiring reparative action? It is both, and to insist otherwise can inhibit faithful ethical response. According to Willis Jenkins, "Climate change is not the sort of problem that can be solved."[6] By this, he meant that climate change is an "unprecedented problem"; part of the ethical task is interpreting and constructing it as a problem.[7]

Expanded and intentional vision is necessary to see anthropogenic climate change as a problem. The scope and scale of the effects of human-generated atmospheric greenhouse gases are global, cross-generational, and enmeshed in transnational

---

[3]Kimberly Nicholas, "Climate Science Basics," https://350.org/science/#warming.

[4]U.S. Energy Information Administration, "What Is the United States' Share of World Energy Consumption?" April 11, 2024, https://www.eia.gov/tools/faqs/faq.php?id=87. Data reflects usage in 2022.

[5]Gil Rendle, *Quietly Courageous: Leading the Church in a Changing World* (Rowman & Littlefield, 2019), 27–8, citing Heifetz.

[6]Willis Jenkins, *The Future of Ethics: Sustainability, Social Justice, and Religious Creativity* (Georgetown University Press, 2013), 17.

[7]Jenkins, 9.

systems of economics and governance. Furthermore, persons who benefit most from our current political and economic arrangements are incentivized to downplay climate change as a problem, even "funding 'climate skeptic' campaigns."[8] In 2015, Pope Francis observed, "Many of those who possess more resources and economic or political power seem mostly to be concerned with masking the problems or concealing their symptoms."[9] Christian morality cannot address what cannot be seen. Thus, Cynthia Moe-Lobeda began her constructive ethical approach to climate change by enabling "moral vision" that "extend[s] beyond interpersonal relationships to social structural and ecological relationships."[10] Viewing the climate crisis as an ethical problem allows us to see that it is caused by structural relationships with a history of injustice.

Understanding the climate crisis as an *ethical* problem requires an expansion of our understanding of ethics. The word *anthropogenic* points to humanity as the primary causal factor, but even those who see climate change as an ethical problem differ on who is to blame for the harm. The devastating effects of climate change are widespread, traumatic, diffuse, and ongoing, resisting easy identification with any specific weather event or human activity. The causal links of a warming planet are difficult to assess. When we recognize patterns of increased global temperatures, frequency and severity of storms and droughts, melting glaciers, and rising sea levels, we are flummoxed, finding fault with everyone yet no one in particular. Jenkins observed: "the accidental powers of humanity generate problems that exceed our moral imagination and defeat our abilities to take responsibility."[11] If ethics is understood as acting responsibly, how are we to take responsibility for climate change?

The moral uncertainty of climate action calls for new ways of doing ethics. Climate change "is a structurally 'wicked problem,' in that what would count as a solution is ecologically and culturally indeterminate."[12] Our lack of certainty about causes, culpability, and solutions complicates attempts at ethical action. Thus, "accepting the inevitable ambiguity of human action … and admitting the complexity inherent in local communities engaging planetary problems," Whitney A. Bauman and Kevin J. O'Brien proposed "an ethics of uncertainty, moving at the pace of ambiguity."[13] They argued against "simple or straightforward answers" to climate change and other aspects of environmental ethics.[14] Four uncertainties illustrate their method: justice,

---

[8]Sean McDonagh, "Part I: Catholic Teaching and the Environment," in *On Care for Our Common Home: The Encyclical of Pope Francis on the Environment, Laudato Si', with Commentary by Sean McDonagh*, by Catholic Church, Pope Francis, 3–142 (Orbis, 2016), 37.

[9]Pope Francis, *Laudato Si': On Care for Our Common Home* (Encyclical Letter, 2015), 26.

[10]Cynthia D. Moe-Lobeda, *Resisting Structural Evil: Love as Ecological-Economic Vocation* (Fortress, 2013), 61.

[11]Jenkins, *The Future of Ethics*, 17.

[12]Jenkins, 20.

[13]Whitney A. Bauman and Kevin J. O'Brien, *Environmental Ethics and Uncertainty: Wrestling with Wicked Problems* (Routledge, 2020), 2–3.

[14]Bauman and O'Brien, 5.

interconnectedness, urgency, and wonder.[15] As we shall see, a trauma-informed approach to the ethics of climate change wrestles with these uncertainties through historical clarity, grounded being, attentive presence, and meaningful participation, respectively.

We must be willing to risk action despite uncertainty and inexperience. Moral actors must try anyway, even though we have never encountered such a problem before. Part of "the task of religious ethics in climate change" is "to turn an inchoate crisis into a real problem" by insightful ethical interpretation and creative moral improvisation.[16] All people of good will, individually and collectively, can and should respond to the climate crisis through thoughtfully informed interpretation and action. Thus, Willis advocated that religious communities adopt pragmatic strategies for addressing climate change despite their technical "incompetence," claiming that "unprecedented problems can drive moral adaption."[17] Some churches have risen to this task.

Discussion Questions

1 What kind of problem has no solution? In two columns, write down ways in which climate change is and is not a problem that can be solved.

2 What kind of ethical problem has both no one and everyone to blame? In two columns, write down ways in which climate change is and is not an *ethical* problem.

3 What do you think about taking action despite moral uncertainty? If so many aspects of climate change are unknown or uncertain, how can action be justified? On the other hand, how can *inaction* be justified?

Ecclesial Witness

Churches can voice an important public witness, calling for changes in energy consumption and reparative action to address the climate crisis. In 1997, Ecumenical Patriarch Bartholomew, "The Green Patriarch" of the Orthodox Church, declared, "for humans to degrade the integrity of Earth by causing changes in its climate, by stripping the Earth of its natural forests, or destroying its wetlands … these are sins." Thus, he urged international cooperation: "we call on the world's leaders to take action to halt the destructive changes to the global climate that are being caused by human activity."[18] One month later, delegates from 160 countries adopted and signed the Kyoto Protocol to reduce global greenhouse gas emissions. Bartholomew's

---

[15]Bauman and O'Brien, 5–11.
[16]Jenkins, *The Future of Ethics*, 20.
[17]Jenkins, 23, 105.
[18]Greek Orthodox Archdiocese of America, "The Greenhouse Effect and the Threat of Climate Change," February 4, 2005, https://www.goarch.org/-/the-greenhouse-effect-and-the-threat-of-climate-change.

witness was not the first and will not be the last time that the church has taken a stance against climate change.

The United Methodist Church drew attention to the deleterious effects of burning coal in 1980, recognizing that the resulting elevated levels of carbon dioxide in the atmosphere "could seriously alter the environment."[19] By the late 1980s, several national churches were investigating climate change, and the United Church of Canada adopted a policy statement in 1989.[20] These initiatives paralleled the establishment of the Intergovernmental Panel on Climate Change (IPCC) by the United Nations and the World Meteorological Organization in 1988.[21] In 1993, the World Council of Churches (WCC) developed a study document, *Accelerated Climate Change: Sign of Peril, Test of Faith*, which the WCC central committee quickly endorsed in a public statement on climate change in 1994.[22] To coordinate their climate witness, a coalition of mainline, evangelical, Catholic, and Jewish organizations in the United States formed the National Religious Partnership for the Environment in 1993.[23] In 2006, a group of progressive evangelical leaders in the United States issued the Evangelical Climate Initiative, a brief but bold public witness that fomented no small amount of pushback within the mostly conservative community of US evangelicals.[24]

John Paul II was the first Roman Catholic pope to speak out about anthropogenic climate change as a problem of "crisis proportions" in his World Day of Peace Message in 1990.[25] Twenty-five years later, Pope Francis wrote an encyclical on the environment, *Laudato Si': On Care for Our Common Home*, in which he made it clear that environmental stewardship and care for the poor are interrelated. He declared, "Climate change is a global problem with grave implications: environmental, social, economic, political and for the distribution of goods. It represents one of the principal challenges facing humanity in our day."[26] His proposal for "an integral ecology" considers environmental, economic, and social dimensions of the climate crisis.[27] The Council of Bishops of The United Methodist Church offered a multidimensional analysis in 2009, recognizing climate change—along with

---

[19]"Energy Policy Statement," in *The Book of Resolutions of The United Methodist Church 1980*, 91–2 (UMPH, 1980).

[20]David G. Hallman, "Ecumenical Responses to Climate Change: A Summary of the History and Dynamics of Ecumenical Involvement in the Issue of Climate Change," *The Ecumenical Review* 49, no. 2 (1997): 134.

[21]Intergovernmental Panel on Climate Change (IPCC), "History of the IPCC," https://www.ipcc.ch/about/history/.

[22]Hallman, "Ecumenical Responses to Climate Change," 136.

[23]Becka A. Alper, "Sidebar: Involvement by Religious Groups in Debates over Climate Change," *Pew Research Center*, November 17, 2022, https://www.pewresearch.org/religion/2022/11/17/sidebar-involvement-by-religious-groups-in-debates-over-climate-change/.

[24]David P. Gushee, *The Future of Faith in American Politics: The Public Witness of the Evangelical Center* (Baylor University Press, 2008), 175.

[25]Pope John Paul II, "Peace with God the Creator, Peace with All of Creation," January 1, 1990, https://www.vatican.va/content/john-paul-ii/en/messages/peace/documents/hf_jp-ii_mes_19891208_xxiii-world-day-for-peace.html.

[26]Pope Francis, *Laudato Si'*, para. 25.

[27]Pope Francis, chapter 4.

poverty, disease, war, and violence—as interrelated threats to the well-being of God's creation.[28] In 2016, a United Methodist public policy resolution continued to draw attention to the problem and the social inequities underlying it. "We understand climate justice not simply as an environmental or economic concern but rather as a deep ethical and spiritual concern that the Church must address so that abundant life is ensured for our children and future generations."[29] The UMC's Social Principles warns about "global warming and climate change" and the role that burning fossil fuels plays in "the consequent warming of the earth's atmosphere."[30] This witness was rooted in longstanding Methodist concern about the environment—and about anthropogenic climate change, in particular.[31]

For churches proclaiming a witness on climate change, up-to-date scientific knowledge informs moral reasoning. Science is a form of reason, one of the standard sources of theological insight, along with scripture, tradition, and experience. For example, the UMC declared no contradiction between science and other sources of wisdom:

> We recognize science as a legitimate interpretation of God's natural world … We reexamine our ethical convictions as our understanding of the natural world increases. We find that as science expands human understanding of the natural world, our understanding of the mysteries of God's creation and word are enhanced … we also believe that theological understandings of human experience are crucial to a full understanding of the place of humanity in the universe. Science and theology are complementary rather than mutually incompatible.[32]

Thus, the debate is not whether to believe the findings of climate scientists. That question is already settled in the affirmative. The challenge is how to interpret the moral and theological implications of climate science in the context of comfort and privilege.

In 2016, the UMC explicitly rejected the legitimacy of climate skepticism, calling it a stance of the privileged to justify their own lifestyles: "Leaders in some developed nations continue to debate, from places of comfort and privilege, the 'reality' of a changing climate in order to perpetuate their polluting ways."[33] Thus, this church called out the chosen ignorance of privileged persons and their willful refusal to see climate change as an anthropogenic moral problem. Humanity's ability to pollute and change Earth's climate has outpaced humanity's ability (or willingness) to imagine that they could produce such global effects. Larry L. Rasmussen, a Lutheran ethicist, soberly reflected, "The rest of nature has no independent life apart from us now.

---

[28]Council of Bishops of the United Methodist Church, *God's Renewed Creation: Call to Hope and Action: Foundation Document*, 2009, https://web.archive.org/web/20220120212523/http://hopeandaction.org/main/wp-content/uploads/2010/03/Foundation-Doc-Eng-Handout-2-col.pdf.

[29]"Climate Change and the Church's Response," in *The Book of Resolutions of the United Methodist Church 2016*, 81–2 (UMPH, 2016).

[30]*The Book of Discipline of The United Methodist Church 2020/2024* (UMPH, 2024), 110–11.

[31]Darryl W. Stephens, *Reckoning Methodism: Mission and Division in the Public Church*, (Cascade, 2024), 140–69.

[32]*The Book of Discipline of The United Methodist Church 2016* (UMPH, 2016), ¶ 160.F.

[33]"Climate Change and the Church's Response," 81–2.

Nature belongs to the empire of its most aggressive species."[34] As it turns out, the climate crisis—including our ability to see climate change as a moral problem and to marshal efforts to address it—is inextricably bound up in structures of empire.

Discussion Questions

1 What does your religious tradition say about climate change? If your church or denomination does not have an official statement, borrow one from another tradition: Presbyterian Social Witness Policy, Evangelical Lutheran Social Statements, Pope Francis's *Laudato Si'*, and so on.

2 Why do some religious traditions reject the idea of anthropogenic climate change as an ethical problem? What theological convictions lead them to dismiss the concern or abdicate moral agency in responding to it?

Empire

Empire shapes moral actors and their worldviews, preventing the kind of collaborative positive social change required to recognize, interpret, and address the moral problem of climate change. As defined by Joerg Rieger, empire consists of "large and ever-changing conglomerates of power that are aimed at controlling all aspects of our lives."[35] Moe-Lobeda named these powers as they relate to the climate crisis—specifically, colonialism, ecological injustice, and neoliberal economic globalization.[36] In fact, argued George Handley, "we can read climate change denial as a form of neo-colonialism."[37] Insofar as Western Christianity has participated in and supported these social systems, it is also part of this empire, this regime of neo-colonialism. The same is true of racism, patriarchy, and a host of other oppressions.

Empire is an exercise of power impacting both colonizer and colonized, albeit in drastically different ways. The United Methodist Social Principles document defines colonialism and neocolonialism:

> Colonialism refers to the practice of establishing full or partial control of other countries, tribes, and peoples through conquest and exploitation. Neocolonialism continues the historic legacy of colonialism by maintaining economic, political, and social control of formerly colonized nations and peoples.[38]

This statement acknowledges the continued impact of these legacies on the denomination's worldwide fellowship and the fact that United Methodism includes

---

[34]Larry L. Rasmussen, "Doing Our First Works Over," *Journal of Lutheran Ethics*, April 1, 2009, https://www.elca.org/JLE/Articles/385#_ednref6.

[35]Joerg Rieger, *Christ and Empire: From Paul to Postcolonial Times* (Fortress, 2007), vii.

[36]Moe-Lobeda, *Resisting Structural Evil*, 27.

[37]George B. Handley, "What Else Is New?: Toward a Postcolonial Christian Theology for the Anthropocene," *Religions* 11, no. 5 (2020): 225, https://doi.org/10.3390/rel11050225.

[38]*The Book of Discipline of The United Methodist Church 2020/2024*, 126.

both the colonizers and the colonized. The church itself is complicit: "We recognize that far from being innocent bystanders, the church has often been deeply involved in colonialism and neocolonialism." Then, the statement calls for education, repentance, and reparation—including "active support for sustainable development initiatives."[39] This is an important witness—and well-intentioned. However, as recent studies in diakonia and mission reveal, the path of "development" is not necessarily empowering to colonized peoples or the lands they inhabit.[40] The UMC's Social Principles document does not address the way in which empire malforms the moral imaginations of the colonizers.

Empire keeps moral actors ignorant and unaware of their culpability, complicity, and potential role in addressing systemic injustices. Mary Elizabeth Moore stated the problem succinctly:

> One of the profound challenges for addressing climate crises is the inadequacy of dominant theologies and world views, intertwined with inadequate relational patterns, as in colonial structures, patterns of dominance of some people over others, emphases on individualism and progress, and the dominance of humans over the land and sea.[41]

To the extent that they uphold climate-damaging structures and practices, Western forms of democracy, capitalism, and Christianity obfuscate rather than elucidate climate change as a moral problem. According to Moe-Lobeda, we suffer "moral oblivion," maintained by structures of power that "normalize and rationalize existing social and ecological conditions."[42] For example, when global capitalism is seen as an inherent feature of modern life, leaders are tempted to adapt to the condition rather than seek solutions. Thus, empire creates a "hegemonic vision" composed of "socially constructed perceptions and assumptions" about reality, possibility, and morality.[43]

Significant factors contributing to impaired moral vision are individualism and racism. The individualistic values and assumptions of Western politics, global capitalism, and Christianity make it difficult to recognize, interpret, and respond to complex, structural problems.[44] Political formation that focuses solely on the individual as a citizen, with certain rights and responsibilities, renders unaccountable the failings of society. Economic formation that focuses solely on the individual as a consumer, with free choice and opportunity, ignores the environmental costs of mass

---

[39]*The Book of Discipline of The United Methodist Church 2020/2024*, 126.

[40]The concept of *conviviality* recenters relationships of trust within cultures overrun by the divisions and individualism created by neoliberal, globalized market economies, offering a liberative corrective to the development model of diakonia. World Council of Churches and ACT Alliance, *Called to Transformation: Ecumenical Diakonia* (WCC, 2022), 29–30. For discussion, see Chapter 1.4.

[41]Mary Elizabeth Moore, "Responding to a Weeping Planet: Practical Theology as a Discipline Called by Crisis," *Religions* 13, no. 3 (2022): 244, 4, https://doi.org/10.3390/rel13030244.

[42]Moe-Lobeda, *Resisting Structural Evil*, 87.

[43]Moe-Lobeda, 88.

[44]See, for example, discussion of "theories of individual autonomy and individual well-being … leading to the overtaking of land for individual gain or the economic gain of industrialists" in Moore, "Responding to a Weeping Planet," 3.

overconsumption. Theology that teaches sin and salvation as issues solely between the individual and God has little to say about the human family and the renewal of creation. In its own distinct way, white racism also contributes to moral blindness, or what Emilie Townes more pointedly termed "willful oblivion."[45] Here, the refusal to recognize or acknowledge race as a social and cultural reality serves to protect some persons to the detriment of others. This "uninterrogated coloredness" is part of the "fantastic hegemonic imagination" identified by Townes.[46] Each of these moral malformations hides power differentials, collective agency, and structural injustice.

This hegemonic imagination prevents people from recognizing the climate crisis as a problem and contributes to continued destruction. Moe-Lobeda identified multiple factors distorting our moral vision, including "privatized morality and the blinders of charity"; self-deception; "denial, guilt, grief"; and "despair or hopelessness and perceived powerlessness."[47] Each of these factors, familiar to persons who work with victim-survivors of trauma, complicates moral response to the climate crisis. The power of empire distorts the moral vision of everyone involved—victims, perpetrators, bystanders—drawing no distinctions. Townes observed, "the fantastic hegemonic imagination is in all of us."[48] When empire's hegemonic vision impairs moral vision, how can we respond to the problem?

To overcome moral oblivion, Moe-Lobeda advocated for "a profound shift in moral consciousness."[49] She named three necessary facets to this shift: structural, relational, and positional. We must learn to "perceive the world as interconnected"; "to perceive reality through the narratives and experiences of subjugated people and peoples"; and to locate ourselves within rather than outside of the rest of God's creation.[50] The lens of social ethics, attuned to the role of institutions and the power of empire, helps with the first. Liberation and feminist theologies help with the second. The third requires decentering the human in our moral and political deliberations. Taken together, this multifaceted moral shift means relating to God, self, neighbor, and the cosmos in new ways. Thus, Rasmussen observed, "We do not save the planet, the planet saves us—this is now the starting point ... The planet's well-being is primary; human well-being is derivative. That is the 'flip' we must make."[51] The crisis of climate change awakens us to the new reality that we must do Christian ethics differently—including the way we bear witness through a trauma-informed approach to Christian ethics.[52]

---

[45]Emilie M. Townes, *Womanist Ethics and the Cultural Production of Evil* (Palgrave Macmillan, 2006), 58.

[46]Townes, 21, 60.

[47]Moe-Lobeda, *Resisting Structural Evil*, 90–106. She names eight factors: "privatized morality and the blinders of charity"; "blessings veiling stolen goods"; "denial, guilt, grief"; "despair or hopelessness and perceived powerlessness"; "unconscious conformity"; "corporate investment in maintaining public moral oblivion"; "uncritical belief in 'growth' as good"; and "moral oblivion embedded in practice."

[48]Townes, *Womanist Ethics*, 21.

[49]Moe-Lobeda, *Resisting Structural Evil*, 119.

[50]Moe-Lobeda, 120.

[51]Rasmussen, "Doing Our First Works Over."

[52]Moe-Lobeda, *Resisting Structural Evil*, 128. She recommended the practice of "ecological-economic-justice literacy," an approach that complements a trauma-informed approach to Christian ethics.

Discussion Questions

1 Structures of empire surround us daily and are difficult to perceive. To gain a clearer perspective, talk with someone from a different culture, race, ethnicity, or nationality. What are you able to discover about empire?

2 How do the ideals of individualism and consumerism shape or distort your ability to understand climate change as a moral problem?

Bearing Witness to Creation

Bearing witness in relation to the Earth is premised on a recognition of the cosmos as God's good creation, capable of receiving, reflecting, and participating in love, justice, and solidarity. Each moment of bearing witness to the traumatic suffering of creation due to climate change challenges the ethics of empire and opens new possibilities for relating to the community of the cosmos (Table 3.2.1).

The hope of resistance to climate violence is grounded in the human capacity to transcend traumatic ruptures of time, space, and community, inviting alternative ways of relating. According to Catholic Social Teaching, only humanity has a "capacity for God"; that is an openness to transcendence.[53] However, Catholic Social Teaching remains anthropocentric, built on an ontological hierarchy that inhibits our ability to see ourselves as part of a creation that is equally valued by God.[54] To be human is to have the capacity to recognize the self in relation to others and others as subjects equal to oneself. The cosmos is God's good creation, bestowed with worth by God. Marjorie Suchocki likewise named the ability to transcend oneself and one's circumstances as a defining feature of humanity.[55] Thus, process theology provides a helpful way to speak about the transcendent and morality while considering the social nature of humanity and the interconnectedness of the natural world.

Understanding oneself in relation to the rest of creation allows for the possibility of morality by providing meaningful choice in relation to climate violence. According to Suchocki, evil is not sin if there is no ability to transcend one's violent tendencies.[56] The reverse is also true. The ability to recognize, remember, empathize, and imagine implicates one in an interconnected world of sin and allows for a moral response. In other words, these four modes of transcendence enable human moral agency. Anthropogenic climate change can be named sinful, unjust, and immoral because of the human ability to *recognize* all of creation as equally good and created by God,

---

[53]Pontifical Council for Justice and Peace, *Compendium of the Social Doctrine of the Church* (USCCB, 2004), paras. 109, 130.

[54]For example, Pontifical Council for Justice and Peace, para. 108. For brief discussions, see McDonagh, "Part I: Catholic Teaching and the Environment," 18–19; and Kevin J. O'Brien, "The Scales Integral to Ecology: Hierarchies in Laudato Si' and Christian Ecological Ethics," *Religions* 10, no. 9 (2019): 511, https://doi.org/10.3390/rel10090511.

[55]Marjorie Hewitt Suchocki, *The Fall to Violence: Original Sin in Relational Theology* (Continuum, 1994), 94.

[56]Suchocki, 94.

TABLE 3.2.1 *Bearing Witness to Non-human Creation*

Perspectival Moment	Mode of Transcendence	Moral Theme	Practice of Social Action	Creation Wisdom (anti-empire)
I. Existence	recognition	dignity	grounded being	intrinsic worth, interrelatedness, awe
II. Present	empathy	love	attentive presence	creatureliness, non-human agency, insistence
III. Past	memory	justice	historical clarity	systemic perspective, countermemory
IV. Future	imagination	solidarity	meaningful participation	wonder, repair, full flourishing of creation

empathize with the suffering of the non-human world, *remember* and interpret the wider circumstances causing the climate crisis, and *imagine* more just relationships between humanity and the rest of creation. Thus, the ability to transcend our violent tendencies supplies both a moral possibility and a moral imperative in response to climate change.

Bearing witness to the suffering of creation requires a trauma-informed approach, aligning moral themes and practices of social action with each mode of transcendence (Table 3.2.1). Reckoning with our created existence, the mode of *recognition* elicits awareness of our common human dignity and the goodness of creation, leading to a practice of grounded being. Reckoning with the present, *empathy* enables our capacity for love of God, self, and neighbor (including non-human creation), leading to a practice of attentive presence. Reckoning with the past, *memory* enables our capacity for justice, seeing patterns and roots of climate violence, leading to a practice of historical clarity. Reckoning with the future, *imagination* enables our capacity for solidarity with victim-survivors of trauma, leading to a practice of meaningful participation in processes of liberation and the full flourishing of all creation. A trauma-informed approach to anthropogenic climate change must therefore *realize* the widespread traumatic suffering in creation, *recognize* the signs and symptoms of the trauma of climate violence, *respond* to this suffering by putting knowledge into action, and *resist* causing further harm to each other and the world in which we live.

An ethical approach does not have to be specifically trauma-informed to resonate with these moments of bearing witness. For example, Mary Elizabeth Moore articulated "four practices that are important to reshaping and deepening practical wisdom for ecological justice: attending, searching, imagining, and communal living and acting."[57] Moore's practices integrate the four social actions identified

---

[57]Moore, "Responding to a Weeping Planet," 9.

in Table 3.2.1. Her practice of "attending" involves reverence for the Earth, and "searching" requires "an attitude of openness, curiosity, and humility" toward the Earth. Both practices overlap with my descriptions of grounded being and attentive presence. Moore's practice of "imagining" involves both historical clarity (reconstructing narratives) as well as meaningful participation in a new future, and "communal living and acting" invokes memory as well as meaningful participation in new forms of community.[58]

From a Wesleyan perspective, bearing witness to creation involves responding to and participating in God's creating, redeeming, and sustaining grace.[59] The first moment recognizes the dignity of humanity and the intrinsic worth of the natural world as grounded in the goodness of creation and God's bestowed worth—an experience of prevenient, creating grace. The second moment, sparked by convicting grace, consists of a loving, attentive presence as we become aware of God's redemptive activity. In this moment, God provokes in us humility (initial repentance) and empathy for the suffering world around us. In the third moment, we respond to justifying grace, fully desiring to participate in God's redemptive activity. Through historical clarity, we reckon with our past, name our complicity in anthropogenic climate change, and respond with repentance in light of God's justice and forgiveness. In the fourth moment, we respond to God's sustaining, sanctifying grace by imagining God's good future in solidarity with the Earth. We find meaningful participation in this future of reconciliation and *shalom* by challenging and redressing structures of climate violence so that all creation may flourish.

Discussion Questions

1   Spend fifteen minutes in nature—uninterrupted and undistracted. Be attuned to all your senses. What do you notice about the flora, fauna, and geology around you?

2   Have you tried to bear witness to the suffering of animals, plants, or the Earth itself? If so, what was it like? If not, what prevents you?

Recognition and Dignity

A trauma-informed response to climate change begins by realizing the widespread existence of traumatic suffering in the world we inhabit. To overcome the relational barriers preventing us from realizing non-human suffering, we must expand the concept of human dignity rooted in the *imago Dei* to recognize the intrinsic worth of all of creation. Humans are not set apart from creation; we participate in an

---

[58]Moore, 9–12.

[59]I suggest the categories *creating, redeeming,* and *sustaining* grace (to parallel and augment prevenient, justifying, and sanctifying grace) as a way of expanding John Wesley's Scripture Way of Salvation to include the divine work in all of creation. Redeeming grace could also be termed renewing grace; sustaining grace could also be called reconciling grace, as evident in 2 Corinthians 5:17–19. See Table 2.1.1 and Theodore Runyon, *The New Creation* (Abingdon, 1998), 222.

interconnected world. Reckoning with created existence expands our moral vision to see God in all that God has made and to be open to the suffering and agency of non-human creation.

Recognizing ourselves and everything in the cosmos as created by God grounds us in the shared experience of being and being in relation to God. The United Methodist Social Principles begins with an affirmation, "all creation belongs to God," recognizing "that we are part of complex ecosystems, all valued by God."[60] Shared human dignity arises from creation: God called humanity "very good." God's love bestows inestimable worth on each person. Yet, God also called every other part of creation "good." And when God arrived incarnate on Earth, it was not just humanity God came to save: "For God so loved the world [*kosmon*] that he gave his only Son" (Jn 3:16). God so loved *the cosmos*. Thus, the UMC asserts: "Created in God's image to live in covenant with God and the world, we honor the dignity of all beings and affirm the goodness of life."[61] The interrelatedness of creation becomes apparent as we recognize ourselves as participants in—rather than exceptional to—created existence.

To realize the widespread traumatic effects of climate change on non-human creation, we must recognize that non-human creation is capable of suffering. For example, Stef Craps, observing a post-humanist turn in trauma studies, noted "attempts to reconceptualize trauma in non-anthropocentric terms and to acknowledge the interconnectedness and entanglement of human and non-human traumas."[62] Likewise, Storm Swain developed an ecological pastoral theology focused on "the ecological body that continues to suffer."[63] Recognizing that the Earth can suffer trauma opens the possibility of bearing witness to non-human creation.

To bear witness to creation's suffering, we must call out forms of "hegemonic vision" that stand in our way. It is a well-worn strategy of powerful groups to assert their dominance over others by dehumanizing them. For example, in his autobiography, Howard Thurman shared a childhood story of being attacked with a pin by a white girl. When he recoiled, she responded, "Oh, Howard, that didn't hurt you! You can't feel!"[64] White racism taught that Black children were not human enough to feel pain, imposing a hegemonic vision outrightly denying Thurman's ability to suffer. Empire often takes the form of racism. Dehumanization usually takes the rhetorical form of putting vulnerable populations in closer proximity to animals, with the assumption that non-human creation cannot suffer pain. Paradoxically, when one is recognized as a victim of trauma, one's agency is often dismissed with the assumption that to be a victim is to be helpless.[65] Victimhood—and bearing

---

[60]*The Book of Discipline of the United Methodist Church 2020/2024*, 109.

[61]*The Book of Discipline of the United Methodist Church 2020/2024*, 107.

[62]Stef Craps, "Climate Trauma," in *The Routledge Companion to Literature and Trauma*, ed. Colin Davis and Hanna Meretoja, 281 (Routledge, 2020).

[63]Storm Swain, "Climate Change and Pastoral Theology," in *T&T Clark Handbook of Christian Theology and Climate Change*, ed. Ernst Conradie and Hilda Koster, 616 (Bloomsbury, 2020).

[64]Howard Thurman, *With Head and Heart: The Autobiography of Howard Thurman* (Harcourt Brace Jovanovich, 1981), 12.

[65]For discussion of the agency of Black women victim-survivors, see Traci C. West, *Wounds of the Spirit: Black Women, Violence, and Resistance Ethics* (New York University Press, 1999), 57.

witness to victimhood—whether human or non-human, is a dangerous location in the context of empire. Recognizing creation as inherently worthy and asserting the agency of victim-survivors require resistance to empire.

Recognizing human interrelatedness with the cosmos expands our moral vision, rendering insufficient traditional understandings of the *imago Dei*. Sallie McFague suggested that ignoring our interrelatedness to the rest of creation provides an "earthly notion of sin"—namely "the refusal to accept our place."[66] The claim that humans are created in the image of God too often functions anthropocentrically, serving both to emphasize humanity's close relation to God and to denigrate the rest of creation. Michael Northcott named this problem as a root sin: "At the heart of the pathology of ecological crisis is the refusal of modern humans to see themselves as creatures, contingently embedded in networks of relationships with other creatures, and with the Creator."[67] Thus, an anthropocentric rendering of the *imago Dei* fuels the idea of "human exceptionalism" in relation to the cosmos.[68] Human exceptionalism then limits our understanding of the dignity and goodness of the rest of creation.

If humanity is to cooperate with the rest of creation to address climate change, we must recognize creation's dignity and agency. For example, contemplating the question, "Who is my neighbor?" H. Richard Niebuhr suggested that *neighbor* includes not only humanity here and now but also "the unborn generations who will bear the consequences of our failures" as well as "animal and inorganic being, all that participates in being."[69] Furthermore, we must welcome these neighbors as partners rather than only wards of our care. The Social Principles document states that "every part of creation" has a role "in healing the whole"—not only humans but also "other sentient and non-sentient beings."[70] Only then can we answer the call "to live in right relationship with the Creator and with the whole of God's creation."[71] We must recognize non-human creation as having intrinsic rather than instrumental worth.

Expanding the notion of *dignity* to encompass the intrinsic goodness of all creation may change the way we see God and ourselves. "Awakening humans to our intrinsic earthiness is essential for a change of perspective," asserted Pamela R. McCarroll.[72] To change the way we see non-human creation, McFague offered the metaphor of Earth as body of God.[73] If we understood incarnation as the divine-self residing *in* creation (panentheism), presumably humanity would not only see the intrinsic worth of non-human creation but also develop a radically expansive view of God. John Wesley wrote provocatively along these lines:

---

[66]Sallie McFague, *The Body of God: An Ecological Theology* (Augsburg Fortress, 1993), 112–13.

[67]Michael S. Northcott, *A Moral Climate: The Ethics of Global Warming* (Orbis, 2007), 16.

[68]Pamela R. McCarroll, "Embodying Theology: Trauma Theory, Climate Change, Pastoral and Practical Theology," *Religions* 13, no. 4 (2022): 294, https://doi.org/10.3390/rel13040294.

[69]H. Richard Niebuhr, with Daniel Day Williams and James M. Gustafson, *The Purpose of the Church and Its Ministry: Reflections on the Aims of Theological Education* (Harper & Brothers, 1956), 38.

[70]*The Book of Discipline of the United Methodist Church 2020/2024*, 109.

[71]*The Book of Discipline of the United Methodist Church 2020/2024*, 109.

[72]McCarroll, "Embodying Theology," 6.

[73]McFague, *The Body of God*. See discussion in Danielle Elizabeth Tumminio Hansen, "The Body of God, Sexually Violated: A Trauma-Informed Reading of the Climate Crisis," *Religions* 13, no. 3 (2022): 249, https://doi.org/10.3390/rel13030249.

The great lesson that our blessed Lord inculcates here ... is that God is in all things, and that we are to see the Creator in the glass of every creature; that we should use and look upon nothing as separate from God ... who pervades and actuates the whole created frame, and is, in a true sense, the soul of the universe.[74]

If God is in all things, then all things can tell us something about God—an idea closely associated with appeals to "traditional wisdom."

Discussion Questions

1   Recognizing the inherent worth and dignity of all of creation—that God called it all "good"—challenges us to expand our understanding of the image of God. What ethical difference does it make to consider every part of creation as valued by God and potentially revealing something about God?

2   What do you know about God through the world around you? Describe a time you have sensed God in nature.

3   Identify as many images of and metaphors for God in the Bible as you can. Which of them expands beyond the human?

From Traditional Wisdom to Creation Wisdom

What is traditional wisdom and how can it help address the climate crisis? So-called "traditional wisdom" about nature is attributed to Indigenous peoples, who are presumed by colonizers to have a closer relationship to the Earth. However, does *traditional wisdom* really belong only to Indigenous peoples, or is it universally accessible? This question is one of epistemology, the study of how we know what we know. A critical examination of the concept exposes hierarchical structures of empire that lessen or erase the dignity of colonized communities and, consequently, non-human creation as well.

The concept of *traditional wisdom* is a colonizing project. It is often contrasted to or considered complementary to knowledge acquired through science, thereby distancing colonized peoples from the truths known by Western civilization. For example, the UMC "affirm[s] the value of science and reason in providing deeper understandings of the origins and functioning of the cosmos" and "also affirm[s] the traditional wisdom found within indigenous communities."[75] This statement also assumes that such wisdom has a positive moral function in relation to non-human creation. For example, the Social Principles document recognizes "indigenous and other sources of communal wisdom" as inherently calling "for air, land, and water to be treated with profound respect."[76] It affirms "the emphasis that native and first peoples have placed on living in harmony and balance with the earth and other

---

[74]*The Book of Discipline of the United Methodist Church 2020/2024*, 109.
[75]*The Book of Discipline of the United Methodist Church 2020/2024*, 114–15.
[76]*The Book of Discipline of the United Methodist Church 2020/2024*, 112.

animals as well as the need to protect the air, land and water."[77] However, by placing colonized people in closer relationship to the Earth, the UMC reinforces a hierarchy (the Great Chain of Being) in which the colonizers understand themselves to be naturally superior to Indigenous persons, animals, plants, and inanimate objects. Thus, when the Social Principles "affirm the wisdom and agency of indigenous peoples and marginalized populations" in determining their own needs in relation to the environment, the gesture sounds paternalistic rather than liberating.

Such a projection of earthy knowledge and kinship onto Indigenous persons and their cultures neither liberates nor edifies. According to Jace Weaver, founding Director of the Institute of Native American Studies at the University of Georgia, such idealization "denies Indian personhood" and actually "contributes to the exploitation of Natives."[78] Thus, uncritical appeals to "traditional wisdom" serve to "other" Indigenous persons and their communities rather than encountering them as complicated moral agents and equal members church and society. While it is generally true that post-industrial societies are less aware of and attuned to their natural environments, romanticizing the relationships that Indigenous and pre-industrial communities have with nature does not allow for mutual learning. Instead of a colonialist view of "traditional wisdom," a more respectful—and educative—approach is for former colonizers to engage Indigenous peoples as equals, collaborators in shared moral projects addressing the problem of climate change.[79] "Traditional wisdom" could be recast, not as "other" but rather as a universally accessible form of practical wisdom attuned to creation.

Creation wisdom refers to our capacity for holistic ways of knowing about ourselves and the rest of the cosmos. Moore offered a definition: "practical wisdom [*phronesis*] is the embodied, accumulating knowledge and ethical insight that arise from human and creaturely experience of the world and the numinous."[80] In this definition, it is our embodied creatureliness that gives us insight into the divine. This definition also resists dualistic notions of mind versus body, spiritual versus material, animal versus human, and the like. Significant features of creation wisdom include an awareness of the interconnectedness of all of creation, a prioritizing of community (in contrast to the neoliberal focus on the individual), practices of learning from the created world (including embodied knowledge), and a sense of awe and recognition of the divine within all of creation. Ecowomanism draws on a specific form of creation wisdom: "the eco-wisdom of women of colour, specifically women of African descent."[81] A broadened understanding of wisdom is part of what Moe-Lobeda described as "critical mystical vision," which includes "seeing ever more fully the sacred Spirit of life coursing throughout creation."[82] Such vision requires "an epistemological realignment from modernity's assumptions regarding knowledge";

---

[77]*The Book of Discipline of the United Methodist Church 2020/2024*, 115.
[78]Jace Weaver, "Introduction," in *Defending Mother Earth: Native American Perspectives on Environmental Justice*, ed. Jace Weaver, 1–28 (Orbis, 1996), 4.
[79]For example, see Mary Elizabeth Moore, *Ministering with the Earth* (Chalice, 1998), 74–7. Also, Moore, "Responding to a Weeping Planet," 7–9.
[80]Moore, "Responding to a Weeping Planet," 5.
[81]Melanie L. Harris, "Doing Justice to Issues of Race?" in *T&T Clark Handbook of Christian Theology and Climate Change*, ed. Ernst Conradie and Hilda Koster, 659–62 (Bloomsbury, 2020), 660.
[82]Moe-Lobeda, *Resisting Structural Evil*, 114.

for many Christians, this knowledge derives from four classical sources: scripture, tradition, experience, and reason.[83] To move beyond anthropocentrism, Moe-Lobeda proposed "a fifth source: *other-than-human voices of the Earth*."[84] I interpret this source as pointing to a universally accessible form of practical wisdom.

Some persons and cultures are more attuned to learning from non-human creation than others. In relation to cultures shaped by overconsumption and empire, Moe-Lobeda claimed, "Moral knowing informed by Earth is unchartered epistemological terrain."[85] While it may be unchartered, it is not absent. Alternative medicine, folk ways, and many other expressions of creation wisdom can be found in the margins of empire. Indigenous cultures and persons of color do not have some special connection to the Earth through so-called traditional wisdom; rather, the systems and mindsets of empire dull the senses. The post-Enlightenment disenchantment of the universe—as imagined and experienced through the lens empire—is a cultural malady in need of healing. Science does not need to be pitted against a hypothesized traditional wisdom, as if only one way of seeing the world could be true. Nor is the critical mode of scientific inquiry a more mature form of culture, as if learning from (rather than about) nature were simply naïve. In the conceptual language of Paul Ricoeur, we can strive for a post-critical naïveté, valuing creation wisdom for the truths it reveals alongside what we know through science.

Every culture has stories of success and failure in loving God's good Earth. Even within white US culture, which I share with Moore and Moe-Lobeda, I find guidance for listening to and with non-human creation: "The ways and wisdom of the more-than-human world provide a template for healthy communication: cooperation, collaboration, reciprocity, complementarity, and generosity. This guidance is available anywhere we find ourselves, even in the starkest environments: we have merely to pay attention, look, and listen."[86] In addition to the wisdom of the world around us, we need to relearn how to listen to the wisdom within us. Embodied knowledge is too little valued and heeded within my culture, one that tends to prioritize abstract, objective viewpoints rather than the particularity of ourselves in this time and place as created beings. To value the insights of creation wisdom, each cultural tradition must be engaged through both critical and appreciative inquiry.

A culture of empire that has lost a sense of connection to the rest of creation can learn through dialogue with other cultures to renounce its colonialist ways. Melanie Harris developed a critical and constructive contribution to conversations about climate change by focusing on ecowomanist wisdom. Harris's project of ecowomanism resists "the logic of domination" characteristic of a colonialist perspective, instead offering "a holistic perspective of all creation" that "emphasizes the relationality between parts of nature."[87] Where Moore described a universal, human capacity,

---

[83]Moe-Lobeda, 243.

[84]Moe-Lobeda, 243, original emphasis.

[85]Moe-Lobeda, 243.

[86]Sharon Browning, Donna Duffey, Fred Magondu, John A. Moore, and Patricia A. Way, *The Little Book of Listening: Listening as a Radical Act of Love, Justice, Healing, and Transformation* (Good Books, 2024), 13.

[87]Melanie L. Harris, "Ecowomanist Wisdom: Encountering Earth and Spirit," in *Planetary Solidarity: Global Women's Voices on Christian Doctrine and Climate Justice*, ed. Grace Ji-Sun Kim and Hilda P. Koster, 239–48 (Fortress, 2017), 242–3.

Harris claimed an epistemology centered on "black women's culture," drawing on "African religious cosmologies … as a mode of resistance to systems of domination inherent in empire."[88] Identifying the characteristics and sources of creation wisdom in each culture—including white US culture—can contribute to an enhanced ethic of response to climate change.

Discussion Questions

1   Consider the idea of *traditional wisdom*. What exotic images come to mind? Now, consider the traditional wisdom of your own family and culture. What similarities and differences do you observe?

2   Animals and plants are attuned and responsive to the world around them, communicating and caring for each other. Consider a pet, other animal, or plant that you know. What knowledge or wisdom can you glean from them?

Empathy and Love

Debate, denial, and despondency are themselves evidence that the climate crisis is experienced traumatically by many people. McCarroll observed that polarized political discourse, climate denial and indifference, and intellectualizing can all be identified as "fight, flight, fright and freeze trauma responses."[89] These responses are the body's survival mechanisms when confronted with existential threat—even threat that we pose to ourselves. One of the complicating aspects of empathetically attending to the suffering of creation is the realization that humanity is both oppressor and victim. Anthropogenic climate change is of our own making, and we suffer trauma because of it. When we bear witness to the traumatic suffering of God's creation, we inescapably bear witness to our own wounds that are too deep to acknowledge otherwise.

Embodied knowledge, a mode of creation wisdom, allows us to bear witness to ourselves and the suffering world in which we are interconnected. Besser van der Kolk emphasized the embodied effects of trauma in his book titled *The Body Keeps the Score*. Our bodies register our traumas long before we are cognitively aware of them. Turning to McCarroll: "Our bodies hold a kind of knowing, the reclamation of which leans towards healing."[90] Integrating what we know intellectually with what our bodies know and bearing witness to the same in the bodies (both animate and inanimate) around us is part of the process of recovery from the trauma of climate change. Is this evidence of vicarious trauma, a result of human empathy for creation's traumatic suffering? Or, is it something more existential? McCarroll insightfully remarked, "What trauma theory helps us notice is that beneath the multivalent ways trauma responses manifest and wreak havoc is a deeper fear from which we are

---

[88]Harris, 240 and 245.
[89]McCarroll, "Embodying Theology," 4.
[90]McCarroll, 6.

desperate to escape—a fear of our own creatureliness, vulnerability, dependence and finitude."[91] We must overcome our fear about being human creatures in order to truly love ourselves and to love our non-human neighbors. Only then will we be able to see God revealed in creation and learn from creation wisdom and God's self-revelation through creation.

Attentive presence to God's created world is necessary for this form of practical wisdom. McFague invoked the term *attention epistemology* to describe this source of embodied knowing.[92] Attentiveness is a form of love, allowing us to know the suffering and trauma of the Earth due to climate change. McFague also asserted, "The distinctive characteristic of Christian embodiment is its focus on oppressed, vulnerable, suffering *bodies*, those who are in pain due to the indifference or greed of the more powerful."[93] A trauma-informed Christian ethic must therefore attend to suffering. We become aware of the interconnectedness of all of creation: "We recognize we are interconnected members of complex ecosystems, intricate webs of life, all of which have their origins in God's gracious act of creation."[94] When we bear witness to the suffering of others, when we pay attention to the suffering of the Earth, when we become aware of the traumatic score that our own bodies keep— this is the beginning of practical, creation wisdom.

Empathy is the mode of transcendence that allows relationships between subjects. "By perceiving the root problem as fear (rather than resistance and refusal, for example) and tapping into compassion, we can break the cyclical hold of trauma reactivity in our relating and existing."[95] The type of empathy required is not the affect-driven failure to make hard decisions in a hostile environment while caving into other people's emotional demands.[96] Nor is it a debilitating compassion in which we take on the feelings of others mired in the depths of trauma, vicariously fighting, fleeing, or freezing alongside them. Rather, empathy is a holistic endeavor in which affect informs reason and reason disciplines affect. According to Suchocki, "self-transcendence through empathy emerges when one relates to the other as the related other who is also a subject."[97] Empathy for non-human creation recognizes the agency of all parts of creation. In relation to the created world, "Love reflects our interconnectivity with other beings."[98] Empathy then allows us to love the cosmos that God so loves.

Love expressed through attentive presence is a bulwark against the reactionary tugs of urgency when bearing witness to this imperiled Earth. Bauman and O'Brien named urgency as one of four significant uncertainties in the work of climate ethics.[99] Urgency can be thought of as a tyranny of the now. There is no time for studied

---

[91]McCarroll, 7.

[92]McFague, *The Body of God*, 49–54.

[93]McFague, 164, original emphasis.

[94]*The Book of Discipline of The United Methodist Church 2020/2024*, 110.

[95]McCarroll, "Embodying Theology," 8.

[96]Edwin H. Friedman, *A Failure of Nerve: Leadership in the Age of the Quick Fix*, rev. ed. (Church Publishing, 2017), 141–67.

[97]Suchocki, *The Fall to Violence*, 40.

[98]McCarroll, "Embodying Theology," 7.

[99]Bauman and O'Brien, *Environmental Ethics and Uncertainty*, 5–11.

reflection of the past and no luxury of planning for the future. Something that is urgent demands all our attention in the present moment. However, for a victim-survivor of trauma, there is only the now. A sense of urgency has little meaning when a traumatic past constantly interrupts the present and persistently impedes the ability to imagine a different future. For a body triggered into survival mode, everything is urgent, and yet no one action takes priority. Survival in the moment is the only priority, the only reality experienced during trauma response. Even when we are not in the throes of survival mode, the structures of modernity simulate this debilitating sense of urgency. The demands of a digitized culture compound the trauma responses we already experience. An incessant news cycle, technology that constantly tracks our whereabouts, a global economy—all these features of our world disrupt natural rhythms of bodies and lifecycles. The urgent exigencies of modern existence claw at the attention we might otherwise spend being attentive to the world around us and to the bodies we are. Empire does not play well with nature.

Natural rhythms are more accurately described as insistent rather than urgent. The insistence of nature during the climate crisis, which requires both long-term solutions and immediate action, challenges our inherited notions of agency and the image of God. One way of constructively responding to the uncertainty of urgency is bearing witness to ourselves and our environment. Whether urgency is imposed by economic and political structures or by traumatic memories, we can ground ourselves in a moment of attentive presence to the insistent patterns of nature. This expression of love can create a sense of safety amid the urgent threats demanding our attention. We may still harbor uncertainties—and we most definitely will not be certain about how to respond to the climate crisis—but we will be fully present and in relationship with others. Then, we may be ready to reckon with our past on the way to imagining a better future.

Discussion Questions

1   How does your embodied knowledge inform you about your moods, desires, and anxieties? Observe the embodied knowledge of a pet or other animal. How do their bodies help them survive and thrive?

2   There is a tension between acting on the urgency of the climate crisis and slowing down to feel the natural rhythms of creation. Both are necessary. How do you navigate this tension?

Memory and Justice

Memory allows us to transcend the present by reckoning with the past causes of the climate-induced suffering we bear witness to today. A trauma-informed approach to the climate crisis seeks to right past harms and restore broken relationships with non-human creation. Thus, historical clarity about anthropogenic climate change equips us to address the climate crisis from a standpoint of justice—albeit a greatly expanded notion of justice.

We gain historical clarity about climate trauma by remembering the interconnectedness of economic, political, and environmental actions. Since the problem of climate change involves multiple systems, such as the economy and government, loving our non-human neighbors requires a systemic perspective. According to Moe-Lobeda, "the norm of neighbor love includes the norm of justice."[100] Justice provides us with a systemic perspective. Thus, Moe-Lobeda reconceptualized the love command as an economic and ecological vocation that attends to systems of oppression and harm. In response to climate change, she named three facets of neighbor-love: compassion, justice, and Earth's well-being.[101] Bearing witness through historical clarity focuses on the justice component of neighbor-love.

The unprecedented nature of climate change complicates our understanding of justice. Jenkins observed, "Received ideas of justice do not anticipate moral agency exercised cumulatively across generational time, aggregately through ecological systems, and nonintentionally over evolutionary futures."[102] For example, justice as fairness, or what is due to each person, is an inadequate conceptual category for the climate crisis. According to Jenkins, "Ethics seems unprepared to address human action as a globalizing aggregate that influences systems through dispersed, cumulative, nonintentional effects."[103] Who is to blame? We are all complicit in patterns of overconsumption and environmental neglect. Drawing on the writing of Iris Marion Young, Jenkins proposed that justice must be recast "as responsibility for the systems through which we belong to each other."[104] Ethical response to climate change—like the cause of the problem itself—is a group project involving all of humanity in relation to the entire Earth.

However, empire works against attempts to recognize and rectify the structural and collective aspects of the current climate crisis. Those most responsible for climate change are the ones who most benefit from the patterns of exploitation causing the problem. Moe-Lobeda termed this situation "the paradox of privilege," stunting individual moral response and hiding oppression.[105] Furthermore, privileged actors often view their economic consumption as virtuous. For example, the neoliberal valuation of growth as an unqualified economic good—even increased spending on fossil fuels—is a significant hurdle to a faithful Christian response to overconsumption and the climate crisis.[106] Individualism and empire make it difficult to address injustices resulting from the well-intentioned efforts of good people. Thus, when people debate about climate change, more is at stake than the physics of a warming planet.

The climate crisis has become a proxy for adjudicating the veracity of competing worldviews. Michael Northcott argued that "climate change represents a challenge not only to energy-led consumerism and unfettered capitalism ... but [also] to the

---

[100]Moe-Lobeda, *Resisting Structural Evil*, 178.

[101]Moe-Lobeda, 201.

[102]Jenkins, *The Future of Ethics*, 1.

[103]Jenkins, 3.

[104]Jenkins, 34.

[105]Moe-Lobeda, *Resisting Structural Evil*, 61–2.

[106]Moe-Lobeda, 102–5, 204–5. See also Herman E. Daly and John B. Cobb Jr., *For the Common Good: Redirecting the Economy toward Community, the Environment, and a Sustainable Future*, 2nd ed., with contributions by Clifford W. Cobb (Beacon, 1994), 62–3.

epistemological and ontological foundations of modern liberalism."[107] The very philosophical basis of Western culture is implicated—as are structures of oppression and privilege, such as white racism. Thus, "the atmosphere has become a political arena in which justice is being renegotiated."[108] This renegotiation, however, is situated in cultures beholden to empire, in which structures of power and privilege are reified and hidden.

Justice in the climate crisis requires the historical clarity to call out oppressive systems and harmful structures. When facing the "fantastic hegemonic imagination" that imposes a single historical interpretation supporting empire, Townes proposed "the strategy of countermemory" as a mode of resistance.[109] Seeking clarity from the subjectivity and particularity of experiences of Black women, she asserted: "Countermemory can open up subversive spaces within dominant discourses that expand our sense of who we are and, possibly, create a more whole and just society in defiance of structural evil."[110] Harris's ecowomanism creatively utilizes Townes's concept of countermemory as a mode of resistance to climate change.[111] According to Harris, "Ecowomanism is an approach to environmental ethics that centres the voices, perspectives and epistemologies of women of African descent."[112] Seeking justice for Black women and the environment, ecowomanism includes multiple steps: narrating and reflecting on experience, intersectional analysis and deep questioning of history, transformation through spiritual activism and dialogue with multiple religious traditions, and linking social justice action with justice for the Earth.[113] Thus, climate justice cannot be separated from racial justice. "From an ecowomanist perspective, to truly repent of the sins of climate change requires a deep, and critical understanding of the multiple ways the abuse of the earth and the abuse and exploitation of black bodies intersect."[114] To be liberative, historical clarity and memory cannot be abstracted from the particularities of the persons seeking clarity and claiming those (counter)memories.

Justice in the context of the climate crisis must consider power differentials, historical patterns of oppression, and inequitable distributions of power.[115] Justice is social, attending to the common good and the well-being of the least well-off neighbors—even and especially when those neighbors are non-human parts of creation. Trauma-informed justice prioritizes the well-being of the victim-survivor, consistent with liberation theologies. It also means exercising individual agency as a contribution to the collective agency required to address the problem of climate change within the context of empire. As Townes asserted about "dismantling the cultural production of evil"—of which the climate crisis is certainly a part, "this must be a group project."[116] Ready for meaningful participation to address the traumas

---

107 Jenkins, *The Future of Ethics*, 43, citing Northcott, *A Moral Climate*, 179.
108 Jenkins, 18.
109 Townes, *Womanist Ethics*, 21.
110 Townes, 23.
111 Harris, "Ecowomanist Wisdom," 245.
112 Harris, "Doing Justice to Issues of Race?" 659.
113 Harris, 661–2.
114 Harris, 660.
115 Moe-Lobeda, *Resisting Structural Evil*, 181.
116 Townes, *Womanist Ethics*, 160.

of climate change, historical clarity about the past can spark our imaginations for the future.

Discussion Questions

1   Empire shapes our perception of history, written from the standpoint of those currently in power. What counter-memories challenge the way you have been taught about individualism versus interconnectedness, privilege versus oppression, or fossil fuels versus free market capitalism?

2   How has the natural environment been treated unjustly? What would justice for the Earth look like?

Imagination and Solidarity

Imagination allows us to transcend ourselves and the present climate crisis by reckoning with the future. Moore defined imagining as "the capacity to discern opportunities and alternate futures."[117] This capacity is a crucial tool in addressing the climate crisis. So much of our denigration of the Earth is tied up in and replicates structures of injustice to which the fantastic hegemonic imagination is beholden and of which it is unaware. Without the transcendent mode of imagination in solidarity with a traumatized Earth, its inhabitants, and its climates, we would be unable to change what currently is to what could be.

Through imagination, we can reconnect with nature and each other, restoring broken relationships and resisting causing further harm. The concept is so important to addressing the climate crisis that the book *Planetary Solidarity: Global Women's Voices on Christian Doctrine and Climate Justice* begins with four chapters on "reimagining."[118] Catherine Keller dedicated an entire book to the task of imagining the climate crisis as an impending apocalypse—not as a scare tactic but as a constructive enterprise: "Like much contemplative practice, [this book] aims through meditation, imagination, and conversation at actualization. Of what is—actually—possible."[119] Imagination taps into our sense of wonder, nurturing our hope for the flourishing of all creation. Imagination allows us to anticipate the surplus of grace found in alternative relationships forged through the suffering of climate change.

Ethical response to the climate crisis must transcend the power of empire, risking solidarity through alternative relationships. Solidarity with victim-survivors is made possible by recognizing their inherent dignity and value, being attentively present with them, and doing the work of historical clarity. Then we can imagine our meaningful participation in collaborative material projects for the common good, the well-being of our neighbors, and the full flourishing of all of creation. Attentive presence to the traumatic effects of climate change calls us to bear witness to the Earth itself: "the

---

[117]Moore, "Responding to a Weeping Planet," 11.
[118]Grace Ji-Sun Kim and Hilda P. Koster, eds., *Planetary Solidarity: Global Women's Voices on Christian Doctrine and Climate Justice* (Fortress, 2017).
[119]Catherine Keller, *Facing Apocalypse: Climate, Democracy, and Other Last Chances* (Orbis, 2021), xv.

earth's traumatized speech can be read as an act of resistance undertaken by the earth to draw our attention to the reality of its traumatization, calling humans out of denial to be witnesses."[120] To bear witness to suffering, though, is risky.

Bearing witness to trauma victim-survivors is a dangerous political act. "Because it seeks justice, *love is a political as well as interpersonal vocation*," asserted Moe-Lobeda. "Jesus' teachings ... apply to social structural spheres of life—political, economic, cultural systems." This is especially true when following Jesus' example of solidarity with the poor and oppressed, the victim-survivors in his community. Thus, Moe-Lobeda warned, "*Neighbor-love may be dangerous*."[121] A trauma-informed approach to climate change takes sides with the most vulnerable parts of the Earth on which we live. Because climate change is a structural problem created by, enmeshed in, and complicated by empire, it is doubly risky.

God's grace offers hope. Rieger's notion of surplus, "anything that points beyond the status quo," provides glimpses of grace beyond the structures of empire.[122] According to Rieger, surplus can be found in alternative relationships, "developed in solidarity with real people whose lives are being destroyed."[123] Surplus can arise when people act in solidarity, exerting collective agency to address structural problems. Jenkins's depiction of faith communities coming together to find pragmatic solutions to unprecedented problems alludes to a similar surplus of grace: "the reality of Christ always exceeds any practice, it exceeds the performance of any project."[124] Rieger observed the existence of an unexpected theological surplus emerging from "alternative relationships among people who are brought together ... often against their will" when faced with economic hardship.[125] "These relationships," claimed Rieger, "can lead to new kinds of solidarity."[126] The same can be said for people facing hardship due to the climate crisis. When these alternative relationships include non-human creation, the potential for surplus is expanded.

Expanding solidarity to include non-human creation takes courageous imagination. If Earth is imagined as a partner in ministry, then we share the work of repairing the world. Moore's vision of "ministering with the earth" is an apt description of this imaginative work, in which we are invited "to participate with God and with the earth in repairing the world"; to do so, she invoked "the Hebrew concept of *tikkun olam* (repair of the world)—a vision of social, political, and religious transformation."[127] This hope depends on both God's gracious action and our response. By "seeing this complexity of our connections to other people," we open ourselves to God's transformation of those relationships and "have a better

---

[120]Tumminio Hansen, "The Body of God, Sexually Violated," 10, drawing on McFague's metaphor of the earth as the body of God.

[121]Moe-Lobeda, *Resisting Structural Evil*, 185, original emphasis.

[122]Joerg Rieger, *No Rising Tide: Theology, Economics, and the Future* (Fortress, 2009), 162; see also Rieger, *Christ and Empire*, 9.

[123]Rieger, *No Rising Tide*, 155.

[124]Jenkins, *The Future of Ethics*, 104.

[125]Rieger, *No Rising Tide*, 162.

[126]Rieger, 162.

[127]Moore, *Ministering with the Earth*, 3–4.

chance of becoming fully human," to use Rieger's framing.[128] Solidarity with the Earth is a path toward creating alternative, life-giving relationships and new forms of community.

Meaningful participation in this good future requires that we join in solidarity with victim-survivors of climate trauma—especially the Earth and its wondrously interconnected geographies and ecosystems. For example, McFague imagined a kenotic, panentheistic theology to counter the power struggles within Western individualistic cultures and the structures of empire. Her theology is kenotic and self-sacrificing, a kind of love that empties self on behalf of others and is thus counter to the prevailing values of US culture.[129] This theology does not draw an identification between God and the world (pantheism) but rather views "the world as living—finding its source and fulfillment—*within* God's very self, the dance of self-emptying love that desires the flourishing of all life" (panentheism).[130] In other words, God is not the sum of creation, rather God is *in* all creation. Thus, McFague offered a "sacramental vision in which the world is a reflection of the divine."[131] This image, she pressed metaphorically by imagining the world as God's body, changes the way we understand life together on this climate-changed Earth. In McFague's "kenotic paradigm ... 'salvation' is ... not a release from punishment for our sins, but a call to relate to all others (from God to homeless persons and the drought-ridden trees) as God would and does."[132] Salvation then becomes a collaborative project between us and God, in which we participate through solidarity with all that God has created.

Imaginatively expanding our moral vision and creating new relationships of solidarity with the Earth as a moral subject has the potential to upend oppressive hierarchies built into inherited cultural values of individualism, capitalism, and androcentric theologies. Rieger concluded a book on the economy with this assertion: "Without seeing the complexity of our connections to other people, including the sever distortions in these connections, we will never be able to transform them in life giving ways."[133] The same can be said for our connections to non-human creation.

Discussion Questions

1   What kind of relationships do you have with the flora and fauna in your neighborhood? What alternative relationships can you imagine?

2   Consider a part of creation that is threatened locally. Now, imagine being in solidarity with that part of creation. How could you meaningfully participate in resisting further harm?

---

[128]Rieger, *No Rising Tide*, 162.

[129]Sally McFague, "Reimagining the Triune God for a Time of Global Climate Change," in *Planetary Solidarity: Global Women's Voices on Christian Doctrine and Climate Justice*, ed. Grace Ji-Sun Kim and Hilda P. Koster, 101–18 (Fortress, 2017), 102.

[130]McFague, 110–11, original emphasis.

[131]McFague, 111.

[132]McFague, 111.

[133]Rieger, *No Rising Tide*, 162.

New Possibilities

Bearing witness to the traumatic suffering of God's creation caused by climate change is a dangerous and necessary social action. Climate change is caused by intersecting systems enmeshed in empire, causing difficulty for realizing, recognizing, responding to, and resisting the traumatic effects. Trauma response requires an awareness of social structures of power and the injustices they cause. However, humanity is both oppressor and victim in this struggle. Ethical action requires individuals working in solidarity with each other and the Earth for the sake of all. Alternative relationships forged out of the trauma of climate change can generate theological surplus, providing new possibilities for solidarity and social action.

Anthropogenic climate change is an ethical challenge in at least two distinct ways. The trauma of climate crisis challenges us to act more ethically in relation to the world around us, and it also challenges the way in which we understand ethics. It is a problem characterized by uncertainties; it must be addressed but cannot be solved. Furthermore, the forces of empire that led to climate crisis also prevent us from seeing and understanding climate change as a structural problem over which humans have some agency—both as cause of suffering and as potential partners in healing. Bearing witness to the suffering of creation in the context of empire requires a reevaluation of inherited understandings of moral agency, suffering, God, sources of wisdom, justice, and solidarity.

Anthropogenic climate change is an unprecedented problem that challenges inherited understandings of ethics. We must be willing to expand our moral vision and to act with ambiguity and uncertainty, for we do not have the luxury of certainty about causes, blame, and corrective action. Since the early 1980s, churches have brought attention to the climate crisis as a moral issue, drawing on multiple sources of wisdom, including scripture and science. Yet, the structures of empire, based on a logic of domination, impair our ability to perceive the climate crisis and to respond. We must learn to relate to ourselves and the world around us differently, seeing the interrelatedness of God's creation.

Bearing witness to the traumatic suffering of creation allows us to perceive and relate to the world through the human capacity for transcendent awareness. This trauma-informed approach also challenges and expands our understanding of Christian ethics. Recognition of non-human parts of the world as moral subjects rather than objects allows us to see the dignity and inherent goodness of creation. Perceiving the suffering of creation—and God's presence within creation—expands our understanding of the image of God beyond human exceptionalism. Furthermore, recognizing the dignity and wisdom of creation confronts us with an epistemological challenge. Learning from the created world is a form of wisdom accessible to all persons and cultures. Creation wisdom can take many forms—eco-womanist, Indigenous, embodied, traditional—and belongs to all who pay attention to their bodies and the bodies around them (both animate and inanimate). Indeed, embodied knowledge is requisite for loving ourselves and our neighbors.

Empathy allows relationship between subjects. It is impossible to have empathy for an object. To empathize with the suffering of creation, we must see ourselves and

God in relationship to the cosmos. This awareness of the subjectivity of the non-human and to see God's image in it allows us to love the world that God so loves. While the climate crisis demands immediate action, our sense of urgency must be tempered by attuning ourselves to the natural rhythms of creation. Love is patient.

Memory provides perspective on what is going on in today's climate-changed world. Memory is necessary for gaining historical clarity on the economic, political, and environmental decisions and practices contributing to the crisis. A systemic perspective incorporates justice as an aspect of loving our neighbors, both human and otherwise. Expanding the notion of justice to ecological systems, including flora, fauna, geography, and atmosphere, challenges inherited worldviews shaped by empire. Not only memory but also countermemory is necessary for the group project of climate justice.

Imagination is vital for addressing an unprecedented problem of global proportions impacting multiple generations. We must be willing to risk alternative relationships with the Earth and other members of God's creation even when we cannot see the possibilities. We can only imagine. Expanding solidarity to include the vulnerable and non-human creation is risky. The danger and uncertainty are aspects of ethical responsibility—choosing a course of action because it is right, not because it is safe, assured, or imposed. Through this meaningful participation in relationships of solidarity with the Earth, we allow for the possibility of transformation, healing, and recovery from the trauma of climate change.

3.3

Abuse and Betrayal

"Say no!" advised her clergy colleague. "Don't even consider a move to Elmsdale Church. You don't want to be in the middle of that mess of a congregation." Pastor Kellie thought to herself, "I wonder what's wrong with them?"

This brief exchange between clergy colleagues challenges the way we see the church, the body of Christ. According to Paul,

> For just as the body is one and has many members, and all the members of the body, though many, are one body, so it is with Christ ... If one member suffers, all suffer together with it; if one member is honored, all rejoice together with it. Now you are the body of Christ and individually members of it.
>
> (1 Cor. 12:12; 12:26-27)

Each Christian is a member of the body of Christ with unique gifts, rejoicing and suffering along with the other members. When one member suffers, all suffer with them. Before we jump too quickly to Christ's resurrection, however, Paul's words to the congregation in Corinth remind us that the church can suffer even now. Each congregation is one manifestation of our incarnate savior who suffered, died, was buried, and rose again.

As a deacon, I have a distinctive perspective on the church and its ministry, viewing it through ministries of word, service, compassion, and justice. Through the diaconate of all Christians, each member participates in these ministries of diakonia (see Chapter 1.4) and can adopt a deacon's viewpoint. Meditating on the gospel of Mark with a deacon's eye, I see a wounded church:

> It was nine o'clock in the morning when they crucified him ... Those who passed by derided him, shaking their heads and saying, "Aha! You who would destroy the temple and build it in three days, save yourself, and come down from the cross!" In the same way the chief priests, along with the scribes, were also mocking him among themselves and saying, "He saved others; he cannot save himself."
>
> (Mk 15:25-32)

This image of Christ crucified contrasts with the way many Christians usually view the church, yet it depicts a reality that many congregations face: the experience of being the wounded body of Christ in need of healing.

The fictional Elmsdale Church scenario provides an entry point for discussing congregational care after spiritual leader misconduct. Elmsdale Church is fortunate to have the clarity of adjudication. In this case, the former pastor was found guilty of sexually exploiting an adult congregant and was removed from ministry. The primary victim and her family experienced some measure of justice, including a formal apology from the church council and judicatory leaders, as well as paid counseling as a form of restitution. Yet, members of the congregation still exhibit a wide array of emotions, and some are in denial about the outcome of the church trial. Parishioners at Elmsdale will likely distrust the next pastor and the judicatory that credentialed her, since a previous pastor proved abusive. Thus, Rev. Kellie would begin her ministry at Elmsdale Church in an atmosphere of mistrust. Every pastor serving after an incident of abuse by a trusted leader faces this reality.

When a person in a position of ministerial leadership, lay or ordained, violates the sacred trust of that office, individuals and entire faith communities must bear witness to the harm. In the case of Elmsdale Church, instead of asking, "What is wrong with them?" a trauma-informed pastor would consider, "What has happened to them?" The former question reinforces a dynamic that shames the congregation; the latter question expresses empathy for the congregation, offering pastoral accompaniment. Changing the question in this manner shifts the emphasis from blame to care. This subtle difference in perspective signals a trauma-informed approach to congregational healing and recovery. Once the primary victims have received crisis triage and harm has been acknowledged,[1] there are longer-term practices that can help the congregation reckon with its shock, grief, complicity, and woundedness. Elmsdale Church can become a healing congregation.

A trauma-informed approach to abuse and betrayal must bear witness to our collective failings as a church. With a deacon's eye for truth and repair, I view the church as the body of Christ, wounded and wounding, at times betrayed by one of its own members—even a leader. In this chapter, we apply the four Rs of trauma-informed response (realize, recognize, respond, and resist—see Chapter 1.2) to situations in which a congregation has been harmed by its own leader. I present *healing congregations* as a trauma-informed response to the abuse of power and

---

[1]Crisis triage, counseling, medical and psychiatric care, as well as holding the perpetrator accountable for the harms done—matters of primary trauma care and juridical intervention—are beyond the scope of this book. Activities of care for the affected congregation should run parallel to assuring the safety and healing of the primary victims and their families, whose needs should be prioritized. The literature on victim assistance and perpetrator accountability in religious contexts includes Heather T. Banis, "Resiliency, Hope, Healing: Victims Assistance Ministry in a Trauma-Sensitive Theological Context," in *Theology in a Post-Traumatic Church*, ed. John N. Sheveland, 17–38 (Orbis, 2023); Lauren D. Sawyer, Emily Cohen, and Annie Mesaros, eds., *Responding to Spiritual Leader Misconduct: A Handbook* (FaithTrust Institute, 2022), https://faithtrustinstitute.org/; and Clergy Sexual Misconduct Information and Resources, https://clergysexualmisconduct.com/.

institutional betrayal often associated with incidents of sexual abuse in ministry. Thus, with more information, Pastor Kellie's clergy colleague might have expressed her concern better by saying, "Elmsdale Church has been wounded by a former pastor and needs a courageous person to lead them in bearing witness to this reality as they seek healing and recovery. Are you prepared for this role?"

Discussion Questions

1   This chapter addresses the disturbing reality of sexual abuse by clergy and other spiritual leaders. Before proceeding, it is important to acknowledge the emotions that this topic elicits in you.

2   Abuse of power can occur in any institutional context. Consider the institutions that shape your life—school, workplace, family, political party, community organizations, and so on. How are persons in power held accountable and the potential for abuse addressed?

Realizing the Extent

One of the most devastating wounds to the body of Christ today is sexual abuse in ministry: when a person in a position of ministerial leadership, lay or ordained, violates the sacred trust of that office by inappropriately crossing intimacy boundaries with a congregant.[2] Sexual abuse by a spiritual leader is an abuse of power. When a church leader engages in sexualized behavior with someone they should be serving in ministry, that leader is no longer serving the best interests of their parishioner but instead exploiting that person and the position of ministerial leadership to gratify their own desires. When a ministerial relationship becomes sexualized, it ceases to be a ministry of the church, and the aftereffects can be devastating not only to the exploited congregant but also to the entire congregation. Bearing witness requires that we realize the extent of abuse and betrayal in churches and recognize the dignity of alleged victims.

Clergy sexual misconduct and harassment are not as rare as we might suppose. In 2008, Diana Garland and Mark Chaves surveyed thousands of women who had attended church at least once in the preceding month. They found that one in thirty-three women reported having been sexually harassed or abused by her own pastor during her adult life.[3] My own denomination, the UMC, handles between 150 and 500 credible allegations of clergy sexual abuse every year in the

---

[2] The term *spiritual leader* encompasses not only clergy but also laypersons, staff, and volunteers in positions of authority representing the church. Sawyer et al., *Responding to Spiritual Leader Misconduct*, 8. See also Clergy Sexual Misconduct Information and Resources, https://clergysexualmisconduct.com/what-is-csm%3F; and Darryl W. Stephens, "Fiduciary Duty and Sacred Trust," in *Professional Sexual Ethics: A Holistic Ministry Approach*, ed. Darryl W. Stephens and Patricia Beattie Jung, 23–33 (Fortress, 2013).
[3] Diana R. Garland, "The Prevalence of Clergy Sexual Misconduct with Adults: A Research Study—Executive Summary," *Baylor University*, n.d., https://socialwork.web.baylor.edu/executive-summary.

United States.[4] Through anonymous surveys of thousands of United Methodist clergy, I have learned that 50 percent report having "served a church where sexual misconduct by a ministerial leader occurred in its history." Extrapolating from this unpublished data, I estimate one in ten United Methodist congregations in the United States is suffering from the after-effects of sexual abuse by a ministerial leader.

When allegations are not handled with the victim's best interests prioritized, the church becomes a second violator. An institution, such as a denomination or congregation, compounds harm through unjust policies and practices and by denying abuses by leaders. In psychological terms, Jennifer J. Freyd developed betrayal trauma theory through the observation that "abuse perpetrated within close relationships is more harmful than abuse perpetrated by strangers because of the violation of trust within a necessary relationship."[5] This is the case when the church and its leadership are the violators. Freyd and co-researcher Carly Parnitzke Smith defined the "institutional action and inaction that exacerbate the impact of traumatic experiences" as *institutional betrayal*.[6]

Institutional betrayal occurs when a church becomes complicit in the abuse instead of protecting its vulnerable members. When a church colludes with perpetrators by ignoring victim-survivors, disbelieving them, or even attacking them, a predictable pattern emerges. Freyd termed this phenomenon *DARVO*: "Deny, Attack, & Reverse Victim and Offender."[7] Through DARVO, truth-tellers are silenced, and perpetrators play the victim. Another term, *betrayal blindness*, describes the tendency of persons within the institution "to preserve the relationships, institutions, and social systems on which they depend" by ignoring the violations rather than risk compromising the institution.[8] When churches choose institutional protection over justice, they enact a form of betrayal that can be worse than the initial violation. Thus, persons abused by the church often suffer twice: once through the initial violation and again when the institution betrays them.[9]

Many denominations and churches have a history of institutional betrayal. When the horrific legacy of church and state-sponsored Indigenous boarding schools comes to light—this is institutional betrayal revealed.[10] When an independent audit of the

---

[4]Sally Badgley Dolch, "Healing the Breach: Response Team Intervention in United Methodist Congregations" (DMin thesis, Wesley Theological Seminary, 2010), 131–2.

[5]Carly Parnitzke Smith and Jennifer J. Freyd, "Institutional Betrayal," *American Psychologist* 69, no. 6 (2014): 577, https://doi.org/10.1037/a0037564, citing Jennifer J. Freyd, *Betrayal Trauma: The Logic of Forgetting Childhood Abuse* (Harvard University Press, 1996).

[6]Smith and Freyd, "Institutional Betrayal," 577.

[7]Center for Institutional Courage, "We Are Making a Call to Institutional Courage," https://www.institutionalcourage.org/the-call-to-courage.

[8]Center for Institutional Courage, "Knowledge Base and Research Priorities," https://www.institutionalcourage.org/knowledge-base-and-research-priorities.

[9]More generally, negative reactions, such as disbelief, to the victim's report are termed the "second wound." Clergy Sexual Misconduct Information and Resources, https://clergysexualmisconduct.com/definitions. See also Krystal Lynne Woolston, "'It Was Like Double Damage': An Exploration of Clergy-Perpetrated Sexual Abuse, Institutional Response, and Posttraumatic Growth" (PhD diss., Montclair State University, 2023).

[10]NICWA, "Department of Interior Releases Federal Indian Boarding School Investigative Report Vol. II," August 20, 2024, https://www.nicwa.org/news/department-of-interior-releases-federal-indian-boarding-school-investigative-report-vol-ii/.

Southern Baptist Convention revealed twenty years of "resistance, stonewalling, and even outright hostility" toward victims and whistleblowers reporting sexual abuse by ministerial leaders to the Convention's Executive Committee—this is institutional betrayal revealed.[11] When decades of child molestation by priests in the Roman Catholic Church are reported, in diocese after diocese around the globe, and along with it, decades of coverup—this is institutional betrayal revealed.[12]

A Case Study of Abuse and Betrayal

The following is a de-identified case study of institutional betrayal—a case similar to Elmsdale but without the benefit of adjudication. Vivian, a church secretary in her mid-40s and a member of the congregation, filed a complaint against her senior pastor, alleging that he coerced her into a sexual relationship, violating the sacred trust of ministry. She admitted that, initially, she thought the relationship was based on genuine and mutual love. It had felt like God intended her to be with this man; she could imagine a wonderful future with him. He admonished her to keep it their secret, explaining how others in the congregation would not understand and that they should wait to tell people when the time was right. Their sexual intimacy went on for nearly a year before she became so uncomfortable with the secrecy that she demanded they make their relationship public. He tried to convince her to keep quiet, saying this was God's plan for their lives. But she told him she could not stay quiet any longer. He then broke things off with her and asked her to resign her position at the church. As a single mother with no other source of income, she faced a dilemma: she needed this job.

Vivian sought help from a victim advocate and discovered the definition of clergy sexual misconduct: "any sexualized behavior (verbal or physical) on the part of a religious leader toward a person under his or her spiritual care."[13] Thus, she learned to identify her pastor's behavior as abuse. It was at this point that she began to realize the extent of his manipulation and coercion: he was the one at fault. She filed a complaint with the bishop alleging clergy sexual misconduct. Meanwhile, she was afraid of losing her job. In fact, the congregation's personnel committee, on a directive from the pastor, dismissed her with two weeks' notice, even as she told them about the pastor's abusive behavior and her complaint to the bishop. When she contested her firing by appealing to the bishop, she received an official letter from the conference's lawyer stating that personnel matters were up to the local congregation to decide, not the bishop.

Vivian left her job, her congregation, and her pastor. The bishop dismissed her complaint as lacking sufficient evidence since there were no witnesses. The pastor

---

[11]Guidepost Solutions, "Report of the Independent Investigation: The Southern Baptist Convention Executive Committee's Response to Sexual Abuse Allegations and an Audit of the Procedures and Actions of the Credentials Committee," May 15, 2022, https://www.documentcloud.org/documents/22031737-final-guidepost-solutions-independent-investigation-report.

[12]See John N. Sheveland, ed., *Theology in a Post-Traumatic Church* (Orbis, 2023).

[13]"Adult Clergy Sexual Misconduct (CSM) Explained," *Clergy Sexual Misconduct Information and Resources*, https://clergysexualmisconduct.com/what-is-csm%3F.

remained in the pulpit, and members of the congregation became divided over who and what to believe. As she began sharing the real reason for her departure with members of the congregation, she was met with a range of responses: disbelief, horror, fear, and compassion, to name only a few. Some members grew in distrust and suspicion of the pastor and others grew in their unfaltering support for his ministerial leadership. The personnel committee, who this time interviewed only male candidates for the job, told the next church secretary nothing about these circumstances and the growing conflicts in the congregation. This case of abuse by a ministerial leader illustrates the damaging and lingering effects of that behavior on a congregation.

Discussion Questions

1   In Vivian's church and employment situation, what went wrong, and when? Name key decision points that caused harm and betrayal.

2   What conditions should be met before one believes an alleged victim reporting abuse? Should any conditions be placed on recognizing the dignity of someone who reports abuse?

3   What is the history of abuse of power in an institution in which you participate, such as a college or university? Conduct internet searches for recent headlines about abuse in similar institutions. What do you realize about the extent of abuse and betrayal in this context?

Recognizing the Signs

Many faith communities have unacknowledged histories of abuse and betrayal. The situation of Elmsdale Church is unusual only in that the offender was found guilty and held accountable. Vivian's congregational situation is more common. Most cases of misconduct by a spiritual leader are unreported, unadjudicated, and unresolved. Many faith communities suffer from unhealed wounds, which do not heal on their own. Symptoms can last for decades in the absence of intentional practices of healing. A trauma-informed leader recognizes the signs of congregational woundedness, even when the details of abuse and betrayal are unknown, and treats alleged victims with empathy and love.

The diverse ways in which individuals within a congregational system experience an adverse congregational event complicate healing and recovery. Stages of grief come into play. Individuals will experience the full range of denial, anger, bargaining, depression, and acceptance—and at different times and to different degrees. Some may empathetically identify with a primary victim. Others may experience compassion fatigue as they care for victim-survivors. Still others may have the courage to bear witness to the community's collective experience of betrayal and resulting woundedness.

A congregation wounded by its own trusted leader also suffers spiritually: the perpetrator is in a position representing God. The very resources that a church typically draws upon—its pastoral leadership, judicatory personnel, and integrity as a community of faith—are thrown into disarray and distrust, hampering recovery. People may question their faith and their beliefs about God. Some people deal with this spiritual dissonance by refusing to believe what happened. Others will want to move toward forgiveness quickly while still others may seek accountability from those in leadership. Some people will withdraw from the congregation, and more will follow if the congregation remains mired in dysfunction rather than healing. Many congregants will distrust the pastoral office and the church that it represents; every spiritual leader becomes suspect after one minister's offense.

In a wounded congregation, laypersons often take sides over what really happened and who is to blame for alleged sexual abuse. Furthermore, when the victim is an adult, congregations are often divided because many people find it difficult to understand how an adult can be a victim, lacking the ability to offer genuine consent to the sexual advances of their pastor. Often victims are blamed, and perpetrators are not held accountable. Even when the abuse is acknowledged, many judicatory personnel mistakenly believe that simply getting rid of the perpetrator (and often also the victim) will solve the problem. However, when a wounded congregation is not assisted in healing, it remains mired in unhealthy patterns long after the initial breach of trust. This type of wound does not go away on its own.

Once, I heard from a church leader dealing with a congregation mired in dysfunction. The presenting issue was a deepening conflict over pastoral leadership—a sure path to congregational decline.[14] This congregation had gone through eight pastors in the past ten years, each one dismissed for different reasons, and all experienced hostility and dissatisfaction from the laity. Unproductive conflict in the congregation is often a surface expression of generalized distrust. My colleague, however, was a trauma-informed leader and knew that congregations express underlying fear and unresolved anxiety through irrational, controlling, and obsessive behaviors, such as:

- Perpetual staff changes
- Lack of appropriate boundaries
- Reluctance to change
- Anger, helplessness, or disconnection under stress
- Withdrawal and isolation from the larger community or judicatory
- Secrecy and lack of transparency in communications
- Overly rigid approach to traditions, roles, and relationships

While many faith communities exhibit one or two of these symptoms, the co-occurrence of so many dysfunctions may indicate an unhealed wound of the community. Conflicts over leadership can become part of the congregational system, possibly due to suspected or confirmed misconduct by a prior ministerial leader.

---

[14]Notably, "serious conflict is a very strong predictor of congregational decline," and conflict over pastoral leadership is the conflict type "most strongly associated with decline." Faith Community Today, "FACTs on Growth 2010 Report," https://faithcommunitiestoday.org/wp-content/uploads/2019/01/FACTs-on-Growth-2010.pdf.

After further investigation, my colleague discovered that a former pastor had left the congregation ten years prior under a cloud of suspicion of sexual misconduct. The case was never adjudicated or addressed publicly, and it remained unresolved. This congregation's unhealed wounds continued to hamper its ministry a decade after the event. Vivian's congregation is heading down a similar path by creating workarounds (e.g., interviewing only male candidates for church secretary) rather than confronting the reality of abuse by the pastor. This wounded body of Christ needs to address not only the pastor's violation but also its subsequent pattern of institutional betrayal. As for my colleague's situation, the congregation needed a process of healing regardless of whether it could be determined who was at fault.

Bearing Witness as Healing Congregations

Individuals and communities suffering from the effects of abuse by a trusted spiritual leader should be intentional about their healing and recovery. Violations can be experienced as trauma, though I have been careful not to equate congregational woundedness with collective trauma.[15] Congregational woundedness may be a form of trauma—but not necessarily. Even when a wounded congregation's experience does not meet the clinical definition of trauma, many of the signs and symptoms may overlap with that of a traumatized victim-survivor. Regardless, a trauma-informed approach to congregational healing does not hinge on a diagnosis of trauma or knowledge of any specific event of abuse or betrayal. To recover vitality, leaders and members of a wounded congregation must bear witness to primary victims and to each other.

It is through a deacon's eye that the church can learn to identify, name, and address the wounds of violation due to abuse in ministry. The prophetic nature of diakonia lends itself to truth-telling. "Diakonia is a permanent challenge, and a constant thorn in the flesh of the church. It challenges the church to ongoing change ..."[16] Healing is a also central part of diaconal identity, helping the church work toward "reconciliation, healing and integrity in [the church's] own life and ... actions."[17] A deacon's viewpoint emphasizes justice and healing—a valuable perspective for a congregation recovering from a prior incident of ministerial abuse. Thus, diakonia can assist the church in the hard work of bringing its own institutional life in line with the gospel. Faith communities require intentional healing to overcome abuse by a spiritual leader.

---

[15]For a compelling argument against overly broad claims of a "traumatized church," see Jennifer E. Beste, "Critical Reflection on the Discourse of a 'Traumatized Church,'" in *Theology in a Post-Traumatic Church*, ed. John N. Sheveland, 39–63 (Orbis, 2023).

[16]Reinhard Böttcher, ed., *Prophetic Diakonia: "For the Healing of the World"* (Lutheran World Federation, November 2002), 25, https://www.episcopaldeacons.org/uploads/2/6/7/3/26739998/prophtcdiak_luth02.pdf.

[17]Böttcher, 28.

TABLE 3.3.1 *Bearing Witness as Healing Congregations*

Perspectival Moment	Mode of Transcendence	Moral Theme	Trauma-Informed Response (SAMHSA)	Stage of Recovery (Herman)	Healing Congregations
I. Existence	recognition	dignity	realize	overcoming relational barriers	realize woundedness and harm
II. Present	empathy	love	recognize (identify and name)	safety	reassert healthy boundaries, truth-listening
III. Past	memory	justice	respond	reconstruction of narrative	community rituals of grief and lament
IV. Future	imagination	solidarity	resist	reconnection and restoration	reconnection, scarring

A deacon's perspective is especially valuable for identifying institutional betrayal in hierarchical systems characterized by clericalism.[18] In all contexts, the church must reconcile the violation committed by trusted leader with the community's historical narrative and self-understanding. According to the authors of *Prophetic Diakonia*,

> A culture of silence regarding violence, and the injustices that underlie it, jeopardizes the churches' prophetic voice and needs to be challenged. An appropriate role of churches is to confront perpetrators of violence, seeking to bring them to repentance, in order to transform and accompany the process of reconciliation and healing.[19]

This process of healing is of utmost importance when the church and its leadership are the perpetrators of injustice and violence. Viewing woundedness with a deacon's eye can assist this process of grieving in healthy ways.

My diaconal view of healing congregations contributes to the model of bearing witness through dignity, love, justice, and solidarity. For each moment of bearing witness in Table 3.3.1, I draw connections between SAMHSA's four Rs of trauma-informed response, Judith Herman's stages of healing and recovery, and practices of healing congregations.[20] First, congregational leaders may begin, as we

---

[18] Julie Hanlon Rubio and Paul J. Schutz, *Beyond "Bad Apples": Understanding Clergy Perpetrated Sexual Abuse as a Structural Problem & Cultivating Strategies for Change* (Fordham University, 2022), https://takingresponsibility.ace.fordham.edu/santa-clara-structural-clericalism/.

[19] Böttcher, *Prophetic Diakonia*, 8.

[20] Other examples of trauma-informed response in ministry include Erik Cave, "Trauma-Informed Ministry with Chris Haughee," September 8, 2022, https://pacnwc.org/trauma-informed-ministry-with-chris-haughee/; and Sawyer et al., *Responding to Spiritual Leader Misconduct*, 79–86.

have in this chapter, by recognizing the dignity of victim-survivors and realizing the widespread occurrence of spiritual leader abuse and institutional betrayal. This moment of realization cannot remain abstract or distant. To overcome relational barriers, the leaders and members must also realize that this congregation has been wounded and that harm has been done to specific individuals.

Second, acting through empathy and motivated by love, trauma-informed leaders can re-establish a greater sense of safety by identifying and naming the violations that caused harm. For healing congregations, this includes reasserting healthy boundaries—especially where boundaries previously had been violated—and engaging in active "truth-listening." Recognizing harm requires listening to and believing the brave messengers of this shocking news—the victims and whistleblowers.

Third, bearing witness through memory requires reckoning with the congregation's past with an eye toward justice. Responding as a trauma-informed community, the congregation must come to terms with what happened. A past that is not fully acknowledged has lasting and binding power over the present. Healing within a congregation allows members and leaders to become co-owners of a common story, bad and good, and no longer stuck in the past dynamics of trauma. Leaders must find ways to re-tell the congregational narrative so that members are neither continually reacting to a past violation nor obsessed with nostalgia for a previous era. Community rituals of grief and lament provide necessary groundwork for reconstructing a congregational narrative.

Fourth, to resist further harm, the congregation must join in solidarity with the most vulnerable, including those who have been most harmed by the abuse and betrayal. By allowing themselves to imagine the vast possibilities of God's good future, the congregation fosters reconnection among congregants and restoration to community of those who have been harmed. Deep wounds, such as trauma, do not disappear, though. Healing produces scars. The idea of *scarring* reminds us that the wounds of abuse and betrayal will always be part of the congregation's identity and, in fact, may equip a wounded congregation to become a healing congregation for others.

Discussion Questions

1   With a study partner or small group, read the cases of Emory and Liam presented in *Responding to Spiritual Leader Misconduct* (Sawyer et al., 82–6) and engage the suggested discussion questions.

2   The phrase *healing congregation* has multiple meanings—the congregation could be a patient in the process of healing or an agent of healing for others. How might these meanings conflict? How might the roles of patient and agent complement each other?

Responding and Resisting as a Community

A trauma-informed leader responds by applying knowledge of trauma through intentional practices of healing and by resisting doing further harm to the community.

Immediate crisis intervention by trained support personnel prioritizes the physical and psychological safety of primary victims, emergency communications, and triage. Once the immediate crisis is addressed, congregational leaders can engage in intentional practices of healing for long-term recovery within a congregation. As discussed in Chapter 1.2, trauma-informed response values safety, trustworthiness, empowerment, collaboration, and cultural and contextual sensitivity, among other things. These values serve as antidotes to the abuse of power, violation of trust, coercion, secrecy, and disempowerment typically characterizing misconduct by a spiritual leader.

Fatih communities can reclaim a long tradition of communal practices to promote healing and recovery after abuse by a spiritual leader. Communal prayers of lament, for example, can address feelings of abandonment, providing recognition of harm and betrayal. Community rituals can address disruption by re-integrating members into shared observances. The practice of storytelling addresses the interruptions caused by abuse and betrayal, providing opportunities for re-narrating the community's history, purpose, and shared experiences. The practice of accompaniment—what we have been calling attentive presence in this book—helps overcome isolation by building solidarity with those who have been marginalized or left out. All of these practices contribute to community building, replacing separation with reconnection and strengthened relationships. These practices so integral to faith communities (more so than other types of institutions) are powerful balms of healing, which is why abuse and betrayal disrupting these practices within a congregation can be so devastating. Additionally, congregational leaders should strive to become trauma-informed in all areas of ministry, such as preaching, pastoral care, evangelism, Bible study, and so on.[21]

The following illustrations depict integrated activities—community rituals and other practices—and do not provide a sequential process of steps to be followed. Each activity must be adapted to the contextual realities of the community and its situation.

Reasserting Healthy Boundaries

Misconduct by a spiritual leader is, by definition, an inappropriate crossing of professional boundaries: a person in leadership has abused the power of the pastoral office. Traumatized individuals and wounded communities need to feel safe to begin healing from a violation. Reasserting healthy boundaries, including transparency of communications, is of foremost importance for re-establishing safety and trust in a community of faith.

---

[21]Elaine A. Heath, *Healing the Wounds of Sexual Abuse: Reading the Bible with Survivors* (Brazos, 2019); Charles Kiser and Elaine A. Heath, *Trauma-Informed Evangelism: Cultivating Communities of Wounded Healers* (Eerdmans, 2023), 121–8; Deborah van Deusen Hunsinger, *Bearing the Unbearable: Trauma, Gospel, and Pastoral Care* (Eerdmans, 2015); Karen A. McClintock, *Trauma-Informed Pastoral Care: How to Respond When Things Fall Apart* (Fortress, 2022); R. Scott Sullender, *Trauma and Grief: Resources and Strategies for Ministry* (Cascade, 2018); Sarah Travis, *Unspeakable: Preaching and Trauma-Informed Theology* (Cascade, 2021).

Healthy boundaries can be reasserted through policies, protocols, communication, and other practices. Safe church policies designed to protect children, youth, vulnerable adults, and those who care for them are essential, even if the violation that occurred involved only adults. Often, it is easier for congregants to understand the need for policies when children are involved, laying the groundwork for more difficult discussions of power and vulnerability among adults. Sexual ethics policies for staff and other ministerial leaders, protocols for handling money and financial auditing, rules for giving and receiving gifts, expectations about time management, and what constitutes a pastoral emergency—all of these are important ways of communicating and establishing healthy boundaries in ministry. Then, these boundaries must be put into practice.

Rituals of Grieving and Lament

The removal of a spiritual leader for misconduct is a type of loss. Whenever a community suffers a significant loss, it is important to allow time for grieving and lament. Rituals of lament provide opportunity for embodied anguish through prayer, song, and art, allowing the community to worship together, transcending differences of opinion and experience.[22] Victim survivors should be included in planning and leadership. During traumatic events, victims are overwhelmed and feel a lack of agency. Collaborating with victim-survivors in the healing process allows them to regain a sense of agency. Trauma specialists refer to survivors' "voice and choice" as essential to healing and recovery.

A complicating factor in the case of misconduct is that persons in the community will grieve different losses and for different reasons. Some may grieve the loss of beloved pastor. Others may grieve the loss of a certain image of God, who should have protected the victims from abuse, or a sense of safety and security in their faith community. Still others may grieve the loss of "the way things used to be"—whatever that may look like to them. Furthermore, sexual misconduct may be surrounded by shame and secrecy due to social stigmas regarding the topic of sexuality. Such complex and multifaceted grieving is aided by rituals of communal lament, in which members of the community may feel permission to question God, express their disappointment and anger in the church, and face the world's brokenness.

Congregational Truth-Telling

Telling and bearing witness to the truth of what happened is essential for coming to terms with a traumatic event. When misconduct by a spiritual leader has not been formally acknowledged through adjudication, the truth-telling is much more difficult. In some cases of unresolved past trauma, the first step is to bring the congregation

---

[22]See Joan Huyser-Honig, "Trauma-Informed Care in Church Worship and Life," *Calvin Institute of Christian Worship*, March 24, 2020, https://worship.calvin.edu/resources/resource-library/trauma-informed-care-in-church-worship-and-life/; and Institute for Collective Trauma and Growth, "Tools for Worship," https://web.archive.org/web/20230701110926/https://www.ictg.org/tools-for-worship.html.

to a realization that the dysfunctions they are experiencing are the result of pastoral misconduct that happened years ago. Only when harm is acknowledged can the congregation bear witness to victim-survivors.

For truth-telling to contribute to healing, the focus and priority must be on hearing from survivors, though no victim should be required to share their story. The congregation can bear witness to survivors, even if there remains division within the congregation. Allowing adult victim-survivors to tell their truths can be empowering when done in a safe environment. Ground rules, covenant of civility, and assurance of appropriate confidentiality should be put in place. This is also not the appropriate occasion for an offender to speak—even penitently. Leaders should collaborate with victim survivors to maximize their choices and allow them voice in planning a communal practice of truth-telling.

Congregational truth-telling may include stories from secondary victims and others negatively affected in the community. For example, cases of spiritual leader misconduct may involve institutional betrayal, in which judicatory leaders compound an initial act of misconduct through lack of transparency, coverup, or complicity. Harmful acts of institutional self-protection may be part of the truth that needs to be told and lamented. Creating a safe space for sharing may also elicit previously untold stories of abuse within the same community. Furthermore, hearing stories of abuse may trigger traumatic memories unconnected to the presenting incident. Faith leaders must be prepared to respond to and support such disclosures and reactions.

Forgiveness and Reconciliation

Forgiveness is only appropriate toward the end of a process of healing, and even then, forgiveness does not mean forgetting or lack of accountability. When a person has egregiously abused the power of the ministerial office, it is in the best interests of everyone, including the offender, not to give them that power again. This kind of accountability is fully consistent with forgiveness and may be the most loving course of action. Victim-survivors should never be forced to forgive an offender. In all cases, it is important not to rush to forgiveness. Likewise, efforts toward reconciliation should not be rushed. In many cases of abuse, reconciliation does not mean that a victim-survivor and offender are able to live harmoniously in the same congregation. Being reconciled with God may be enough. A congregation can reconcile itself to its past while still holding the offender accountable.

Integrating a Painful Past into the Congregational Narrative

For healing, a congregation must integrate the traumatic experience into its congregational narrative. Integrating a painful past into the congregational story requires long-term work. Outside facilitators can provide expertise and skills to guide a congregation through this journey.

There are many creative ways that communities of faith have learned to come to terms with their traumatic pasts. Creating a shrine or physical space of remembrance can assist with healing. Ritually reclaiming adulterated spaces in the building can provide survivors a sense of psychological and spiritual safety. Removing physical reminders, such as a photograph of the offending pastor, might be part of the reclaiming of space. Intentional rituals of remembrance on significant dates, anniversaries, or events can help the congregation reclaim the narrative while acknowledging the past. Creating a congregational timeline is another way of remembering traumatic events while not allowing them to define the congregation's narrative.

Discussion Questions

1   Have you ever considered doubts and questions about God to be a form of prayerful speech? Choose a psalm of lament and read it aloud with a group. Discuss how the psalmist's faith in God allows for expressions of anguish.

2   What does forgiveness mean in your faith community? How are memory and accountability incorporated into practices of forgiveness?

A Portrait of Courage

One of the challenges associated with abuse in ministry is that the church must tell the truth to and about itself. Healing begins with truth-telling, and, indeed, truth-telling is one of the primary gifts of the diaconate.[23] Breaking the silence surrounding an incident of abuse by a ministerial leader is the only way to give voice to what really happened and to re-empower the victim-survivor and the congregation itself. Sexual misconduct often begins as a secret, with all the appeal, allure, and danger that secrets harbor. When a survivor is empowered to speak the truth about what happened, to name the abuse, and to identify it as a violation, then the secret is dispelled, and a healing process can begin. A wounded congregation must be similarly empowered to name past abuse and acknowledge the wound in need of healing. This is important for the community of faith as well as the primary victim-survivors.

Healing congregations requires courage. Freyd and colleagues offered a vision of courage to counter betrayal. *Institutional courage* is a response that "includes institutional accountability, transparency, making reparations where needed, and a commitment to being responsive to its members."[24] Their ten principles of institutional courage include complying with criminal and civil codes, accountability, transparency, and apology.[25] These guidelines illumine an alternative to institutional betrayal, allowing the church to become a supporter of victim-survivors. Likewise,

---

[23]"To Love and Serve the Lord: Diakonia in the Life of the Church," *The Jerusalem Report of the Anglican–Lutheran International Commission (ALIC III)*, 2013, 17, https://lutheranworld.org/resources/publication-love-and-serve-lord-diakonia-life-church.

[24]Center for Institutional Courage, "Knowledge Base and Research Priorities."

[25]Jennifer J. Freyd, "When Sexual Assault Victims Speak Out, Their Institutions Often Betray Them," *The Conversation*, January 11, 2018, https://theconversation.com/when-sexual-assault-victims-speak-out-their-institutions-often-betray-them-87050. See also Susan M. Shaw, "Institutional Betrayal, Institutional Courage and the Church," *Baptist News Global*, July 26, 2022, https://baptistnews.com/article/institutional-betrayal-institutional-courage-and-the-church/.

Marie Fortune, founder of the FaithTrust Institute, offered seven elements of justice-making, including truth-telling, acknowledging the violation, and compassion for victims.[26] Freyd's framework of institutional courage and Fortune's elements of justice-making allow us to see the possibilities for the church to be an agent of healing and justice.

The case of the Anabaptist Mennonite Biblical Seminary illustrates the courage required for truth-telling in community. This wounded and wounding institution held a special service to acknowledge and apologize to the victims of John Howard Yoder, a former professor, on March 22, 2015. Some of the women who had been sexually violated by Yoder were able to tell their stories publicly for the first time. What is so remarkable is that the institution finally, decades after the fact, acknowledged Yoder's abuse of over 100 women and offered an apology to them. The then-current seminary president, Sara Wenger Shenk, had not been part of the institution during Yoder's time on faculty. Nevertheless, she confessed on the institution's behalf: "What was done to you … was grievously wrong … It should never have been allowed to happen. We failed you. We failed the church. We failed the Gospel of Jesus Christ."[27] This communal confession is just one part of a much larger task of reckoning with Yoder's tainted legacy.[28]

Shenk's apology illustrates Fortune's second element of justice-making: acknowledging the violation. Fortune explained, "Simple though it is, verbal acknowledgement conveys a depth of understanding and compassion that cannot be accomplished in any other way."[29] Often this requires the assistance of judicatory leaders courageous enough to acknowledge the reality of sexual abuse in the church. Healing requires that the institutional church and its judicatory structures be forthright about specific violations and acknowledge the harm done.

Fortune's third element of justice-making is compassion. It takes bold leadership to reestablish ministerial trust where it has been violated. In the best cases, a trained Response Team can facilitate a congregational disclosure meeting in partnership with the bishop and other judicatory personnel.[30] Such a team, composed of persons with specific skills and expertise in handling sexual trauma, can help members of a congregation work through their reactions, feelings, and responses to the news of

---

[26]Marie M. Fortune, *Is Nothing Sacred? When Sex Invades the Pastoral Relationship* (Harper & Row, 1989), 114–15. For discussion of Fortune's justice-making agenda, see Lauren D. Sawyer, "A Sacred Trust: The Spiritual Community's Duty," in *Spiritual Healing from Sexual Violence: An Intersectional Guide*, ed. Debra Meyers and Mary Sue Barnett, 5–22 (Routledge, 2023), https://doi.org/10.4324/9781003323631-2.

[27]Michelle Sokol, "Mennonite Seminary Apologizes to Victims of Famed Theologian John Howard Yoder," *National Catholic Reporter*, April 9, 2015, http://ncronline.org/news/accountability/mennonite-seminary-apologizes-victims-famed-theologian-john-howard-yoder. On the process and significance, see Sara Wenger Shenk, "Repairing the Moral Canopy after Institutional Betrayal," in *Liberating the Politics of Jesus: Renewing Peace Theology through the Wisdom of Women*, Studies in Anabaptist Theology and Ethics 2, ed. Elizabeth Soto Albrecht and Darryl W. Stephens, 169–87 (T&T Clark, 2020).

[28]Karen V. Guth, *The Ethics of Tainted Legacies: Human Flourishing after Traumatic Pasts* (Cambridge University Press, 2022), 222–33.

[29]Fortune, *Is Nothing Sacred?*, 115.

[30]"Response Team Ministry for Sexual Misconduct," in *The Book of Resolutions of The United Methodist Church 2020/2024*, 359–61 (UMPH, 2024); Sawyer et al., *Responding to Spiritual Leader Misconduct*, 103–4.

sexual misconduct by one of their pastoral leaders. A team member may also be assigned to accompany the alleged victim through the process of reporting and adjudication. A ministry of listening and being present with those suffering in the body of Christ bears witness to the victim's dignity, expressing compassion during a difficult process of justice-seeking, and builds the foundation for solidarity.

Toward Healing

Justice and compassion in response to sexual abuse in ministry are vital practices for mission in a hurting world. Not a week goes by that I do not read a news headline about some form of sexual assault or violation by persons with power—church leaders, professional athletes, political leaders, entertainment celebrities, or military personnel—in institutions unwilling or unable to address these offenses with compassion and justice. Soon after Shenk's courageous apology on behalf of Anabaptist Mennonite Biblical Seminary, *The New York Times* reported credible allegations from multiple women of sexual harassment by a professor at the Yale School of Medicine.[31] The report described a pattern of sexually harassing behaviors and complaints over a period of decades, during which the school failed to offer compassion and justice. This school and many other institutions in our society need a model for compassion and justice, a way toward healing.

A congregation seeking to address its own woundedness as the body of Christ must ready itself to receive the transformative healing offered by the Great Physician. Just as the practice of radical hospitality is a rebuttal to an inquiry by the Pharisees and scribes of Jesus' day, who asked, "'Why does he eat with tax collectors and sinners?'" my suggestion to tend to wounded and ailing congregations echoes his answer: "When Jesus heard this, he said to them, 'Those who are well have no need of a physician but those who are sick'" (Mk 2:16-17). For a congregation to be the bearer of this Good News, it must trust in the Great Physician and seek healing for its ailments. Only through its own healing can a congregation become a healing congregation for others.

Churches can model God's healing presence through acts of truth and repair. It is through a deacon's eye for compassion and justice that we can identify, name, and attend to the church's need for healing, so that it can again bear witness to the Good News of Christ Jesus. The work of healing congregations is transformative. When a wounded congregation becomes a healing congregation, the wounded body of Christ becomes an agent of grace in the world. The church's authenticity tending to its own woundedness is essential to being a credible and reliable witness to the Gospel in a world in which domestic violence, sexual abuse, and violence against women and children continue to be the existential reality for millions of persons. The ministry of healing is a moral imperative for the body of Christ, wounding and wounded. " ... Now you are the body of Christ and individually members of it."

---

[31]Tamar Lewin, "Seven Allege Harassment by Yale Doctor at Clinic," *The New York Times*, April 13, 2015, https://www.nytimes.com/2015/04/14/us/former-yale-medical-professor-accused-of-sexual-harassment.html?partner=rss&emc=rss&_r=1.

Congregations can heal after misconduct by a spiritual leader. Chances are good that all faith leaders will at some point serve after misconduct, whether they realize it or not. Elmsdale Church is not alone in its struggle. It can yet become a healthy community through intentional, healing practices guided by Pastor Kellie or another trauma-informed pastor.

Discussion Questions

1 Consider a faith community with which you are familiar. What are some scars that allow this community to be an agent of healing for others?

2 Bearing witness can be appropriate in times of natural disaster, war, epidemics, and other community-wide experiences of collective woundedness. Consider how the institutions that shape your life participated in healing practices in the aftermath of a recent disaster. What practices contributed to community healing? What wounds have yet to heal?

Conclusion: Strengthening Moral Community

This book has provided an inductive journey from love to justice, from individual faith to political action. We began with the question, "How shall we love our neighbors in traumatic times?" The initial answer was for individuals and faith communities to become trauma-informed.

By bearing witness to suffering and striving for solidarity with victim-survivors, we can join in God's action for a more just world. The Christian moral life is about participation in God's mission of renewal and reconciliation, in solidarity with the oppressed, motivated, and empowered by the Holy Spirit. Ethical discipleship and church's moral witness are our grace-enabled responses to human suffering, systemic injustice, and a hurting world. We cannot claim to love our neighbors and fail to bear witness to their suffering. To bear witness is to transcend our individual selves, as kin in community. Bearing witness is premised on recognizing each person as having dignity equal to our own. Bearing witness also provides tools to critique ourselves and the church when we fall short. Bearing witness to each other, we can learn to love our neighbors—human and non-human—and seek justice in solidarity. Together, as neighbors of many faiths, we can imagine God's will for a more just world and join in bringing it about. We can contribute to the repair of the world.

To conclude this journey, I invite us to consider trauma-informed Christian ethics as a project of strengthening moral community under adverse circumstances. We have refined the concept of bearing witness, introduced in Chapter 1.3, throughout the chapters of this book. This constructive work has heightened our awareness of the theological and political aspects of Christian social ethics. When we bear witness to individual survivors, we become aware of the social nature of suffering and the dynamics of domination allowing it. Trauma-informed ethics is ultimately the work of a community of persons bearing witness to traumatic suffering as a political problem.[1] Such an approach is essential in a time when the foundations of democracy are under attack.

---

[1] On this theme, see Elizabeth Soto Albrecht, "The Politics of Suffering and JustPraxis," in *Liberating the Politics of Jesus: Renewing Peace Theology Through the Wisdom of Women*, ed. Elizabeth Soto Albrecht and Darryl W. Stephens, 53–66 (T&T Clark, 2020).

Refined in the Struggle

Bearing witness is a complex task to be worked out in context and community. We have modeled this task through engagement with multiple theological lenses and ethical challenges. Table 4.1 provides a comparison of theological themes and ethical emphases discussed throughout this book. As we encountered diverse moral issues, our conceptual toolbox grew in complexity. In particular, the contemporary challenges in Part Three of this book helped us refine the moral themes of bearing witness. The following brief discussion summarizes key learnings for the purpose of prompting deeper discussion about Christian social ethics.

The moral theme of dignity, theologically grounded in prevenient grace and humanity as created in the image of God, entails commitments to equality, reciprocity, and human rights when viewed through the lens of diakonia. Contemporary challenges further refine the theme of dignity. Traci West's resistance and disruptive ethics demand attention to diversity, difference, and shared humanity when considering dignity in patriarchal and racist contexts. In the context of empire, creation wisdom expands dignity to include the intrinsic worth and interrelatedness of the entire cosmos, eliciting a sense of awe as we ponder God in non-human creation. When addressing abuse of power and institutional betrayal, healing congregations recognize dignity by realizing the woundedness and harm caused to the community and its members.

The moral theme of love finds theological footing in convicting grace, humility (initial repentance), and care for the vulnerable. Through the lens of diakonia, love insists on seeing, listening to, and ensuring the availability of basic goods for our neighbors. West's ethics sees particularity and embodied wisdom as aspects of love, while creation wisdom is insistent on recognizing non-human agency and our own creatureliness as members of a vast creation. Love in situations of abuse and institutional betrayal is expressed by reasserting healthy boundaries and listening to victim-survivors as truth-tellers.

The moral theme of justice—rooted in justifying grace, repentance, and reparation— prompts reflection on and judgment about forms of restitution from a perspective of diakonia. Resistance and disruptive ethics employ an intersectional power analysis as a tool of justice, while creation wisdom brings a systemic perspective to critique structures of empire, engaging countermemories as we reckon with the past. Justice in healing congregations relies on community rituals of grief and lament.

The moral theme of solidarity finds theological company in sanctifying grace, holiness, and reconciliation. The liberating service of diakonia expresses solidarity through action, collaboration, and reconciliation, while West's antiracist ethic leans into reciprocal learning, strategic alliances, and human freedom as touchstones for solidarity. Creation wisdom counters empire through wonder, projects of repair, and the full flourishing of all creation. Healing congregations strive toward the solidarity of reconnection even as scarring witnesses to the remainder of healed wounds.

Our understandings of dignity, love, justice, and solidarity are thus specified and complexified as we confront multifaceted ethical challenges in today's world. These moral themes are not fixed in abstraction but are animated with the throes of life. Faced with additional contemporary challenges, the moral themes of bearing witness

TABLE 4.1 *Theological Themes and Ethical Emphases Summarized*

Moral Theme	Liberating Service (diakonia) Table 1.4.1	Wesleyan Theological Themes Table 2.1.1	Resistance and Disruptive Ethics (West) Table 3.1.1	Creation Wisdom (anti-empire) Table 3.2.1	Healing Congregations Table 3.3.1
dignity	equality, reciprocity, human rights	image of God, prevenient grace	diversity, difference, shared humanity	intrinsic worth, interrelatedness, awe	realize woundedness and harm
love	seeing, listening, ensuring basic goods	humility, convicting grace, care for vulnerable	embodied wisdom, particularity	creatureliness, non-human agency, insistence	reassert healthy boundaries, truth-listening
justice	reflecting/ judging, restitution	justifying grace, repentance, reparation	intersectional power analysis	systemic perspective, counter-memory	community rituals of grief and lament
solidarity	acting, collaboration, reconciliation	sanctifying grace, holiness, reconciliation	reciprocal learning, strategic alliances, human freedom	wonder, repair, full flourishing of creation	reconnection, scarring

will be further refined. For it is *en la lucha* (in the struggle) that a liberating Christian ethics finds meaning.[2] One such struggle demanding a trauma-informed approach to Christian ethics is the threat of tyranny.

Discussion Questions

1   Reflecting on your journey in reading this book, how was your understanding of *dignity* stretched and deepened through each column in Table 4.1? What about your understandings of love, justice, and solidarity?

2   In the Preface to this book, you were asked to name the most pressing moral issues facing your community. Choose one of these issues: How might struggling with this issue further refine your understanding of the moral themes of bearing witness?

Against Tyranny

Now, I bring this book full circle. In the Introduction, we encountered the work of Judith Herman, specifically through her book, *Truth and Repair*. Bearing witness to survivors of trauma during a career spanning fifty years, Herman found herself inevitably engaged in issues of justice and equality. She blazed the trail of modern trauma studies by arguing that "the suffering of traumatized people is a matter not only of individual psychology but also, always, of social justice."[3] From trauma survivors, she learned that they need to be seen, heard, believed, and cared for by the wider community. They also need strong allies who will support their efforts to reclaim a sense of agency and develop a missional purpose for their life. So, she posited a final stage of trauma recovery focused on justice (3). In this section, I follow Herman's argument identifying bearing witness as a political action against tyranny.

Justice is a matter of right relationship. Thus, justice involves not only the trauma survivor but also bystanders, perpetrators, and social structures. Bystanders who fail to bear witness to victim-survivors contribute to "the social ecology of violence" that is trauma (Herman, 3). As bystanders, we either bear witness or bear responsibility—often both. When survivors envision justice, they see right relationships restored in ways much different from the ways civil and criminal courts typically understand justice. Herman's book *Truth and Repair* offers details about the kind of "healing justice" sought by survivors (9).

Justice, from the perspective of my informants, was not centered on the question of the offender's fate; it was first and foremost about their *own* recovery. In their view, the primary obligation of the moral community was to help repair the harm

---

[2]Ada María Isasi-Díaz, *En la Lucha / In the Struggle: Elaborating a Mujerista Theology* (Fortress, 2004).
[3]Judith L. Herman, *Truth and Repair: How Trauma Survivors Envision Justice* (Basic Books, 2023), 1.

that had been done to *them*... healing a damaged relationship, not primarily between victims and offenders but rather between victims and the bystanders in their communities.

(Herman, 131)

In other words, healing justice is about bearing witness to the survivor and supporting their healing through repaired relationships. This vision of justice is premised on the existence of moral community.

Those who bear witness to trauma become the survivor's moral community. Herman defined *moral community* as "a community to which the individual belongs and which she trusts to come to her aid when she is hurt" (50). As we have seen, trauma ruptures community and relationships. Healing, therefore, involves repair of community and relationships. When a victim's anger is transformed into a shared sense of righteous indignation within the community, the victim-survivor feels not only vindicated but also respected (47). Such empathetic indignation strengthens moral community, contributing to healing and repair (47, 53).

Moral community requires a shared sense of justice. Herman posited a type of justice built on "the democratic principle of equality" (39). Her emphasis on equality is consistent with the first moment of bearing witness presented in this book, recognizing human dignity, which grounds our commitment to human rights. Equality does not mean treating everyone the same. Consider, for example, the preferential option for the poor in Roman Catholic Social Teaching and the secular assertion that the measure of a society is how it treats its most vulnerable members. Thus, the ideal of equality requires an understanding of fairness when social, economic, and other actual inequalities shape the context in which trauma occurs. On this topic, Herman cited John Rawls, who formulated a sophisticated conception of justice as fairness, asserting, "Social and economic inequalities are to be arranged so that they are ... to the greatest benefit of the least advantaged."[4] Inequality is a contextually fluid rather than static reality, and inequalities are due to many factors. In situations of trauma, the person experiencing the trauma is "the least advantaged"—the person with the least power in that situation. Thus, justice as fairness dictates that the trauma victim-survivor's healing needs to be prioritized as a matter of democratic equality.

The opposite is the case in societies shaped by structures of tyranny, defined as unfair treatment by people wielding power over others (Herman, 25). Coercion, control, and violence provide the means of dominance. Structures of patriarchy, racism, and other forms of oppression form the social structures supporting tyranny. One requirement for people in power to benefit from tyranny is for bystanders to remain silent and compliant (Herman, 35). Conversely, when bystanders bear witness to trauma and abuse under systems of tyranny, they are thrust into the political spotlight as a threat to the dominant order. To bear witness to victim-survivors of trauma in patriarchal and racist societies is to engage in a political act of defiance. Thus, to form moral community in solidarity with victim-survivors of trauma is to advocate for democracy over tyranny.

---

[4]Herman, 42; John Rawls, *A Theory of Justice*, rev. ed. (Belknap, 1999), 266.

Discussion Questions

1 When have you witnessed or experienced moral community, as described by Herman?

2 What difference would it make to contemporary political discourse if every member of society understood themselves as a member of the same moral community?

Sending Forth

The work of trauma-informed response involves all sectors of society engaging head, heart, and hands. This book has assisted with the intellectual task of learning about trauma and ethics. The practice of bearing witness, however, involves the entire self in relationship. Empathy, for example, must be heartfelt, not just cognitively understood. Furthermore, bearing witness to survivors of trauma is a community effort. We can learn about trauma and practice bearing witness individually, but we must work together to become fully trauma-informed. When we bear witness to someone else's suffering, we enter into a relationship with that person in community. Bearing witness is also a material endeavor, involving our hands and feet.

Moral community is forged in the collective struggles of everyday life. I am convinced that many of the ills dividing society have root in unhealed experiences of individual and collective trauma. We do not have to wait for an official diagnosis, though. The ethics of bearing witness, like trauma-informed response, consists of best practices appropriate for loving all of our neighbors, not just those whom we suspect have a history of trauma. This effort requires full participation; we must invest our lives in each other. In polarized times, the bonds of democratic society depend not on intellectual argumentation about public policy or even heartfelt testimony about the truth of our own experiences. Rather, moral community depends on our willingness to roll up our sleeves and join hands in collaborative projects of shared material concern. True liberation comes through solidarity.

May you go forth bearing witness to the stories and sufferings of those around you. May you transcend your selfish interests through recognition, empathy, memory, and imagination. May you learn and practice dignity, love, justice, and solidarity. And, through God's grace, may you do so in the company of others, forging and strengthening moral community for the common good and the full flourishing of all creation. May it be so. Amen.

WORKS CITED

Addy, Tony. "Community Practice and Critical Community Research: Perspectives from Conviviality and the CABLE Approach." *Diaconia* 10, no. 2 (2020): 161–79. https://doi.org/10.13109/diac.2019.10.2.161.

Addy, Tony. "Seeking Conviviality: A New Core Concept for the Diaconal Church." In *The Diaconal Church*, edited by Dietrich et al., 158–70. Regnum Books International, 2019.

Addy, Tony, ed. *Seeking Conviviality: Reforming Community Diakonia in Europe*. Lutheran World Federation, 2014. https://www.interdiac.eu/resources/seeking-conviviality-reforming-community-diakonia-in-europe.

Adichie, Chimamanda Ngozi. "The Danger of a Single Story." *TEDGlobal*, 2009. https://www.ted.com/talks/chimamanda_ngozi_adichie_the_danger_of_a_single_story.

Alexander, Michelle. *The New Jim Crow: Mass Incarceration in the Age of Colorblindness*. New Press, 2012.

Alper, Becka A. "Sidebar: Involvement by Religious Groups in Debates over Climate Change." *Pew Research Center*, November 17, 2022. https://www.pewresearch.org/religion/2022/11/17/sidebar-involvement-by-religious-groups-in-debates-over-climate-change/.

Amer, Yasmin, and Andrea Asuaje. "A Respite Center Helped Her Heal. Now She's Helping Other Refugees Overcome Their Trauma." *WBUR*, October 22, 2019. https://www.wbur.org/kindworld/2019/10/22/place-of-respite.

Amer, Yasmin, and Andrea Asuaje. "There's a Lot of Tragedy at the Southern Border. There's Also Profound Compassion." *WBUR*, October 25, 2019. https://www.wbur.org/kindworld/2019/10/25/lifelines-series.

American Humanist Association. "Humanism and Its Aspirations: Humanist Manifesto III, a Successor to the Humanist Manifesto of 1933." https://americanhumanist.org/what-is-humanism/manifesto3/.

Ammerman, Nancy T. "Golden Rule Christianity: Lived Religion in the American Mainstream." In *Lived Religion in America: Toward a History of Practice*, edited by David D. Hall, 196–216. Princeton University Press, 1997.

Ampony, Godwin, Martin Büscher, Beate Hofmann, Félicité Ngnintedem, Dennis Solon, and Dietrich Werner, eds. *International Handbook on Ecumenical Diakonia: Contextual Theologies and Practices of Diakonia and Christian Social Services—Resources for Study and Intercultural Learning*. Regnum Books International, 2021.

Baldwin, Jennifer. *Trauma-Sensitive Theology: Thinking Theologically in the Era of Trauma*. Cascade, 2018.

Bauman, Whitney A., and Kevin J. O'Brien. *Environmental Ethics and Uncertainty: Wrestling with Wicked Problems*. Routledge, 2020.

Benhabib, Seyla. *Situating the Self: Gender, Community, and Postmodernism in Contemporary Ethics*. Routledge, 1992.

Bennett, John Coleman. *Social Salvation: A Religious Approach to the Problems of Social Change*. Charles Scribner, 1948.

Beste, Jennifer Erin. *God and the Victim: Traumatic Intrusions on Grace and Freedom.* Oxford University Press, 2007.

Birrell, Pamela J., and Jennifer J. Freyd. "Betrayal Trauma: Relational Models of Harm and Healing." *Journal of Trauma Practice* 5, no. 1 (2006): 49–63. https://doi.org/10.1300/J189v05n01_04.

Block, Elizabeth Sweeny. "White Privilege and the Erroneous Conscience: Rethinking Moral Culpability and Ignorance." *Journal of the Society of Christian Ethics* 39, no. 2 (2019): 357–74.

Bloom, Paul. *Against Empathy: The Case for Rational Compassion.* HarperCollins, 2016.

Bogart, Anne. "Bearing Witness." *SITI*, February 18, 2016. https://web.archive.org/web/20160228005129/http://siti.org/content/bearing-witness.

The Book of Discipline of The United Methodist Church 2016. UMPH, 2016.

The Book of Discipline of The United Methodist Church 2020/2024. UMPH, 2024.

The Book of Resolutions of The United Methodist Church 1980. UMPH, 1980.

The Book of Resolutions of The United Methodist Church 1984. UMPH, 1984.

The Book of Resolutions of The United Methodist Church 1992. UMPH, 1992.

The Book of Resolutions of The United Methodist Church 1996. UMPH, 1996.

The Book of Resolutions of The United Methodist Church 2000. UMPH, 2000.

The Book of Resolutions of The United Methodist Church 2008. UMPH, 2008.

The Book of Resolutions of The United Methodist Church 2012. UMPH, 2012.

The Book of Resolutions of The United Methodist Church 2016. UMPH, 2016.

Boston University School of Theology Anna Howard Shaw Center. "2013 Women in the World Conference." http://www.bu.edu/shaw/events/women-in-the-world-conference/2013-women-in-the-world-conference/.

Böttcher, Reinhard, ed. *Prophetic Diakonia: "For the Healing of the World."* Lutheran World Federation, November 2002. https://www.episcopaldeacons.org/uploads/2/6/7/3/26739998/prophtcdiak_luth02.pdf.

Bratnober, Carolyn. "Traci C. West: Disruptive Activism, Ministry, and Scholarship." In *Challenging Bias against Women Academics in Religion,* Women in Religion, vol. 2, edited by Colleen D. Hurting, 105–24. Atla Open Press, 2021. https://doi.org/10.31046/atlaopenpress.46.

Brock, Rita Nakashima, and Gabriella Lettini. *Soul Repair: Recovering from Moral Injury after War.* Beacon, 2013.

Brock, Rita Nakashima, and Rebecca Ann Parker. *Proverbs of Ashes: Violence, Redemptive Suffering, and the Search for What Saves Us.* Beacon, 2001.

Browning, Sharon, Donna Duffey, Fred Magondu, John A. Moore, and Patricia A. Way. *The Little Book of Listening: Listening as a Radical Act of Love, Justice, Healing, and Transformation.* Good Books, 2024.

Bstan-'dzinrgya-mtsho, Dalai Lama XIV. *Ethics for the New Millenium.* Riverhead, 1999.

Buber, Martin. *I and Thou,* 2nd ed. Scribner, 1958.

Burke, Tarana. "Me Too Is a Movement, Not a Moment." TEDWomen, 2018. https://www.ted.com/talks/tarana_burke_me_too_is_a_movement_not_a_moment?language=en.

Cannon, Katie G. *Black Womanist Ethics.* American Academy of Religion Academy Series 60. Scholars Press, 1988.

Carpenter, C.C.J., Joseph A. Durick, Hilton J. Grafman, Paul Hardin, Nolan B. Harmon, George M. Murray, Edward V. Ramsage, and Earl Stallings, "Alabama Clergymen's Letter to Dr. Martin Luther King, Jr." April 12, 1963. https://teachingamericanhistory.org/document/letter-to-martin-luther-king/.

Cave, Erik. "Trauma-Informed Ministry with Chris Haughee." September 8, 2022. https://pacnwc.org/trauma-informed-ministry-with-chris-haughee/.

CDC. "About Child Sexual Abuse." 2024. https://www.cdc.gov/child-abuse-neglect/about/about-child-sexual-abuse.html.

CDC. "About the CDC-Kaiser ACE Study." 2021. https://www.cdc.gov/violenceprevention/aces/about.html.

CDC. "Prevalence of Adverse Childhood Experiences among U.S. Adults—Behavioral Risk Factor Surveillance System, 2011–2020." 2023. https://www.cdc.gov/mmwr/volumes/72/wr/mm7226a2.htm.

Center for Institutional Courage. "Knowledge Base and Research Priorities." https://www.institutionalcourage.org/knowledge-base-and-research-priorities.

Center for Institutional Courage. "We Are Making a Call to Institutional Courage." https://www.institutionalcourage.org/the-call-to-courage.

Central Conference of American Rabbis. "The Guiding Principles of Reform Judaism." https://www.ccarnet.org/rabbinic-voice/platforms/article-guiding-principles-reform-judaism/.

Chopp, Rebecca S. "Theology and the Poetics of Testimony." *Criterion* 37, no. (1998): 2–12.

Clayton, Susan, Christie Manning, Kirra Krygsman, and Meighen Speiser. *Mental Health and Our Changing Climate: Impacts, Implications, and Guidance.* American Psychological Association and ecoAmerica, 2017. https://www.apa.org/news/press/releases/2017/03/mental-health-climate.pdf.

Clergy Sexual Misconduct Information and Resources. https://clergysexualmisconduct.com.

Collins, John N. *Diakonia Studies: Critical Issues in Ministry.* Oxford University Press, 2014.

"A Common Word between Us and You." October 13, 2007. https://www.acommonword.com/downloads-and-translations/.

Cooper-White, Pamela. *The Cry of Tamar: Violence against Women and the Church's Response.* Fortress, 1995.

Cooper-White, Pamela. *The Cry of Tamar: Violence against Women and the Church's Response,* 2nd ed. Fortress, 2012.

Cooper-White, Pamela. *Shared Wisdom: Use of the Self in Pastoral Care and Counseling.* Fortress, 2004.

Copeland, M. Shawn. "'Wading through Many Sorrows': Toward a Theology of Suffering in Womanist Perspective." In *A Troubling in My Soul: Womanist Perspectives on Evil and Suffering,* edited by Emilie M. Townes, 109–29. Orbis, 1993.

Cordner, Christopher. "What Did Iris Murdoch Mean by 'Attention'?" *ABC Religion & Ethics.* Australian Broadcasting Corporation, July 11, 2019. https://www.abc.net.au/religion/iris-murdoch-and-the-meaning-of-attention/11301690.

Council of Bishops of the United Methodist Church. *God's Renewed Creation: Call to Hope and Action. Foundation Document.* 2009. https://web.archive.org/web/20220120212523/http://hopeandaction.org/main/wp-content/uploads/2010/03/Foundation-Doc-Eng-Handout-2-col.pdf.

Council of Bishops of the United Methodist Church. "A Statement from the Council of Bishops as We Embark on a Journey toward Healing Relationships with Indigenous Peoples." April 30, 2012. https://web.archive.org/web/20200921061104/https://www.epaumc.org/archives/2012-general-conference/2012/04/act-of-repentance-and-healing-for-indigenous-persons/.

Courtois, Christine A. "First, Do No More Harm: Ethics of Attending to Spiritual Issues in Trauma Treatment." In *Spiritually Oriented Psychotherapy for Trauma,* edited by Donald F. Walker, Christine A. Courtois, and Jamie D. Aten, 55–75. American Psychological Association, 2015. https://doi.org/10.1037/14500-004.

Crain, Margaret Ann. *The United Methodist Deacon: Ordained to Word, Service, Compassion, and Justice.* Abingdon, 2016.

Craps, Stef. "Climate Trauma." In *The Routledge Companion to Literature and Trauma*, edited by Colin Davis and Hanna Meretoja, 275–84. Routledge, 2020.

Crawford, S. Cromwell. "Ethical Foundations for Hindu Bioethics." *Dialogue & Alliance* 17, no. 2 (2003): 81–92.

Curran, Charles. "Humanae Vitae: Fifty Years Later." *Theological Studies* 79, no. 3 (2018): 520–42. https://doi.org/10.1177/0040563918784769.

Daly, Herman E., and John B. Cobb Jr. *For the Common Good: Redirecting the Economy toward Community, the Environment, and a Sustainable Future*, 2nd ed., with contributions by Clifford W. Cobb. Beacon, 1994.

Davidson, Shannon. "Trauma-Informed Practices for Postsecondary Education: A Guide." Education Northwest, 2017. https://educationnorthwest.org/sites/default/files/resources/trauma-informed-practices-postsecondary-508.pdf.

"Declaration of Independence: A Transcription." National Archives. https://www.archives.gov/founding-docs/declaration-transcript.

De La Torre, Miguel A. *Doing Christian Ethics from the Margins*, 3rd ed. Orbis, 2023.

De La Torre, Miguel A. *Embracing Hopelessness*. Fortress, 2017.

DIAKONIA World Federation Executive Committee. "Diaconal Reflections: How We Experience Our Diaconal Calling in Our Diversity." 1998. https://web.archive.org/web/20160411170755/http://www.diakonia-world.org/files/theologiepapier98english.pdf.

Dietrich, Stephanie, Knud Jøregensen, Kari Karsrud Korslein, and Kjell Nordstokke, eds. *The Diaconal Church*. Regnum Books International, 2019.

Dietrich, Stephanie, Knud Jøregensen, Kari Karsrud Korslein, and Kjell Nordstokke, eds. *Diakonia as Christian Social Practice: An Introduction*. Regnum Books International, 2014.

Doctors without Borders/Médecins Sans Frontières. "What Guides Us." https://www.doctorswithoutborders.org/who-we-are/principles/bearing-witness.

Dolch, Sally Badgley. "Healing the Breach: Response Team Intervention in United Methodist Congregations." DMin thesis, Wesley Theological Seminary, 2010.

Dyck, Sally. "Eight Principles of Holy Conferencing: A Study Guide for Churches and Groups," 2012. http://mnumc-email.brtapp.com/files/eefiles/documents/holy_conferencing_study_guide_2012.pdf.

Faith Community Today. "FACTs on Growth 2010 Report." https://faithcommunitiestoday.org/wp-content/uploads/2019/01/FACTs-on-Growth-2010.pdf.

Falcke, Heino. "The Ecumenical Assembly for Justice, Peace and the Integrity of Creation." *The Ecumenical Review* 56, no. 2 (2004): 184–91.

Felitti, Vincent J., Robert F. Anda, Dale Nordenberg, David F. Williamson, Alison M. Spitz, Valerie Edwards, Mary P. Koss, and James S. Marks. "Relationship of Childhood Abuse and Household Dysfunction to Many of the Leading Causes of Death in Adults: The Adverse Childhood Experiences (ACE) Study." *American Journal of Preventive Medicine* 14, no. 4 (1998): 245–58.

Field, David N. *Bid Our Jarring Conflicts Cease: A Wesleyan Theology and Praxis of Church Unity*. Foundery, 2017.

Fortune, Marie M. *Is Nothing Sacred?: When Sex Invades the Pastoral Relationship*. Harper & Row, 1989.

Fowler, James W. "Faith Development Theory and the Postmodern Challenges." *The International Journal for the Psychology of Religion* 11, no. 3 (2001): 159–72. https://doi.org/10.1207/S15327582IJPR1103_03.

Francis, Pope. *Laudato Si': On Care for Our Common Home*. Encyclical Letter, 2015.

Francis, Pope, and Sheikh Ahmad Muhammad al-Tayyeb. "Document on Human Fraternity for World Peace and Living Together." February 4, 2019. http://www.vatican.va/content/francesco/en/travels/2019/outside/documents/papa-francesco_20190204_documento-fratellanza-umana.html.

Freyd, Jennifer J. "When Sexual Assault Victims Speak Out, Their Institutions Often Betray Them." *The Conversation*, January 11, 2018. https://theconversation.com/when-sexual-assault-victims-speak-out-their-institutions-often-betray-them-87050.

Friedman, Edwin H. *A Failure of Nerve: Leadership in the Age of the Quick Fix*, rev. ed. Church Publishing, 2017.

Galatzer-Levy, Isaac R., Charles L. Burton, and George A. Bonanno. "Coping Flexibility, Potentially Traumatic Life Events, and Resilience: A Prospective Study of College Student Adjustment." *Journal of Social and Clinical Psychology* 31, no. 6 (2012): 542–67. https://doi.org/10.1521/jscp.2012.31.6.542.

Garcia, Sandra E. "The Woman Who Created #MeToo Long before Hashtags." *The New York Times*, October 20, 2017. https://www.nytimes.com/2017/10/20/us/me-too-movement-tarana-burke.html.

Garland, Diana R. "The Prevalence of Clergy Sexual Misconduct with Adults: A Research Study—Executive Summary." https://socialwork.web.baylor.edu/executive-summary.

General Board of Church and Society. "Church and Society Ethnic Local Church Grant Supports Middle East Migrants." https://www.umcjustice.org/news-and-stories/church-and-society-ethnic-local-church-grant-supports-middle-east-migrants-869.

General Board of Global Ministries. "Sacred Native American Lands Will Be Returned to Wyandotte Nation." August 26, 2019. https://www.umcmission.org/share-our-work/news-stories/2019/august/sacred-native-american-lands-will-be-returned-to-wyandotte-nation.

Georgia Occupational Therapy Association. "Awards and Recognitions: Linda Stephens Scholarship." https://www.gaota.com/recognitions-awards.

Grant, Jacquelyn. "The Sin of Servanthood and the Deliverance of Discipleship." In *A Troubling in My Soul: Womanist Perspectives on Evil and Suffering*, edited by Emilie M. Townes, 199–218. Orbis, 1993.

Greek Orthodox Archdiocese of America. "The Greenhouse Effect and the Threat of Climate Change." February 4, 2005. https://www.goarch.org/-/the-greenhouse-effect-and-the-threat-of-climate-change.

Gühne, Christine. "Diaconia in Contexts of Traumatisation—An Introduction." In *The Diaconal Church*, edited by Dietrich et al., 452–5. Regnum Books International, 2019.

Guidepost Solutions. "Report of the Independent Investigation: The Southern Baptist Convention Executive Committee's Response to Sexual Abuse Allegations and an Audit of the Procedures and Actions of the Credentials Committee." May 15, 2022. https://www.documentcloud.org/documents/22031737-final-guidepost-solutions-independent-investigation-report.

Gushee, David P. *The Future of Faith in American Politics: The Public Witness of the Evangelical Center*. Baylor University Press, 2008.

Gustafson, James M. "Conclusion: The Relation of Other Disciplines to Theological Ethics." In *Intersections: Science, Theology, and Ethics*, 126–47. Pilgrim, 1996.

Gustafson, James M. *Ethics from a Theocentric Perspective: Volume One: Theology and Ethics*. University of Chicago Press, 1981.

Guth, Karen V. *The Ethics of Tainted Legacies: Human Flourishing after Traumatic Pasts*. Cambridge University Press, 2022.

Habermas, Jürgen. *Moral Consciousness and Communicative Action* (Studies in Contemporary German Social Thought). Translated by Christian Lenhardt and Shierry Weber Nicholsen. MIT Press, 1990.

Hahn, Heather. "Church Ratifies Women's Equality Amendment." *UM News*, November 6, 2019. https://www.umnews.org/en/news/church-ratifies-womens-equality-amendment.

Hallman, David G. "Ecumenical Responses to Climate Change: A Summary of the History and Dynamics of Ecumenical Involvement in the Issue of Climate Change."

The Ecumenical Review 49, no. 2 (1997): 131–41. https://research.ebsco.com/linkprocessor/plink?id=831c9230-743d-3012-8569-02c6cc785070.

Halpern, Cynthia. *Suffering, Politics, Power: A Genealogy in Modern Political Theory.* State University of New York Press, 2002.

Handley, George B. "What Else Is New?: Toward a Postcolonial Christian Theology for the Anthropocene." *Religions* 11, no. 5 (2020): 225. https://doi.org/10.3390/rel11050225.

Haque, Umair. "Why Our First Responsibility Is Bearing Witness." *Medium,* May 26, 2018. https://medium.com/on-eudaimonia/why-our-first-responsibility-is-bearing-witness-2e493c4d3fd.

Harris, Melanie L. "Doing Justice to Issues of Race?" In *T&T Clark Handbook of Christian Theology and Climate Change,* edited by Ernst Conradie and Hilda Koster, 659–62. Bloomsbury, 2020.

Harris, Melanie L. *Ecowomanism: African American Women and Earth-Honoring Faiths.* Ecology and Justice Series. Orbis, 2017.

Harris, Melanie L. "Ecowomanist Wisdom: Encountering Earth and Spirit." In *Planetary Solidarity: Global Women's Voices on Christian Doctrine and Climate Justice,* edited by Grace Ji-Sun Kim and Hilda P. Koster, 239–48. Fortress, 2017.

Harvey, Jennifer. *Dear White Christians: For Those Still Longing for Racial Reconciliation,* 2nd ed. Eerdmans, 2020.

Hauerwas, Stanley. *The Peaceable Kingdom: A Primer in Christian Ethics.* University of Notre Dame Press, 1983.

Heath, Elaine A. *Healing the Wounds of Sexual Abuse: Reading the Bible with Survivors.* Brazos, 2019.

Henry, O. "Gifts of the Magi." In *Collected Stories,* edited by Paul J. Horowitz, 760–3. Dorset, 1995.

Herman, Judith Lewis. *Trauma and Recovery: The Aftermath of Violence—From Domestic Abuse to Political Terror,* 2nd ed. Basic Books, (1992)2015.

Herman, Judith Lewis. *Truth and Repair: How Trauma Survivors Envision Justice.* Basic Books, 2023.

Hinson-Hasty, Elizabeth L. "Introductory Comments for Panel on Niebuhr and Feminism." *Niebuhr Society, Annual Meeting of the American Academy of Religion,* Chicago, November 17, 2012.

Hollenbach, David, *The Global Face of Public Faith: Politics, Human Rights, and Christian Ethics.* Georgetown University Press, 2003.

Hunsinger, Deborah van Deusen. *Bearing the Unbearable: Trauma, Gospel, and Pastoral Care.* Eerdmans, 2015.

Huyser-Honig, Joan. "Trauma-Informed Care in Church Worship and Life." *Calvin Institute of Christian Worship,* March 24, 2020. https://worship.calvin.edu/resources/resource-library/trauma-informed-care-in-church-worship-and-life/.

"In Protest of LGBTQ Treatment in UMC, Phil Wogaman Surrenders Clergy Credentials." *UM-Insight,* May 31, 2017. http://um-insight.net/in-the-church/ordained-ministry/in-protest-of-lgbtq-treatment-in-umc-phil-wogaman-surrenders/.

Institute for Collective Trauma and Growth. "Tools for Worship." https://web.archive.org/web/20230701110926/https://www.ictg.org/tools-for-worship.html.

Intergovernmental Panel on Climate Change (IPCC). "History of the IPCC." https://www.ipcc.ch/about/history/.

Iosso, Christian, Darryl W. Stephens, and Roger A. Willer. "Prospects for Ecumenical Ethical Witness: Confronting Climate Degradation." *Ecumenical Review* 70, no. 4 (2018): 772–87. https://doi.org/10.1111/erev.12400.

Isasi-Díaz, Ada María. *En la Lucha / In the Struggle: Elaborating a Mujerista Theology.* Fortress, 2004.

Isasi-Díaz, Ada María. "Kin-dom of God: A Mujerista Proposal." In *In Our Own Voices: Latino/a Renditions of Theology*, edited by Benjamín Valentín, 171–89. Orbis, 2010.

Isasi-Díaz, Ada María. *La Lucha Continues: Mujerista Theology*. Orbis, 2004.

Jacobs, Jill. "The History of 'Tikkun Olam.'" *Zeek: A Jewish Journal of Thought and Culture*, June 2007. http://www.zeek.net/706tohu/.

Jenkins, Willis. *The Future of Ethics: Sustainability, Social Justice, and Religious Creativity*. Georgetown University Press, 2013.

Jenkins, Willis. "Working with Politics." In *T&T Clark Handbook of Christian Theology and Climate Change*, edited by Ernst M. Conradie and Hilda P. Koster, 70–82. T&T Clark, 2020.

Jennings, Theodore W., Jr. *Good News to the Poor: John Wesley's Evangelical Economics*. Kingswood, 1990.

John Paul II, Pope. "Peace with God the Creator, Peace with All of Creation." January 1, 1990. https://www.vatican.va/content/john-paul-ii/en/messages/peace/documents/hf_jp-ii_mes_19891208_xxiii-world-day-for-peace.html.

Jones, Serene. *Trauma + Grace: Theology in a Ruptured World*, 2nd ed. Westminster John Knox, 2019.

Jones, Tamsin. "Bearing Witness: Hope for the Unseen." *Political Theology* 17, no. 2 (2016): 137–50. https://doi.org/10.1080/1462317X.2016.1161300.

Jung, Patricia Beattie, and Aana Marie Vigen, eds., with John Anderson. *God, Science, Sex, Gender: An Interdisciplinary Approach to Christian Ethics*. University of Illinois Press, 2010.

Keefe-Perry, L. Callid, and Zachary Moon. "Courage in Chaos: The Importance of Trauma-Informed Adult Religious Education". *Religious Education* 114, no. 1 (2019): 30–41. https://doi.org/10.1080/00344087.2018.1435989.

Keller, Catherine. *Facing Apocalypse: Climate, Democracy, and Other Last Chances*. Orbis, 2021.

Kim, Grace Ji-Sun, and Hilda P. Koster, eds. *Planetary Solidarity: Global Women's Voices on Christian Doctrine and Climate Justice*. Fortress, 2017.

Kim, Grace Ji-Sun, and Susan M. Shaw. *Intersectional Theology: An Introductory Guide*. Fortress, 2018.

King, Martin Luther Jr. *A Testament of Hope: The Essential Writings and Speeches of Martin Luther King, Jr.*, edited by James Melvin Washington. HarperSanFrancisco, 1986.

Kinghorn, Warren. "Combat Trauma and Moral Fragmentation: A Theological Account of Moral Injury." *Journal of the Society of Christian Ethics* 32, no. 2 (2012): 57–74. doi: https://doi.org/10.1353/sce.2012.0041.

Kiser, Charles, and Elaine A. Heath. *Trauma-Informed Evangelism: Cultivating Communities of Wounded Healers*. Eerdmans, 2023.

Knotts, Alice G. *Fellowship of Love: Methodist Women Changing American Racial Attitudes, 1920–1968*. Kingswood, 1996.

Kristof, Nicholas D., and Sheryl WuDunn. *Half the Sky*. Alfred Knopf, 2009.

Kübler-Ross, Elisabeth. *On Death and Dying*. Simon & Schuster/Touchstone, 1969.

Lachman, Vicki D. "Compassion Fatigue as a Threat to Ethical Practice: Identification, Personal and Workplace Prevention/Management Strategies." *MEDSURG Nursing* 25, no. 4 (2016): 275–8. https://www.nursingworld.org/globalassets/docs/ana/ethics/compassionfatigue.pdf.

Lartey, Emmanuel Y. *In Living Color: An Intercultural Approach to Pastoral Care and Counseling*, 2nd ed. Jessica Kingsley, 2003.

Lebacqz, Karen. *Six Theories of Justice: Perspectives from Philosophical and Theological Ethics*. Augsburg, 1986.

Lewin, Tamar. "Seven Allege Harassment by Yale Doctor at Clinic." *The New York Times*, April 13, 2015. https://www.nytimes.com/2015/04/14/us/former-yale-medical-professor-accused-of-sexual-harassment.html?partner=rss&emc=rss&_r=1.

Lovin, Robin W. *Christian Ethics: An Essential Guide*. Abingdon, 2000.

Lovin, Robin W. *Christian Realism and the New Realities*. Cambridge University Press, 2008.

Lovin, Robin W., and Joshua Maudlin, eds. *Theology as Interdisciplinary Inquiry: Leaning with and from the Natural and Human Sciences*. Eerdmans, 2017.

Lutheran World Federation. *Mission in Context: Transformation, Reconciliation, Empowerment: An LWF Contribution to the Understanding and Practice of Mission*. Lutheran World Federation, 2004. https://lutheranworld.org/resources/publication-mission-context-transformation-reconciliation-empowerment.

Maddox, Randy L. *Responsible Grace: John Wesley's Practical Theology*. Kingswood, 1994.

Marshall, Ellen Ott. *Introduction to Christian Ethics: Conflict, Faith, and Human Life*. Westminster John Knox, 2018.

Maté, Gabor. "Foreword." In *In an Unspoken Voice: How the Body Releases Trauma and Restores Goodness* by Peter A. Levine, Kindle, loc. 163–209. North Atlantic, 2010.

Matheson, Kimberly, Ajani Asokumar, and Hymie Anisman. "Resilience: Safety in the Aftermath of Traumatic Stressor Experiences." *Frontiers in Behavioral Neuroscience* 14 (2020): 9–10. https://doi.org/10.3389/fnbeh.2020.596919.

McCann, I. Lisa, and Laurie Anne Pearlman. "Vicarious Traumatization: A Framework for Understanding the Psychological Effects of Working with Victims." *Journal of Traumatic Stress* 3, no. 1 (1990): 131–49. https://doi.org/10.1002/jts.2490030110.

McCarroll, Pamela R. "Embodying Theology: Trauma Theory, Climate Change, Pastoral and Practical Theology." *Religions* 13, no. 4 (2022): 294. https://doi.org/10.3390/rel13040294.

McClintock, Karen A. *Trauma-Informed Pastoral Care: How to Respond When Things Fall Apart*. Fortress, 2022.

McCracken, Vic, ed. *Christian Faith and Social Justice: Five Views*. Bloomsbury, 2014.

McDonagh, Sean. "Part I: Catholic Teaching and the Environment." In *On Care for Our Common Home: The Encyclical of Pope Francis on the Environment, Laudato Si', with Commentary by Sean McDonagh*, edited by Catholic Church, Pope Francis, 3–142. Orbis, 2016.

McFague, Sallie. *The Body of God: An Ecological Theology*. Augsburg Fortress, 1993.

McFague, Sallie. "Falling in Love with God and the World: Some Reflections on the Doctrine of God." *Ecumenical Review* 65, no. 1 (2013): 17–34.

McFague, Sallie. "Reimagining the Triune God for a Time of Global Climate Change." In *Planetary Solidarity: Global Women's Voices on Christian Doctrine and Climate Justice*, edited by Grace Ji-Sun Kim and Hilda P. Koster, 101–18. Fortress, 2017.

Menakem, Resmaa. *My Grandmother's Hands: Racialized Trauma and the Pathway to Mending Our Hearts and Bodies*. Central Recovery, 2017.

Mescher, Marcus. *The Ethics of Encounter: Christian Neighbor Love as a Practice of Solidarity*. Orbis, 2020.

Michelson, Tzvi, and Avraham Kluger. "Can Listening Hurt You? A Meta-Analysis of the Effects of Exposure to Trauma on Listener's Stress." *International Journal of Listening* 37, no. 1 (2021): 1–11. https://doi.org/10.1080/10904018.2021.1927734.

Močnik, Nena. "Re-Thinking Exposure to Trauma and Self-Care in Fieldwork-Based Social Research: Introduction to the Special Issue." *Social Epistemology* 34, no. 1 (2020): 1–11. https://doi.org/10.1080/02691728.2019.1681559.

Moe-Lobeda, Cynthia D. *Resisting Structural Evil: Love as Ecological-Economic Vocation*. Fortress, 2013.

Moore, Mary Elizabeth. *Ministering with the Earth*. Chalice, 1998.

Moore, Mary Elizabeth. "Responding to a Weeping Planet: Practical Theology as a Discipline Called by Crisis." *Religions* 13, no. 3 (2022): 244. https://doi.org/10.3390/rel13030244.

Ms. Foundation for Women. "More to Do: The Road to Equality for Women in the United States." Special Report, 2013.

Muke, Nagaju. "Diaconia in Traumatised Societies: Learning from the Rwandan Context." In *The Diaconal Church*, edited by Dietrich et al., 456–67. Regnum Books International, 2019.

Naef, Rahel. "Bearing Witness: A Moral Way of Engaging in the Nurse-Person Relationship." *Nursing Philosophy* 7, no. 3 (2006): 146–56. https://doi.org/10.1111/j.1466-769X.2006.00271.x.

National Association of Evangelicals. "For the Health of the Nation: An Evangelical Call to Civic Responsibility." *National Association of Evangelicals*, 2024. https://www.nae.org/for-the-health-of-the-nation/.

National Council of Churches of Christ in the USA. "A 21st Century Social Creed," 2007. https://nationalcouncilofchurches.us/christian-unity/a-21st-century-social-creed/.

Navarrete, Tweedy Sombrero. "In Ministry as a Native American." *Response*, November 2017. https://web.archive.org/web/20210517152213/https://www.unitedmethodistwomen.org/news/in-ministry-as-a-native-american.

Nessan, Craig L., and Darryl W. Stephens, eds. *Diaconal Studies: Lived Theology for the Church in North America*. Regnum Books International, 2024.

Nicholas, Kimberly. "Climate Science Basics." https://350.org/science/#warming.

NICWA. "Department of Interior Releases Federal Indian Boarding School Investigative Report Vol. II." August 20, 2024. https://www.nicwa.org/news/department-of-interior-releases-federal-indian-boarding-school-investigative-report-vol-ii/.

Niebuhr, H. Richard. "The Grace of Doing Nothing." In *An Eerdmans Reader in Contemporary Political Theology*, edited by William T. Cavanaugh, Jeffrey W. Bailey, and Craig Hovey, 254–8. Eerdmans, 2012.

Niebuhr, H. Richard. *Radical Monotheism and Western Culture: With Supplementary Essays*. Harper & Row, [1943]1970.

Niebuhr, H. Richard. *The Responsible Self: An Essay in Christian Moral Philosophy*. HarperSanFrancisco, [1963]1978.

Niebuhr, H. Richard, with Daniel Day Williams and James M. Gustafson. *The Purpose of the Church and Its Ministry: Reflections on the Aims of Theological Education*. Harper & Brothers, 1956.

Niebuhr, Reinhold. *Moral Man and Immoral Society: A Study in Ethics and Politics*. Charles Scribner's Sons, [1932]1960.

Nkulu-N'Sengha, Mutombo. "Bumuntu Memory and Authentic Personhood: An African Art of Becoming Humane." In *Memory and the Narrative Imagination in the African and Diaspora Experience*, edited by Tom Spencer-Walters, 295–336. Bedford, 2011.

Noley, Homer. *First White Frost: Native Americans and United Methodism*. Abingdon, 1991.

Nordstokke, Kjell, ed. *Diakonia in Context: Transformation, Reconciliation, Empowerment: An LWF Contribution to the Understanding and Practice of Diakonia*. Lutheran World Federation, 2009. https://lutheranworld.org/resources/document-diakonia-context-transformation-reconciliation-empowerment.

Nordstokke, Kjell. *Liberating Diakonia*. Tapir Akademisk, 2011.

Northcott, Michael S. *A Moral Climate: The Ethics of Global Warming*. Orbis, 2007.

Nouwen, Henri J. M. *The Wounded Healer: Ministry in Contemporary Society*. Doubleday, 1972.

Nowlin, Matt, Jeramy Townsley, Jay Colbert, and Sharon Kandris. "The Inequalities behind COVID-19 Disparities for African Americans in Indianapolis." *SAVI*, May 15, 2020. https://www.savi.org/the-inequalities-behind-covid-19-disparities-for-african-americans-in-indianapolis/.

O'Brien, Kevin J. "The Scales Integral to Ecology: Hierarchies in Laudato Si' and Christian Ecological Ethics." *Religions* 10, no. 9 (2019): 511. https://doi.org/10.3390/rel10090511.

Oehler, Carolyn Henninger. *Steps toward Wholeness: Learning and Repentance*. General Commission on Christian Unity and Interreligious Concerns. UMC, 2000.

Oliver, Kelly. "Witnessing, Recognition, and Response Ethics." *Philosophy & Rhetoric* 48, no. 4 (2015): 473–93. http://muse.jhu.edu/article/602490.

Omi, Michael, and Howard Winant. "Racial Formations." In *Race, Class, and Gender in the United States: An Integrated Study*, 10th ed., edited by Paula S. Rothenberg with Kelly S. Mayhew, 13–19. Worth, 2014.

Park, Crystal L., Joseph M. Currier, J. Irene Harris, and Jeanne M. Slattery. *Trauma, Meaning, and Spirituality: Translating Research into Clinical Practice*. American Psychological Association, 2017.

Park, HiRho. *Develop Intercultural Competence: How to Lead Cross-Racial and Cross-Cultural Churches*. General Board of Higher Education and Ministry, 2018.

Park, HiRho, and Susan Willhauck, eds. *Breaking through the Stained Glass Ceiling: Women Pastoring Large Churches*. General Board of Higher Education and Ministry, 2013.

Parliament of the World's Religions. "Towards a Global Ethic: An Initial Declaration of the Parliament of the World's Religions." *Council for a Parliament of the World's Religions*, 2018. https://web.archive.org/web/20210817123530/https://www.global-ethic.org/wp-content/uploads/2020/12/WEE_2018.pdf.

Peters, Rebecca Todd. *Solidarity Ethics: Transformation in a Globalized World*. Fortress, 2014.

Poling, James Newton. *Rethinking Faith: A Constructive Practical Theology*. Fortress, 2011.

Pontifical Council for Justice and Peace. *Compendium of the Social Doctrine of the Church*. USCCB, 2004.

PTSD UK. "Trauma: It's More Than Just 'Fight or Flight.'" https://www.ptsduk.org/its-so-much-more-than-just-fight-or-flight/.

Rambo, Shelly. "Foreword." In *Feminist Trauma Theologies: Body, Scripture & Church in Critical Perspective*, edited by Karen O'Donnell and Katie Cross, xv–xviii. London: SCM, 2020.

Rambo, Shelly. "How Christian Theology and Practice Are Being Shaped by Trauma Studies." *The Christian Century*, November 1, 2019. https://www.christiancentury.org/article/critical-essay/how-christian-theology-and-practice-are-being-shaped-trauma-studies.

Rambo, Shelly. *Spirit and Trauma: A Theology of Remaining*. Westminster John Knox, 2010.

Rambo, Shelly. "Trauma, Transformation, and Transcendence." In *Conflict Transformation and Religion: Essays on Faith, Power, and Relationship*, edited by Ellen Ott Marshall, 155–71. Palgrave Macmillan, 2016.

Ramsay, Sharon. "Bearing Witness: Listening to Others Allows God to Show Up," *Presbyterian Record* 140, no. 10 (2016): 22.

Rasmussen, Larry L. "Doing Our First Works Over." *Journal of Lutheran Ethics*, April 1, 2009. https://www.elca.org/JLE/Articles/385#_ednref6.

Rasmussen, Larry L. *Earth Community, Earth Ethics*. Ecology & Justice series. Orbis, 1996.

Rawls, John. *A Theory of Justice*, rev. ed. Belknap, 1999.

Rendle, Gil. *Quietly Courageous: Leading the Church in a Changing World*. Rowman & Littlefield, 2019.

Richey, Russell E., Kenneth E. Rowe, and Jean Miller Schmidt. *The Methodist Experience in America: A History, Volume I*. Abingdon, 2010.

Rieger, Joerg. *Christ and Empire: From Paul to Postcolonial Times*. Fortress, 2007.

Rieger, Joerg. *No Rising Tide: Theology, Economics, and the Future*. Fortress, 2009.

Rivera, Mayra. *The Touch of Transcendence: A Postcolonial Theology of God*. Westminster John Knox, 2007.

Roberts, Gary L. *Massacre at Sand Creek: How Methodists Were Involved in an American Tragedy*. Abingdon, 2016.

Robinson, Elaine A. *Godbearing: Evangelism Reconceived*. Pilgrim, 2006.

Ross, Karen, Megan K. McCabe, and Sara Wilhelm Garbers. "Christian Sexual Ethics and the #MeToo Movement: Three Moments of Reflection on Sexual Violence and Women's Bodies." *Journal of the Society of Christian Ethics* 39, no. 2 (2019): 339–56.

Rubio, Julie Hanlon, and Paul J. Schutz. *Beyond "Bad Apples": Understanding Clergy Perpetrated Sexual Abuse as a Structural Problem & Cultivating Strategies for Change*. Fordham University, 2022. https://takingresponsibility.ace.fordham.edu/santa-clara-structural-clericalism/.

Runyon, Theodore. *The New Creation*. Abingdon, 1998.

Saiving Goldstein, Valerie. "The Human Situation: A Feminine View." *The Journal of Religion* 40, no. 2 (1960): 100–12.

Salasin, Susan. "Sine Qua Non for Public Health." *National Council Magazine*, no. 2 (2011): 18.

Sawyer, Lauren D. "A Sacred Trust: The Spiritual Community's Duty." In *Spiritual Healing from Sexual Violence: An Intersectional Guide*, edited by Debra Meyers and Mary Sue Barnett, 5–22. Routledge, 2023. https://doi.org/10.4324/9781003323631-2.

Sawyer, Lauren D., Emily Cohen, and Annie Mesaros, eds. *Responding to Spiritual Leader Misconduct: A Handbook*. FaithTrust Institute, 2022. https://faithtrustinstitute.org/.

Scharen, Christian, Aana Marie Vigen, with contributors. *Ethnography as Christian Theology and Ethics*. Continuum, 2011.

Schreiter, Robert J. "Reconciliation and Healing as a Paradigm for Mission." *International Review of Mission* 94, no. 372 (2005): 74–83. https://doi.org/10.1111/j.1758-6631.2005.tb00487.x.

Scott, David W. *Crossing Boundaries: Sharing God's Good News through Mission*. Wesley's Foundery, 2019.

Shaw, Susan M. "Institutional Betrayal, Institutional Courage and the Church." *Baptist News Global*, July 26, 2022. https://baptistnews.com/article/institutional-betrayal-institutional-courage-and-the-church/.

Shay, Jonathan. "Casualties." *Daedalus* 140, no. 3 (Summer 2011): 179–88.

Sheveland, John N., ed. *Theology in a Post-Traumatic Church*. Orbis, 2023.

Shin, Wonchul, and Elizabeth M. Bounds. "Treating Moral Harm as Social Harm: Toward a Restorative Ethics of Christian Responsibility." *Journal of the Society of Christian Ethics* 37, no. 2 (2017): 153–69.

Singh, Simran Jeet. "On the Anniversary of His Birth, a Reflection on the Life of Guru Nanak." *Religion News Service*, November 30, 2020. https://religionnews.com/2020/11/30/550-years-after-his-birth-a-reflection-on-the-life-of-sikhisms-founder-guru-nanak/.

Smith, Carly Parnitzke, and Jennifer J. Freyd. "Dangerous Safe Havens: Institutional Betrayal Exacerbates Sexual Trauma." *Journal of Traumatic Stress* 26, no. 1 (2013): 119–24. https://doi.org/10.1002/jts.21778.

Smith, Carly Parnitzke, and Jennifer J. Freyd. "Institutional Betrayal." *American Psychologist* 69, no. 6 (2014): 575–87. https://doi.org/10.1037/a0037564.

Sokol, Michelle. "Mennonite Seminary Apologizes to Victims of Famed Theologian John Howard Yoder." *National Catholic Reporter*, April 9, 2015. http://ncronline.org/news/accountability/mennonite-seminary-apologizes-victims-famed-theologian-john-howard-yoder.

Soto Albrecht, Elizabeth, and Darryl W. Stephens, eds. *Liberating the Politics of Jesus: Renewing Peace Theology through the Wisdom of Women*. Studies in Anabaptist Theology and Ethics. T&T Clark, 2020.

Souza, Raymond J.de "The 'Doctrine of Discovery' and the Catholic Church." *National Catholic Register*, April 4, 2023. https://www.ncregister.com/commentaries/the-doctrine-of-discovery-and-the-catholic-church.

Stephen Ministries St. Louis. "History of Stephen Ministries." https://www.stephenministries.org/aboutus/default.cfm/721.

Stephens, Darryl W. "Fiduciary Duty and Sacred Trust." In *Professional Sexual Ethics: A Holistic Ministry Approach*, edited by Darryl W. Stephens and Patricia Beattie Jung, 23–33. Fortress, 2013.

Stephens, Darryl W. *Methodist Morals: Social Principles in the Public Church's Witness*. University of Tennessee Press, 2016.

Stephens, Darryl W. *Reckoning Methodism: Mission and Division in the Public Church*. Cascade, 2024.

Streets, Frederick. "Social Work and a Trauma-Informed Ministry and Pastoral Care: A Collaborative Agenda." *Social Work & Christianity* 42, no. 4 (2015): 470–87. https://nacsw.org/Publications/SWC/SWC42_4WEB.pdf.

Substance Abuse and Mental Health Services Administration (SAMHSA). "Double Jeopardy: COVID-19 and Behavioral Health Disparities for Black and Latino Communities in the U.S." (Submitted by OBHE). https://www.samhsa.gov/sites/default/files/covid19-behavioral-health-disparities-black-latino-communities.pdf.

SAMHSA. "SAMHSA's Concept of Trauma and Guidance for a Trauma-Informed Approach." HHS Publication No. (SMA) 14–4884. SAMHSA, 2014. https://store.samhsa.gov/product/SAMHSA-s-Concept-of-Trauma-and-Guidance-for-a-Trauma-Informed-Approach/SMA14-4884.

SAMHSA. "Spotlight: Building Resilient and Trauma-Informed Communities—Introduction." SMA17-5014, February 2017. https://store.samhsa.gov/product/Spotlight-Building-Resilient-and-Trauma-Informed-Communities-Introduction/SMA17-5014.

SAMHSA. "Trauma-Informed Care in Behavioral Health Services." Treatment Improvement Protocol (TIP) Series 57. HHS Publication No. (SMA) 13-4801. SAMHSA, 2014.

Suchocki, Marjorie Hewitt. *The Fall to Violence: Original Sin in Relational Theology*. Continuum, 1994.

Sullender, R. Scott. *Trauma and Grief: Resources and Strategies for Ministry*. Cascade, 2018.

Swain, Storm. "Climate Change and Pastoral Theology." In *T&T Clark Handbook of Christian Theology and Climate Change*, edited by Ernst Conradie and Hilda Koster, 615–26. Bloomsbury, 2020.

Swidler, Leonard J. "The Movement for a Global Ethic." *Journal of Ecumenical Studies* 53, no. 1 (2018): 1–11. https://doi.org/10.1353/ecu.2018.0005.

Thurman, Howard. *With Head and Heart: The Autobiography of Howard Thurman*. Harcourt Brace Jovanovich, 1981.

Thurman, Howard. "The Sound of the Genuine." *The Spelman Messenger* 96, no. 4 (1980): 14–15. https://radar.auctr.edu/islandora/object/sc.001.messenger%3A1980.03/.

"To Love and Serve the Lord: Diakonia in the Life of the Church." *The Jerusalem Report of the Anglican–Lutheran International Commission (ALIC III)*, 2013. https://lutheranworld.org/resources/publication-love-and-serve-lord-diakonia-life-church.

Townes, Emilie M. *Womanist Ethics and the Cultural Production of Evil*. Black Religion / Womanist Thought / Social Justice Series. Palgrave Macmillan, 2006.

Travis, Sarah. *Unspeakable: Preaching and Trauma-Informed Theology*. Cascade, 2021.

Trimiew, Darryl M. *Voices of the Silenced: The Responsible Self in a Marginalized Community*. Pilgrim, 1993.

Tumminio Hansen, Danielle Elizabeth. "The Body of God, Sexually Violated: A Trauma-Informed Reading of the Climate Crisis." *Religions* 13, no. 3 (2022): 249. https://doi.org/10.3390/rel13030249.

The United Methodist Hymnal: Book of United Methodist Worship. UMPH, 1989.

United Methodist Development Center. "UMC Pastor Working to Improve Lives of Women in Nigeria." https://web.archive.org/web/20170212221039/http://umcdc.paramoredev. com/stories/umc-pastor-working-to-improve-lives-of-women-in-nigeria.

United Nations. "Universal Declaration of Human Rights." https://www.un.org/en/about-us/ universal-declaration-of-human-rights.

U.S. Energy Information Administration. "What Is the United States' Share of World Energy Consumption?" April 11, 2024. https://www.eia.gov/tools/faqs/faq.php?id=87.

United States Conference of Catholic Bishops (USCCB). *Forming Consciences for Faithful Citizenship: A Call to Political Responsibility from the Catholic Bishops of the United States, with New Introductory Note.* USCCB, 2024. https://www.usccb.org/sjp/forming-consciences-faithful-citizenship.

United States Conference of Catholic Bishops (USCCB). "Seven Themes of Catholic Social Teaching." 2005. https://www.usccb.org/resources/seven-themes-catholic-social-teaching.

United Women in Faith. "Charter for Racial Justice in an Interdependent Global Community." https://uwfaith.org/what-we-do/serve-and-advocate/racial-justice/.

United Women in Faith. "Faith Talks with Cindy Johnson." *Podcast*, August 30, 2019. https://www.spreaker.com/episode/faith-talks-with-cindy-johnson–18959362.

United Women in Faith. "Faith Talks with Grace Musaka." *Podcast*, November 7, 2019. https://www.spreaker.com/episode/faith-talks-with-grace-musaka–20006424.

United Women in Faith. "Grace Musuka." https://uwfaith.org/wp-content/uploads/2023/08/ RegionalMissionaryBios.pdf.

United Women in Faith. "Office of Deaconess & Home Missioner." 2025. https://uwfaith. org/what-we-do/deaconess-and-home-missioner/.

UNY Communications. "The Principles of Holy Conferencing." July 8, 2016. http://www. unyumc.org/news/article/the-principles-of-holy-conferencing.

van der Kolk, Bessel A. *The Body Keeps the Score: Brain, Mind, and Body in the Healing of Trauma.* Penguin, 2014.

Vasko, Elisabeth T. *Beyond Apathy: A Theology for Bystanders.* Fortress, 2015.

Walker, Alice. *In Search of Our Mother's Gardens: Womanist Prose.* Harcourt, 1983.

Weaver, Jace. "Introduction." In *Defending Mother Earth: Native American Perspectives on Environmental Justice*, edited by Jace Weaver, 1–28. Orbis, 1996.

Wells, Samuel. *A Nazareth Manifesto: Being with God.* John Wiley & Sons, 2015.

Wesley, John. *John Wesley's Sermons: An Anthology*, edited by Albert C. Outler and Richard P. Heitzenrater. Abingdon, 1991.

West, Traci C. *Disruptive Christian Ethics: When Racism and Women's Lives Matter.* Westminster John Knox, 2006.

West, Traci C. *Solidarity and Defiant Spirituality: Africana Lessons on Religion, Racism, and Ending Gender Violence.* New York University Press, 2019.

West, Traci C. *Wounds of the Spirit: Black Women, Violence, and Resistance Ethics.* New York University Press, 1999.

Wijlens, Myriam, and Vladimir Shmaliy, eds. *Churches and Moral Discernment: Volume 1: Learning from Traditions*, Faith and Order Paper No. 228. WCC, 2021.

Williams, Jeffrey. *Religion and Violence in Early American Methodism: Taking the Kingdom by Force.* Indiana University Press, 2010.

Williams, Layton E. *Holy Disunity: How What Separates Us Can Save Us.* Westminster John Knox, 2019.

Wink, Walter. *Jesus and Nonviolence: A Third Way.* Facets Series. Fortress, 2003.

Wogaman, J. Philip. *Surrendering My Ordination: Standing Up for Gay and Lesbian Inclusivity in The United Methodist Church.* Westminster John Knox, 2018.

Wolcott, Rick. "Remembrance, Repentance and Restoration: Denomination Returns Entrusted Land to the Wyandot/te Nation." *East Ohio Conference News*, September 24, 2019. https://eocumcnews.com/2019/09/24/remembrance-repentance-and-restoration-denomination-returns-entrusted-land-to-the-wyandot-te-nation/.

Wolterstorff, Nicholas. *Justice: Rights and Wrongs*. Princeton University Press, 2008.

Woolston, Krystal Lynne. "'It Was Like Double Damage': An Exploration of Clergy-Perpetrated Sexual Abuse, Institutional Response, and Posttraumatic Growth." PhD diss., Montclair State University, 2023.

World Council of Churches and ACT Alliance. *Called to Transformation: Ecumenical Diakonia*. WCC, 2022. https://www.oikoumene.org/resources/publications/ecumenical-diakonia.

World Council of Churches, Pontifical Council for Interreligious Dialogue of the Roman Catholic Church, and the World Evangelical Alliance. *Christian Witness in a Multi-Religious World: Recommendations for Conduct*, 2011. https://www.oikoumene.org/resources/documents/christian-witness-in-a-multi-religious-world.

World Day of Prayer Committee of Zimbabwe. "Rise! Take Your Mat and Walk." https://worlddayofprayer.net/zimbabwe-2020.html#/.

World Day of Prayer International Committee. https://worlddayofprayer.net.

World Day of Prayer USA. http://www.wdp-usa.org.

INDEX OF SUBJECTS

INDEX OF PERSONS